IMMORTAL
SELF

IMMORTAL SELF

A JOURNEY TO THE HIMALAYAN VALLEY OF THE AMARTYA MASTERS

AARAVINDHA HIMADRA

BOULDER, COLORADO

Sounds True
Boulder, CO 80306

© 2018 Aaravindha Himadra

Sounds True is a trademark of Sounds True, Inc.

Published 2018

Cover design by Jennifer Miles
Book design by Beth Skelley

Cover image © kpzphoto / Alamy Stock Photo

Printed in Canada

Cataloging-in-Publication data for this book is available
from the Library of Congress

ISBN (paperback): 978-1-68364-113-1
ISBN (ebook): 978-1-68364-114-8

10 9 8 7 6 5 4 3 2 1

In loving memory of Master Phow,
who left his body behind in 2011 at the age of 164.

A special acknowledgment must go to Ashayrah,
who worked ceaselessly in nearly every
aspect of getting this book into print.

Thank you, beautiful and beloved Ashayrah,
for your determined and selfless generosity.

~

CONTENTS

PREFACE

A LETTER TO THE READER

I wrote this book from memory and the notes I took while on my sojourn to the Valley of the Immortals. Initially I intended the account to be no more than a personal record of my stay there, but as time wore on my perspective changed and I decided to share it openly with the world.

It was 2006 when I left for India to begin this journey, but I waited for another six years before I fully put it into words. I have no doubt that what I have recorded here will be highly controversial for some and an affirming balm for others. I invite you to read this account on whatever level speaks to you. My interest only lies in offering the profound value of the spiritual truths within, and I invite you to allow them to open your heart and mind to what is yet possible.

The Amartya tradition—the lineage of masters written about in this book—is rarely thought of today, and whatever references you might find typically view them as an ancient legend. A few fortunate beings have known of their existence, but all who do will certainly bear the same level of intimate confidence that I have and won't—under any circumstance—expose their whereabouts against their will. For the diligent, it may still be possible to find a few traces of their existence in shastra, or sacred scripture, and possibly through old stories that tell of them. Those who see the beauty and value contained in this book can—through their own sincerity in searching out the truth in themselves—connect directly with the masters without needing to physically visit them.

The Himalayas are a vastly expansive region, larger in size and far more remote in body than most major countries. An inexhaustible number of secrets are hidden in those mountains, and for a while yet will continue to stay that way.

I recommend that you read these pages slowly, particularly in the second half of the book. In so doing, the knowledge entailed within will awaken a hidden part of your own journey and possibly even inspire a few lost memories of your own spiritual past. Those who read humbly and with an open heart will clearly gain the most—and will also feel the masters of this tradition coming in secret to stir awake those sacred inner realizations you have long hungered for.

Aaravindha Himadra

INTRODUCTION

Listen with care to those delicate whispers—
those fine-spun musings
that promise to turn your unsung passions to song.
Urge to life that waiting wisdom hidden inside
your humblest of feelings.
For only in earnest humility will you find that
  rightful setting
where your destiny can wake.

The air was humid and heavy; the sun was blisteringly hot. A patchwork of smoky shadows and pulsing hues created a motley background behind the sweltering horde of shoppers. Beyond a spread of green lentils, red chili peppers, and open-ended rice burlaps, past a long curtain of pink, saffron, and blue saris hanging wilted in the windless heat, where the air dulled to a muted haze, a pair of supersized buses unloaded an energetic mob of Japanese tourists. The square's main exit was now gridlocked with sightseers.

I chose to follow the overflow streaming into the less congested parts of the square. Less than a block ahead, beyond a lengthy row of canopied stalls, a narrow alleyway crowned with a muddle of tattered electrical lines promised the nearest escape. Having spent my entire morning combing through an endless mix of beaded malas, music cassettes, and assorted tourist junk, a relaxed lunch in the shade of my hotel piazza seemed idyllic. That is, until one last temptation caught my eye—a finely crafted Tibetan jacket. An unlikely find in a music stall stocked with drums and sitars.

Masked in a barter-readied indifference, I mulled over a possible strategy to acquire the jacket. But just as I was about to engage in the bargaining, a vague sense of being watched pulled my attention back to the crowd. It didn't take long to spot him: standing on the opposite side of the square, a tall, slender man wrapped in a single piece of purple linen had his eyes locked on me. On cue, the instant our eyes met he began walking toward me.

Here in Delhi, dressed in an American-made white shirt and blue jeans, I no doubt came off as an obvious tourist mark. I had already been approached a number of times this morning and was in no mood for another scammer working his con. I looked around. The crowd was thick—a possible cover for me to slip away.

But I hesitated. There was something intriguingly different about this man. His approach was almost supernatural. As he came closer, the shoulder-tight crowd unwittingly parted, seemingly choreographed under the invisible hands of a mysterious puppeteer. Was I the only one seeing this?

A plainly carved, shoulder-high staff swung like a pendulum in perfect stride with his lanky brown legs. In a blink, his pace narrowed the gap between us, eliciting in me an annoyed feeling of being deliberately cornered. Towering above me, his head inked out the sun. Thin glimmers of light fanned through the feathery outer wisps of his dove-white hair.

Blue eyes, I thought. *Not a native Indian!*

A subtle appraisal passed between us. And then, as if to confide a secret, he leaned in and brought his face a bit too close, saying in a half-whisper, "If you're ready and if you're willing, I've come to guide you home!"

"Do I know you?" I asked. "Have we met?"

A telltale smile spread across his face, but he said nothing. I stepped back reactively. The booth's edge resisted with a sharp jab to my hip. I envisioned slipping by him, but the intrigue held me in place. There was something curiously alluring about this man: his confidence, his steady focus, and a subtle trace of something mysterious glinting in his eyes. I couldn't recall having ever met him before, but he seemed oddly familiar. And then something truly strange began to happen: the air around us changed, becoming faintly electric.

The intrigue was building. This wasn't just some chance encounter. He definitely knew me! But how? And why couldn't I remember him?

There are times in life when the hand of fate shows up unpredictably. I've come to relish those moments—their sudden and unanticipated entrance—too elusive or quick for me to just brush aside or react habitually. More often than not, I've discovered in them a heavenly genius at work. I strongly suspected that this might be one of those times.

I soon found myself caught up in a perplexing sensation that time was somehow slowing to a crawl. The spaces between my thoughts were longer than usual. I was now too fascinated to resist. I chose to let go, which immediately stirred up an almost paranormal sense of yearning, both painful and puzzlingly hopeful. It was similar to a feeling I once had as a child when returning home after a long trip away.

The stranger's face started to change, becoming mystifyingly surreal—dreamlike. *This is happening too quickly,* I thought. So quickly that I nearly lost my balance. Peering up into the black centers of his eyes made it even more surreal, producing a peculiar sense of falling into another realm.

In a snap, the environment around us fell completely silent, as if someone had just flipped a switch on the world. And then something else happened: I could see him in a new way, much differently than I had earlier. There was an extraordinary depth of goodness reflected in his face, so pure I couldn't imagine having ever doubted him!

My thoughts decreased; my usual mental chatter had fallen to a complete hush. Oddly, the residual silence swallowed all sense of separation that had previously demarcated us as two. I felt strangely exposed, and yet I felt somehow secure. I was exactly where I should be.

It was apparent now; there weren't any tricks or riddles to his offer. His invitation wasn't merely a request, it was a cue: a kind of prompt that was intended to evoke something in me, something I must have forgotten. An echo of something he had said earlier kept resurfacing in my mind: *if you are ready . . . if you are ready . . . if you are ready . . .* There was a genuine sincerity there. And an undeniable sense that my answer would be somehow life changing.

His eyes were amazingly radiant. This was no ordinary man; this was a person of extraordinary spiritual development. It was all so obvious now. He was a true master, a mystic!

A gentle touch of something evocative and unexplainable washed over me—a whisper of light that called to me, asking me to close my eyes and listen. The moment I did, a window opened. Through it came a streaming mosaic of partial images—broken fragments of a vague and distant memory. Not from my childhood or anything else from this life, but something older, from a prior time. I started to recall pieces of a long-forgotten era, moments of another life beyond my normal reach. What stood out most was a growing sense that at that time, so very long ago, I had made a promise—a yet-to-be-fulfilled promise. I wasn't entirely sure what that promise was, but I knew it had to be the key reason why this master had come: to call it back into my awareness! Except now, the resulting allure around this promise had caused everything else I thought important in my life to fall pale.

The yearning I had felt and the call of that unrequited promise were one and the same. Only one other desire remained—the desire to go with him to the home he promised to guide me to. I wanted to drop everything, to let everything I had been doing in my life fall away. I so very much wanted to go, but I knew I couldn't. Not yet! I was barely a young man, and I hadn't yet accomplished what I had promised to do.

New thoughts sprang to life, spinning wildly, filling the silence with a mounting sense of pressured anguish, but at the same time I was deeply grateful for what I'd just discovered.

The world around me seemed more distant now, like a passing dream. A moment of dizziness nearly tipped me off my feet. I grabbed the edge of the booth. I focused on my breath and used it to calm my mind. Out of the blue, this had all happened so incredibly fast.

"One day . . ." I whispered. I said it again out loud. "One day."

I sensed he already knew my answer; he knew it before he'd asked. He knew I needed to hear myself say it, to feel my conviction—to feel this promise come back to life.

I edged out my final answer, "No, I'm not ready. Not yet!"

He straightened his body, passed his staff to his free hand, and then reassuringly placed his right hand on my shoulder. An otherworldly look of compassion blossomed in his eyes, touching my heart in a way that could only be described as timeless.

"Thank you," I said softly. "I won't forget this."

He nodded. "Very well. We will wait."

It was over! Without another word, he turned and walked off as easily as he'd come. The clamor of the market rushed back with a roar.

I watched him disappear through the crowd. This gentle master had given me a glimpse of something far more significant than I had imagined my life would be. He had broken my world open, and I now stood directly in life's pulse, ready to follow whatever demands it would bring.

I promised myself to keep this encounter secret. I would share it with no one. At least not yet.

1

A SECOND INVITATION

I saw the impossible—
the ghostly vision of a longhaired man dressed in white,
sitting cross-legged and weightless
in the air directly in front of me.

The life-warming southwesterly winds had finally arrived, painting the San Juan Islands green. Winter was over. The drab display of comatose shrubs and branches had burst into song, padding the countryside with clouds of white and cranberry-pink blossoms—a picture-perfect setting for my forest retreat. I pitched my tent on a quiet mossy knoll beneath a canopy of tall Douglas firs and brawny-armed madrone trees I'd stocked my refuge with a sleeping cot, a small table for candles, some incense, and a velvety purple armchair.

The morning was young and the air sweetly crisp. It smelled of rich earth and pine, sprinkled with a delicate aroma of the nearby sea. At dawn I had let myself glide into the satisfying feeling of meditative silence. Time had yielded to the timeless. Then something peculiar occurred. It began as little more than a pulsing glimmer, a silky sparkle that faded in and out beneath my eyelids. I thought to pay it no mind, but upon hearing a curious crackle in the air, I worked open my eyes. A rush surged through me. I saw the impossible—the ghostly vision of a longhaired man dressed in white, sitting cross-legged and weightless in the air directly in front of me.

Since childhood, I had sensed them a thousand times—a distant group of extraordinary masters. Following that invitation in the Delhi market, their influence had grown progressively more pronounced. Lately, scarcely a day would go by when I didn't sense them. But not since that day in the market had I seen one of them with my eyes open.

Not through the use of words, but with an unmistakable and deliberate transmission of thought, the master said, "We request that you will now come to our Himalayan valley!"

Then, in a blink, his apparition evaporated, leaving in its place nothing more than a diffused stream of sunlight spilling in through my tent window. After more than twenty-five years, my second invitation had come, as abrupt and unexpected as the first.

But unlike that first invitation, this one created a few previously unimagined challenges. It failed to convey where to go! I'd often thought of traveling there, but I had no idea of how to find their home without a guide or instructions. I knew only that they live hidden somewhere in the remote Himalayas.

These masters are a nearly forgotten legend, and rarely has anyone found them on their own. I hoped more information would somehow come, but I suspected that I might be reliant on my own methods—methods I was yet unsure of.

Everyone in this world is blessed with some kind of talent and purpose. When one's talent and purpose find each other, everything in life that's meant to be seems to fit together. I discovered the talent part early. However, as a child I struggled with my talent incessantly, most often when it contrasted with the learned boundaries provided by my schooling, friends, or family. I wrestled to adjust my unusual perception of things to my conservative-minded social surroundings. Eventually I learned to direct my talent into service for others. Thereafter my worries of it not fitting into the mainstream world became irrelevant; I had found the second part of the formula—a purpose.

During my journey to the Himalayas, I learned that my particular talent was once referred to as *saumedhika drishti*, a seer's ability. Specifically, saumedhika drishti refers to a perceptual sensitivity best used as a kind of transcendental divining tool—most useful in retrieving information or knowledge that relates to one's spiritual direction in life.

I had never applied my talent in any other manner. I was now considering using it as a compass tuned to a distant and yet unknown location. Up until now, I had been wholly content with my talent as it was. But now, for the first time in my life, I struggled with the real possibility that my abilities might not be enough. Despite the various unknowns that loomed before me, I felt convinced—even with all its potential challenges—that the coming journey was a vital and necessary part of my life's destiny. I was determined. One way or another, I would find a way to answer the invitation of these mysterious masters. And I would follow this path, regardless of the uncertainties.

2

THE LETTER

I saw myself standing in a green landscape
surrounded with tall white-capped mountains.
It was a peaceful and lovely world
where I instantly knew I had once lived.

After an inconclusive year of sketchy research and planning, I booked a flight to Delhi. I was relying solely on my intuition and saumedhika drishti to show me the right path, and for the first few days everything moved along far better than expected. However, today was different.

After acquiring my last travel permit from the Sikkim House, my every step seemed increasingly burdened with a pressing sense of puzzling urgency. By early afternoon, the ensuing restlessness became too obvious to ignore. Having long ago learned not to deny my natural intuitive markers, I abandoned my afternoon sightseeing plans and headed back to my hotel.

Upon entering the hotel foyer, I was struck with a curious wave of attention. Surrounded by suited foreign businessmen and traveling dignitaries, I alone seemed to draw a discreet yet undeniable extra amount of notice. On detecting my uneasiness at being studied, the staff tamed their whispers and shifted their glances, but only to feign a clumsy air of indifference. My curiosity roused, I searched the length of the lobby. I spotted the concierge waving me over from his station, offering me an opportune moment to walk past the scrutiny.

The concierge carefully withdrew an ivory linen envelope from a narrow drawer but hesitated its release just long enough to tell me that a *baba*, a holy man, had left it. For some unknown reason, this baba had been dressed in white and had chosen not to wait.

"Dressed in white?" I asked. Babas typically wore saffron, the color of fire, to symbolize the burning away of impurities. "You're certain he was a baba?" I asked.

The concierge peered over the top of his gold-rimmed glasses and offered me a mildly pretentious nod. "Undeniably, sir! Dressed in white—and most certainly a baba!"

"He must have made quite an impression."

"Excuse me, sir?" he replied.

"On your staff. They seem to have taken an unusual interest in my return. I assume that must be why?"

The concierge directed his gaze into a censuring glare toward two of his porters as they hurried by. Returning his attention to me, he said, "Our sincere apology, sir. It's an uncommon event—a holy man of such obvious tenor entering our hotel. We rarely see anyone other than the usual business men and such."

"No need to apologize. I'm actually relieved. This all makes sense now."

Was this it, my hoped-for contact? I was thrilled at the prospect! After studying the envelope—shorter than average length, with an old-world texture—I slumped back into a burgundy leather club chair, kept private between two overhanging palms. I looked over to see the concierge still studying me inconspicuously through the corner of his eye. *Obvious tenor,* I thought to myself, while I ripped open the envelope's short end with my hotel key. Inside was a single leaflet smelling strongly of incense:

> Shri Aaravindha, namaste. Greetings. We have commenced
> preparations for your arrival. We recommend that you
> follow this secure route.

My eyes immediately shot to the finish. Hmm. No signature. Just the simple salutation, *jai.*

What remained of the letter seemed particularly odd. It felt a bit reserved and said very little, only laying out a puzzling new travel plan. Over the past year I had taken great care in studying maps in search of possible locations where I intuited, but more often imagined, the masters might be. I managed to catch occasional glimpses during meditation, mostly of a hidden Himalayan valley, but in the end I couldn't say for certain if I'd actually sensed anything of real value. Hopeful, I settled on a hypothetical region, but I knew that I hadn't really determined anything concrete.

This new route proposed in the letter didn't reveal much at all; it stopped short of providing me with anything I could follow once I reached the mountains. However, in its final leg, it did end in an area in which I had originally intended to *begin* my journey—in Varanasi. From there, I had planned to catch an overnight train to Sikkim, and in Sikkim I had hoped to trek stealthily into an eastern Himalayan divide, where I believed I might find the means to begin my trek toward the approximate region I sought to find. My plans were rough, sketchy at best, and with no real correlation to anything substantial.

Maybe in Varanasi they will contact me again? Could that be why the directions ended there?

The letter presented a curious new setback—the first part of the route digressed a long way south before heading north. It didn't make sense. Rereading the letter only amplified an unsettling sense that something new and peculiar was afoot. My eyes kept returning to the same two words: *secure route*.

There must be a reason. Had I failed to see something, some sort of threat? Should I be concerned?

I traced my steps back to the beginning of my journey. I was well aware that the Himalayan masters lived in seclusion and that they didn't want anyone uninvited to know of their whereabouts. But it didn't seem reasonable that this route had anything to do with that. I had been especially careful in keeping private any details involving my plans. Even now, with the exception of the masters, only two people knew exactly where I was. Both were in the United States, and both were sworn to confidentiality.

But this puzzling roundabout direction and the odd use of *secure*—there had to be more to it. If this letter was from my contact and was meant to convey some type of warning, it still didn't explain why the masters wanted me to follow this out-of-the-way southerly route, particularly now. In New Delhi, the temperature had risen above 41 degrees Celsuis, or 106 degrees Fahrenheit, and traveling through the Rajasthan desert would be like driving through an oven. A popular daily newspaper had reported the weekend's heat-related death toll in the region of the new route: over one hundred people had perished.

I contemplated the possibility of just bypassing the southern stretch, to go directly to Varanasi. But even the slightest thought of wavering rang out disturbingly wrong. This letter's arrival, here and now, was nothing short of miraculous. If the masters had gone to the trouble of sending it so far, carried in the hands of a holy man, their reason for setting this odd route must be a good one! That was good enough for me.

With the help of the concierge, I commissioned a professional driver. Atmaraj was a fit, smartly dressed man with a '50s-style, oiled-back haircut. Initially he appeared a bit too young—unseasoned and in his early twenties—but after a frank conversation Atmaraj convincingly assured me that he'd been driving the lower routes for years and knew them better than most. We agreed on a fair price and I hired him for the duration.

After a few quiet laps in my hotel pool, I searched for an out-of-the-way spot on a rooftop terrace for my evening meditation. The grinding sounds of the city hushed to a murmur, becoming almost mesmeric, as if the city's gods were secretly casting a sedative spell.

Facing the hazy setting sun, I nestled into a comfortable wrap-around wicker armchair. Closing my eyes, I yielded to the inward pull and sank like a rock into a soundless depth. But my meditation wasn't meant to be. Barely ten minutes in, I was vaguely distracted by a delicate flutter of something foreign that brushed through my awareness. The stir evoked a feeling that I wasn't alone. I sensed a watching presence, not in my surroundings but perplexingly half-veiled beneath the causal inner folds and muted whispers that live amid the first stir of thoughts. Clearly someone was crossing over there to touch my awareness. I flashed back to the time of my second invitation—was this experience going to form into another possible contact?

I waited in quiet repose but soon realized that unlike the second invitation, which arrived as a kind of phenomenal apparition, this time the other being remained elusive and tenuous at best, veiled inside an obscurity of silence. Watching the way silence watches, my perceptions expanded to touch that subtle inner vastness where common thoughts become altogether superfluous.

Then, as gentle as a sigh, a delicate thread of something subtly alluring lifted through the silence. It attracted me to a kind of mental passageway that seemed to open to another world.

I've been here before, I thought, *in the Delhi market over a quarter of a century ago.*

I let myself go, dropped into an effortless abandon, and then surfaced again as a young man living in a past life in a time very long ago. A trainload of images started flashing in and out of my awareness. And then I saw myself standing in a green landscape surrounded by tall white-capped mountains. It was a peaceful and lovely world where I instantly knew I had once lived. This was their hidden valley, where I had been raised as a son to one of the masters I was presently on my way to see.

Pieces fell into place perfectly. A vivid chain of memories, conversations, choices, and finally realizations all came together to reveal my primary reason for having left the valley. A moment later, an even deeper memory surfaced: that of an unrequited vow, a promise I had made long before that life in the valley. It was the same promise I recalled when the master in the Delhi market had helped me first sense it. My circle of remembrance was about to find completion. A surge of anticipation and excitement flooded my body, so strong it nearly roused me out of my meditative state.

I now realized that I had remembered that promise then, when I had lived in that valley as a young man, and it had deeply influenced me in that particular life. At some point, its call had become too compelling to ignore. And though I knew I wasn't in the right life to fully answer it, I had chosen to leave the valley at the age of eighteen to begin my quest to bring it to completion.

When the master in the Delhi market had alerted me to my memory of that promise, I had vaguely sensed that it was yet to be fulfilled. And though I didn't fully understand it then—not in its entirety—I've continued to feel it calling me, even in my present life.

My thoughts flashed back to when I told the master in Delhi that I wasn't ready. At the time, I felt it was too soon, that I couldn't go with him. I sensed I had something left to complete. I now knew what that something was. The vow was bound to an ancient divination, to a prophecy that foretold the coming circumstances of our present era, the twenty-first century. It foretold of a time when our world would pass into an unavoidable and tumultuous period of upheavals and struggles that would be fueled by a dark cloud of collective greed, corruption, and social denials. And though this isn't an altogether new theme in our world, these events would be far more impactful on our world than at any other time in our history. They would inevitably lead to a global onslaught of cataclysmic incidents that would threaten humanity's survival across the globe. A daunting and exceedingly dangerous revolution in our world's economic and human social environment would ensue. Humanity would be compelled to make an unprecedented shift in its ethical motivations, bringing on another shift that would optimally pave the way for a monumental global healing, leading to the potential genesis of a far more evolved age.

Since the visit from that master, I had devotedly assigned my saumedhika drishti efforts toward the retrieval of our world's long-forgotten spiritual knowledge. But until now I hadn't fully realized the unseen force compelling me. It was clear now! The retrieval of that knowledge was an essential part of my vow.

I was about to end my meditation when another memory broke through. Initially it was just a word; I heard the name Krishnalila. It was as if the presence that had come to visit my meditation had intentionally stirred it up in my mind. It wasn't long before the name invoked a broader memory that quickly developed to become remarkably vivid. Approximately one year after leaving my Himalayan home, I had befriended a gentle, compassionate sage who was living on Sikkim's western border near an area called the Five Treasures of the Great Snow. When I first encountered him, he was lecturing his devotees, a group of mountain locals to whom he taught that it was the duty of every fortunate man and woman to alleviate the suffering and hopeless circumstances of the less fortunate. And though he was older and far worldlier than I, after a series of long conversations he became one of my first students.

Then, in a sudden flash, my mysterious watcher vanished. I was once again alone in my meditation.

After that experience, Atmaraj and I pushed south for a few days through Rajasthan's sun-scorched, red-brown cities, finally arriving in Udaipur. After enjoying a day or two of rest, we would change directions and follow the route north-northeast, traveling first through the blue city, Jodhpur, and then head on through Agra. From there, we would stop only briefly to view the Taj Mahal, and then head directly to the city famous for its Kama Sutra temples, Khajuraho. In Khajuraho, I planned to catch a flight to Varanasi, and in Varanasi I would wait.

Hopefully another message would arrive to further instruct me. If for any reason more guidance failed to appear, my contingency plan was to simply follow my original, self-intuited route. I would catch a train to Sikkim, and if in Sikkim a message failed to arrive, I'd slip into the mountains and try to divine my way to their home—an unsettling prospect at best. If that intimidating circumstance did come to be, my departure into the Himalayas would have to be a surreptitious one. Slipping into the deeper mountains through Sikkim is forbidden. Nonetheless, I now had an unwavering sense that I'd find a way, one way or another.

After an early breakfast of chapattis, herbed eggs, and a hot cup of masala chai, I chose to spend my morning touring the historical parts of Udaipur, and later in the evening finish up with a quiet boat ride to the famous Taj Lake Palace for dinner. But first I planned to explore the surrounding countryside and possibly a few ruins.

The day burned hot, but nonetheless passed quickly. On our way back to Udaipur, through the car's passenger side window, I sighted the distant remnants of an alluring hilltop citadel. To avoid the heat, Atmaraj decided to wait with the car in the shade of a large jambul tree, a species of native plum. I set off alone, the way I actually preferred it. I scaled a scrappy stone path up to the ruin's disintegrating forward entry. Here the hot air formed into a determined upsurge of warm drafts, pushing small fragments of dust ever higher against the ruin's tall, craggy perimeter. Time had swallowed most of the walls, entombing them in a thick bramble of shrubs and roots, but the entrance was still traversable. In the center, amid a sunken gray courtyard, stood the doleful vestige of a crumbling, roofless temple. No doubt once quite lovely, it was now little more than an eerie reminder of a long-forgotten realm.

My maps didn't show it; this ruin must not have qualified as a tourist interest. By the look of it, no one had been here for a long time. I followed what had once served as a hallway that ran the length of the temple, which at its end opened to what was most likely the main chamber. Along the sunny side of the room stood an enduring stairway, worn but still sturdy enough to bear my weight. It led to a partially collapsed second-story wall. I found an ideal perch in a small window—a great place to take in the view of the setting sun. The sky was a vivid ocean blue, which is rare in India. A sparsely forested landscape stretched into the horizon as far as I could see. On a forward ridge, a row of lanky tall trees cast long, bluish shadows over a cluster of plump red boulders, and then pushed on to create a row of imaginary sentinels that rose to throw ghostly shadows against a nearby parapet.

The place conjured up one of those unexpected déjà vu moments, promising a memory that doesn't quite form. The setting was an ideal spot to mull over my plans. After the long, pressured drive from Delhi, I decided to set aside all concerns for time. I would relax here till dusk to greet the first rising stars before heading back down the trail. Atmaraj would be fine; there was water and plenty of snacks in the trunk. As the temperature started to drop, an occasional stone would complain with a crack. With the rise of heat slowing, the wind shifted to a whisper. The untroubled serenity was entrancing. Along the outer wall, the flights of hundreds of long-tailed swallows performed in-sync spirals in the now softer upsurges of warm air. Their airborne tricks so charmed me, I soon lost myself in that euphoric allure where nature summons the soul to share in her penchant for inventive play. Maybe it was merely my forgotten sense of time or the calling expanse of the distant landscape that seemed to stretch on forever, but for some reason a hint of nostalgia swept over me, quietly rekindling my memory of the fondness that I had once held for my past-life friend, Krishnalila.

That had to be it! Krishnalila. An instant later, I glimpsed myself standing on a hillside above a rocky desert oasis; below was a small ashram nestled up against a rocky bluff. Krishnalila was somewhere nearby in the Rajasthan desert! Of course. My earlier vision now made sense! For some reason, the masters wanted me to find him.

Fired up with enthusiasm, I barreled down the mountain. By the time I reached the car, reality had set in. Without any idea of where to begin, how could we find Krishnalila in this enormous desert and amid the grueling heat?

3

JJ

It appeared that we'd run down another dead end.
I was about to thank the men and head back to the car
when a short elderly man wearing a sleeveless, orange,
oil-stained T-shirt
pushed his way to the front.
Raising an arthritic arm, he pointed with bent fingers
to a little shack down the road—
the shack closest to the camel.

Too hot to sleep, the night passed slow and uncomfortable. The heat wasn't the only reason I couldn't sleep—I wrestled with a foreboding sense that had dogged me ever since I had read the letter in Delhi. Not yet convinced that I shouldn't be concerned about some kind of threat, and for lack of a solution, I decided to divert my concerns to the greater task that now loomed before me—one laden with a daunting uncertainty.

There was so little to go on to help me find Krishnalila—nothing more than a brief mental flash of an oasis and a feeling that had been strong enough to convince me he was somewhere nearby. Sudden and strong urges such as this weren't new to me. Most often they panned out, though not always, and this could be one of those times. I was willing to accept the possibility that I had misread the vision, but I was determined to at least try. If nothing else, I earnestly believed I was exactly where the masters wanted me to be.

I was aware of the potential dangers ahead. Driving through the desert backcountry when the temperatures were so extreme seemed foolhardy. When I told Atmaraj about my plan to search this southern part of the desert, he offered me little more than a discouraging scowl. His plan had been to pass through the hottest stretches of the desert as quickly as possible, searching for relief from the heat in the cities along the way. After treating him to an especially fine breakfast at my hotel, he found his adventurous side and agreed to give it his best. We loaded up the car with an ice chest and an assortment of supplies and headed north.

We explored a wide diversity of sandy, potholed country roads, most eventually fading to dust or simply coming to an abrupt end. Making our search all the more difficult, the previous rainy season had given rise to a web of flash floods that had laid waste to most of the backroad bridges. By midafternoon, Atmaraj's sense of adventure began to wane. After hours of searching the hot barren landscape, he slipped into an emotional vortex, particularly after changing a flat tire, which gave us no spare in risky territory. Atmaraj channeled his edginess into any excuse to complain. Specifically, he bemoaned the ongoing quarrels with his boss who had chosen to overlook the aged and worn condition of his car. Most of the other drivers in his company had been issued newer ones.

Our white '68 Ambassador diesel was chock-full of that kind of pre-high-tech personality reminiscent of an old Bogart movie. This particular Ambassador had been embellished with an Eastern flavor. Beneath a glitzy gold tassel hanging from the rearview mirror, a small white Nandi bull was glued to the faded dashboard, blessing our view with a gaudy charm. Next to Nandi, the head of a colorful spring-necked Krishna rocked in tempo to the ticks and rattles of the straining air conditioner.

"In all sincerity," I interjected, "I really like this car."

But he wouldn't have it. "Too old, too noisy!" He grumbled. "I should be driving a Bolero or one of those sky-roof Toyotas like the other drivers have!"

I decided to let it be. Soon Atmaraj began to purposely miss fewer potholes. Having to repeatedly brace myself, I also became increasingly weary. But just when we were about to turn back, a rundown little village, built haphazardly up against a mirage-like hillside, sprang into view.

Nudging Atmaraj's arm, I suggested, "Maybe we'll find some information here—maybe a clue, something. Let's give it a try."

It crossed my mind that I might have been wrong about his name. Krishnalila was the name I had once known him by. Or was it? I wasn't entirely sure. We'd already asked more than a dozen times using that name—at roadside teahouses, with goat herders and indigenes walking along the road, even with a stoned baba in the fork of an old shade tree—but each inquiry ended in vain. It didn't seem logical that he'd still use Krishnalila, but it was the only name I had to go on. And there had to be a reason I had heard it. Although earlier in the day another one came to me: Baba Vishram. My thoughts had been drifting, my mind dazed by the bland landscape stretching on and on into nowhere, when it struck me like lightning, catching me completely unaware. Once the name Baba Vishram landed, it stayed with me, buzzing behind my thoughts like a fly caught in a bowl of honey. However, like my other thoughts, the name was extinguished the moment we stepped out of the comfort of our car's air conditioning and we were engulfed in a blast of scorching desert heat. Not good, I thought to myself.

Atmaraj had managed his misgivings admirably but now, tapping a dusty thermometer glued to the cracked side-view mirror, his face clearly betrayed him. And rightfully so. In a pained tone he declared, "Forty-five degrees Celsius, sir." The word *sir* coming off more like a question than a report. This level of heat was dangerous.

I understood his alarm. It seemed ludicrous to travel the desert like this, so far off the beaten path, with no spare tire to boot. Few would have been foolish enough to travel the desert back roads in this extreme heat.

"Alright," I said, "This is our last stop. Then we'll head back and find an air-conditioned hotel—one with a pool!"

In front of us stood a patched together row of broken-down repair shops. Most were assembled from a mishmash of rust-tarnished storage containers. A few were open-ended, the rest fitted with awkwardly mounted wooden doors. Warped cardboard, stained brown from the sun, was layered beneath frayed plastic tarps that canopied a haphazard collection of metal poles and crooked wooden posts. Resting beside the huts was a graveyard for discarded auto parts, mostly tires and old engine blocks—all half-buried amid a bunch of rusty, red oil barrels. Closer to the road, under a flimsy canopy that shaded an open-air counter that belonged to a desolate tea stand, three men sat like melting candles on a rickety collection of chairs. But something else caught my attention. Farther up the road, a camel rested on his belly beneath a pair of sunburnt shade trees.

Just outside the tea stand, a short, stiff-necked man with a leathery face came out of the shade to greet us. He pulled a worn-looking glass bottle of Coke from an eroded, dust-covered Pepsi machine. Using an opener tied to the machine's side, he peeled back its cap, wiped some sand off its neck with his shirtsleeve, and handed it to me. I hesitated but accepted, hoping my willingness to buy something might open a door to some information. A broken-toothed smile spread across his face, forcing a pair of dimples to recede into his bristly cheeks. The abrasive look and texture of the bottle gave it away—a bootleg refill. One appalling sip and my suspicions were realized. Its unbearably warm syrupy-sweet aftertaste compelled me to make a second mistake—to try washing the taste away with what turned out to be an even more acrid lime soda. I diplomatically handed both bottles to Atmaraj, who far less tactfully poured them out into the sand. He and the old man exchanged a few testy protests in the local dialect.

Curiosity had persuaded a few more men to come out of their slumber. No doubt these fellows rarely saw a fair-haired foreigner stop here, if ever. Within a few minutes, eight men braved the heat and gathered around. Atmaraj hit it off straightaway—with everyone except the scowling old soda man. Aside from one bashful fellow, wearing nothing more than a dusty pair of scruffy black slacks, each of the remaining men came forward to ask me the same question: "Where from?" Apparently everyone wanted his own answer.

After ordering a decent-tasting chai, I asked about an oasis and a man named Krishnalila, and for the first time tried out the name Baba Vishram. No one responded. An awkward collection of stares hung in the air. I looked at Atmaraj; he didn't seem the least bit surprised. Annoyingly, he offered me a smug glower to tell me I undoubtedly appeared a bit zany, and not just to him.

It appeared that we'd run down another dead end. I was about to thank the men and head back to the car when a short, elderly man wearing a sleeveless, orange, oil-stained T-shirt pushed his way to the front. Raising an arthritic arm, he pointed with bent fingers to a little shack down the road—the shack closest to the camel.

Atmaraj interpreted: "He says . . . maybe that family can help. They're part of an old desert clan."

Just outside the shack was a dust-covered little boy, no older than three, entirely oblivious to my arrival. He sat cross-legged in the sand, stacking a collection of small, red clay stones into an old, frayed car tire. He wore an undersized T-shirt and no pants, fully rapt in his play. Inside the shade of the shack's front door stood a young girl wearing a tattered red dress and orange blouse, her face airing an expression of contentment as she worked on braiding a strip of multicolored cloth that was tied to a rusty nail in the wall. Unlike her younger brother, the moment she saw me her face suddenly transformed into wide-eyed uncertainty. A younger girl came running up to a small torn screen window and then ducked back out of view the instant our eyes met. A few seconds later, one of her shiny brown eyes appeared through a small knothole in the wall. Before I could say anything to the older girl, the hurried movements of a young boy, maybe eleven years old, caught my attention.

Running excitedly down a trash-littered hillside, still fifty feet away, he called out in excellent English, "Hello sir, hello sir . . . where you from?" Once he came closer, I answered. "America! I live beside the Pacific Ocean, near Canada."

"Very nice hair, sir. Long hair, long life." I fought the urge to laugh—I'd already heard the line a half dozen times since coming to India. And while it wasn't all that long, it was apparently long enough and blond enough to stand out as a novelty where black and henna red were the norm.

Out of breath, the boy shot me his hand, fingers spread wide. "My name is JJ."

I shook his hand. "JJ. What do the *J*s stand for?" I asked.

A brief look of confusion crossed his face. After a quick tilt of his head, he pointed to his chest, "My name is JJ, sir!" Holding up two fingers, he slowly added, "Two *J*s, sir!"

"A nickname?" I asked. He didn't answer.

His sparkling dark eyes beamed with the purity of an unspoiled life. Shiny black hair framed his delicate features and narrow copper face. The tails of his oversized checkered shirt hung low over his knee-frayed blue jeans rolled up at the cuffs. His clothes were clearly secondhand but clean. A small, colorful beaded necklace—red, blue, and black—along with the way he combed his hair told me he cared about his looks.

I asked to speak with his parents. He said they had left on a pilgrimage—a Hanuman *Yatra*. He told me that as a part of their devotional piety, they had opted to leave their camel behind and travel on foot.

"So whom can I speak with?" I asked. "I'm looking for some information concerning someone living out there in the desert."

"I am boss now!" he declared, grinning proudly. "You can ask me!"

"You speak pretty good English!" I said. He looked pleased.

He told me he had learned English working as a part-time camel boy in a nearby resort. He was the only working member of his household. Work was scarce. His father often left to find jobs in the Jodhpur outskirts but at present was unemployed.

I asked JJ if he had ever heard of someone named Krishnalila living in an oasis somewhere nearby. He didn't answer.

I asked a second time and again he didn't answer.

I glanced at Atmaraj, "Do you think he understood my question?"

I turned back to JJ. "Do you know where an oasis is—an oasis where a holy man is living, could be a baba? His name is Krishnalila."

"Oasis?" he asked.

I asked Atmaraj, "Can you help? I think he doesn't know the meaning of the word *oasis*."

Atmaraj interjected: "*Azara!*"

JJ nodded. "Ah, azara!" Instead of answering my question, he asked, "You want rent my camel? I can rent you camel ride—very good price!"

I looked over at the camel resting on its belly in the shade. "A bit too hot for that right now, JJ." I repeated my question: "Krishnalila. Have you heard of this holy man living in a nearby azara?"

"Yes sir," he said. "I give good price—you rent camel?"

"What?" I asked. "Did I hear you correctly? Did you just say yes, you know of a holy man in the desert? Or did you mean yes, you understood me?"

"Yes, man in desert, sir! You want rent camel? Sir, you can please tell me your name? Then you rent camel ride?"

I shifted back to Atmaraj. "I think he just told me he knows!"

Atmaraj was flush with disbelief, as if his waning lack of enthusiasm had slapped him in the face.

"Atmaraj," I asked, "he did say yes, didn't he?" He asked JJ in Hindi. With another minor tilt of his head, JJ answered, "*Ji-han!*"

Atmaraj's palms turned up in wonder. "Yes, sir, I believe he did!"

Stunned, it took me another moment to fully gather my thoughts. "JJ, this is *really* good news that you've heard of him." I looked over to the camel. "I'm not sure yet about renting your camel. But I might if Krishnalila's azara is nearby. Is it far? Can you and your camel take me there?"

After excitedly assuring me he knew where the azara was, and that he could indeed take me there, events transpired quickly. He told me it wasn't possible to go there in just one day. It would likely take one and a half, possibly two days.

I asked him if he could leave his home that long, and if so, who would care for his sisters and his little brother. He assured me that his oldest sister and one of the community members would, and then he did his best to convince me we should leave as soon as possible to take advantage of the cooling hours. I agreed.

While Atmaraj and I made a plan to reconnect after a few days, I garnered out what supplies I might need from the trunk of the car. JJ ran off to speak with the neighboring elders, returning with a beam of excitement.

"They watch my house, brother, and sisters. We can go now!"

4

A SHADOW

My mind was reeling,
hunting frantically for an explanation.
It has to be this thing, this creature, I told myself.
Somehow it was manipulating my thoughts.
But what, or who, can do that?

While I was adjusting my body to the shape of the saddle, JJ prodded the camel to his feet. After a final tweak to my stirrups, JJ, agile as a monkey, climbed up behind me on the saddle's second tier. Easing up the reins, he barked a command, gave the camel a nudging kick, and we were off.

I had packed sparingly, bringing only a small amount of food and just enough water to last a few days. I questioned if I should have packed more when I noticed that JJ had brought even less: no more than a small plastic bottle and a half-eaten pack of Bubbaloo gum. My concern lessened when he stood up in the saddle to pluck a few plums from a nearby tree. This desert wasteland was foreign to me—harsh and threatening—but to JJ it was home.

I had my misgivings; it seemed foolish to ride out into the desert like this, and JJ was just a boy. But I nonetheless had a strong sense that he knew how to get along. He had my trust.

Providence has a way of showing up when least expected. This sudden jaunt into the desert didn't leave much room for planning. All I had going was a subtle sense that this had to be right, so it was vital that I held to that feeling and not let anything slide by unnoticed.

Fortunately, since my arrival in India, each new day fell into place like the turn of a tumbler. I still had to listen carefully, but with every new step my sensitivities seemed to heighten. The key was to give them no resistance, to yield to their urge, their pace, their offer.

For the first hour we rode in near silence, the only sounds being the camel's grunts, the soft sigh of sand bristling over the desert floor, and JJ's occasional commands: "Billy!" (the camel's name) and a goading, "Eh, eh."

Little by little, as the sun began to sink toward the hazy, dust-burdened skyline, JJ's confidence in navigating our way seemed to wane. On the crown of a small hill, JJ brought Billy to a halt. He hesitated, looked down as if he wasn't sure of what to say, and then in his cracked, preadolescent voice, JJ confessed.

"I not sure, sir. Not sure where holy man live." He pointed hesitantly toward a distant set of hills and said in a manner that sounded like something stuck between asking and affirming, "Maybe that way?"

"I can't say I'm surprised," I replied. JJ avoided eye contact. "It's fine," I said. "We've made a commitment to do this. It's still possible—we might yet find the azara!"

JJ's eyes brightened. He started to respond, but I didn't really hear it. I was suddenly distracted. A sense of uneasiness washed over me. Instinctively I stood up in my stirrups and scanned the horizon behind us. With the exception of a few withered brown shrubs and Billy's footprints trailing off into a blur, everything appeared utterly lifeless. And while nothing indicated a reason for concern, I nonetheless felt an undeniable sense that something was amiss. I was about to ask JJ if he felt it too, when he worriedly interjected, "You angry with me, sir?"

I scanned the horizon again, this time more carefully in every direction. *Was it behind us, ahead, or was I just imagining it?*

"No," I answered. "Really, JJ, I'm not angry! If you think it's that way," I said, nodding in the direction he'd previously pointed to, "then let's go that way."

JJ broke into an endearing smile. His eyes glistened with sunlight; his spark of enthusiasm had returned. In that brief moment, he reminded me of long ago, when as a child I too believed a little hope and a good start was enough to make things happen.

We left all vegetation behind and descended the sandy side of the hill, entering a sea of wavelike dunes that seemed to indicate we were now in the true desert. Billy's feet dug deep into the soft sand—a bit like riding on a cloud. But there was something else to be attentive to now. Our light was fading. Soon it would be pointless to continue on.

"We should look for a place to camp, somewhere with a little cover," I said. JJ agreed.

It wasn't long—less than one hour—when we came across a clustered rock landmass that floated on the sand like a boulder island. In the distance it had the appearance of a small city. We'd already passed a number of smaller clusters, but this was by far the most promising. Racing against the fading light, we rushed to circumnavigate its perimeter, searching for some kind of an enclosure—ideally a recessed hollow to shelter us from the rising winds. Mission in hand, JJ impulsively passed me the reins, slid down the camel's back, and charged ahead, his feet kicking up sand as he ran. I quickly realized that managing Billy wasn't much different than handling a horse. I followed JJ's footsteps to where he had disappeared behind a cluster of tall, wind-sculpted boulders.

A short distance ahead, JJ reappeared. "Sir! Sir!" he yelled. "Maybe here? Come look, maybe here?" Too enthused to wait, he darted back out of view.

I dismounted to lead Billy between two bulbous-shaped rocks into a partly shaded patch of earth, encircled in a perimeter of smaller rocks and diverging passageways. JJ was standing in the mouth of a narrow cave, wearing a heroic grin. The cave's interior ran about ten meters back under a bulky stack of red dolomite boulders.

Despite its obvious advantage as a shelter and JJ's enthusiasm, I wasn't entirely convinced. My previous sense of uneasiness had stayed with me. Prompted by that lingering apprehension, I wasn't yet certain a cave with only one way in and out was a good idea. I considered setting up camp just outside the entrance, under the stars, and using the cave only if needed. But that plan was blown away by the first burst of stinging sand that whipped around our ankles—there would be no sleeping in that.

JJ wrenched free a half-buried branch and waved it wide-eyed above his head. "To use in cave. Look for snake, maybe scorpion!"

Our search unearthed nothing more fearsome than a few homely lizards and the dusty scent of dry earth. JJ attended to Billy while, for the sake of creating a camp-like ambiance, I set off to gather firewood. Once alone, my previous uneasiness surfaced again, even more intensely—too intensely to ignore. I scrambled up the tallest stack of boulders I could find, which gave me an extensive view in every direction. But again, I saw nothing. Except for a lone, scrawny desert rat scurrying along between the rocks and a pair of forlorn dust devils whirling aimlessly along the skyline, there simply wasn't anything to see. I did, however, spot a dead lightning-struck tree—perfect for our firewood.

The cave wasn't really a cave in the classic sense. It was more a crevice. Two massive boulders leaned in to touch each other, creating a skyward fissure that ran its distance and exposed a narrow section of star-lit sky. The fissure would work well as an escape for our smoke and sparks. The evening cooled, but only a little. Our fire was small but burned brightly.

We laid our blankets out near the farthest wall from the entrance and then relaxed back to share a leisurely dinner—two papayas and some curried rice that I'd brought along in a resealable baggie. JJ told me everything he could think of about his job as a camel boy and his burning desire to own a cell phone, and then he shared a few stories about his friends. As the light faded along with our fire, JJ listened drowsily with his head resting on my shoulder as I spun a tale about my wife, Ashayrah, whom I described as a golden-haired, green-eyed princess living on a magical emerald isle surrounded by a vast blue ocean on the other side of the world. With his last nod into sleep, he managed to murmur a few fading words, "I never see ocean, only desert." He fell asleep a few seconds later when I set his head down on his blanket.

The night had stolen away the last of the twilight; the dark was gripping. We were out of wood and only a few small glimmering embers still smoldered in the sand. I pushed a hand through the sand, searching for the edge of my blanket when, without warning, an abrupt scraping sound shot through the blackness from the side of the cave's entrance. The sound so startled me that an unnatural rush of adrenaline shot through my veins. The improbability of something or someone entering our cave unnoticed had caught me completely off guard.

My hands darted to my pockets searching for my lighter. Then I remembered—I'd stashed it in my daypack, now out of reach on a rock shelf next to the entrance. Conceivably, something had just fallen over, something that had been leaning against the wall, possibly my pack? But my intuition told me otherwise. Entirely unable to see, I stretched my hearing into the darkness. I could feel something there. Something or someone had definitely entered our cave! I froze into silence It seemed like the rational thing to do.

I calmed my breath to better hear. Something was obviously there; it was skulking quietly across the entrance side of the cave. My hands searched the sand for a rock, anything I might use as protection if something came close enough to threaten us. But no luck. I found nothing but handfuls of sand.

A split-second later, an even louder sound broke the silence, possibly the crack of a brittle stone under a foot. JJ jumped awake; he'd heard it too. He clutched my shirt tight-fisted, fearfully pressing his small frame into mine, his face so close I could feel his breath on my neck. We both jumped back when a large, ghostlike shadow darted across the cave entrance.

Any hope I had that this creature might be harmless was instantly dashed when a startling, deep snarl splintered the quiet. Little JJ pushed even harder into my ribs. The sound was unlike any animal I had ever heard. Judging by its depth and strength, it was unmistakably large. And without a doubt, large meant dangerous.

Cautiously, I used the back of my arm to push JJ behind me. He tugged nervously on my sleeve. I leaned in to let him whisper in my ear. "Sir, maybe leopard, maybe tiger; very bad, *very bad*!" His whisper nonetheless echoed glaringly loud off the hard rock walls.

I whispered back, "Shh . . . I don't know. I don't think so. Try not to make any sudden moves! And stay behind me!"

I knew that this couldn't be a leopard; leopards were now entirely confined to the higher elevation Aravalli and Vindhyan forests. And tigers had long ago gone extinct in this part of Rajasthan. And yet I couldn't completely rule out the possibility. That snarl clearly wasn't human, but neither did it sound anything like a big cat. For a brief moment a dim red glint flashed through the dark, maybe the dying glow of an ember reflected in a pair of eyes? The angle of the reflection affirmed an unnerving and surprising height. No, this clearly wasn't a cat. It was at least as tall as a large man!

A loud and sudden hiss cut through the air—deep and fierce. My muscles tensed, bracing for whatever might come next. But what came was effectively unreal: the temperature started to drop, the warmth shifting toward cold unbelievably fast. An eerie feeling swept over me—a feeling I hadn't felt for a very long time, not since I was a small child.

JJ was sobbing in fear, his warm tears falling on my shoulder then seemingly turning to ice in the cold. Between his sobs I could hear a whispered chant: "Om Ganesh, Om Siva, Shri Ram, Shri Ram." JJ was calling for help the only way he knew how.

I wanted to console him and possibly prepare him for an escape if an opportunity arose, but something alarmingly confusing was affecting my thoughts. I had expected a physical presence, something that made sense, but instead that something was invading my thoughts. It was an unexplainable sensation, like cold fingers digging into my mind. I tried to shake it loose, to pull my thoughts free, but it only got worse, more intense, followed by a string of strange new sensations. Bizarre sensory apparitions replaced reason with dark visions: images of demonic faces and grotesquely distorted bodies. The blackness around me was being transformed into a cauldron of horrors. Against my will I was being pulled into a formless abyss filled with hideous imaginings, and I was losing ground.

None of this made any sense! My mind was reeling, hunting frantically for an explanation. *It has to be this thing, this creature,* I told myself. Somehow it was manipulating my thoughts. *But what, or who, can do that?*

I knew I had to find a way to untangle myself from its influence, to somehow let it all pass through me. But my every effort was met with more intensity. My awareness shot back to JJ. I suddenly felt the rise of a new kind of fear, one I hadn't felt before. JJ needed me! A chilling voice drove its way into my thoughts: *How could you let this happen? You should have been more careful! This is your fault!*

Suddenly it dawned on me. These weren't my thoughts! They were a part of the assaulting influence, a weakening distraction meant to throw me more off balance. The entity meant to trap me in guilt, to cause me to obsess on how I could have let an innocent boy fall into danger, and precisely when I most needed my wits. And now my every attempt to break free from the relentless onslaught of darkening impressions was met with more confidence-thieving doubts that forced their way into my mind, assaulting me with an increasing torrent of horridly repulsive images strangely reminiscent of those that had haunted me between the ages of three and six, when the night had become a place to fear.

I remembered my utter sense of hopelessness when I had tried to tell my parents, or anyone else, about my experiences. Time and again I was told the same thing: "Those dreams aren't real. There's nothing to fear. It's just your imagination. They're just dreams." But they weren't just dreams. The nightmares weren't just nightmares. They were real. But no one had listened, no one had believed me, and no one had understood my cries for help. So I was left to endure my haunting alone.

Until one icy, full-moon night when it finally ended. My father was away working the night shift; the rest of my family was sound asleep. I had just started to dream, when out of the blue a gentle touch on my arm pulled me awake. Opening my eyes, I saw a silent figure standing over me. I instinctively pulled my blanket over my head, leaving just one eye uncovered. His body was luminous—a mysterious vision in the dark. An unearthly blue radiance silhouetted his form. The moonlight coming in through my bedroom window created just enough of a glow to light his eyes. At first I was afraid, but an unforgettable glimmer of kindness passed through those eyes, melting my fear away the instant they settled on mine. The love in his gaze filled every cell and fiber of my being with a gentle calm. I knew without a doubt he'd come to help! Although no words were spoken, I clearly heard his promise: "What those dark forces want from you can never be taken!"

From that day on, the attacks stopped. That was my first glimpse of one of the mysterious masters—an introduction that has stayed with me ever since.

Now, hiding in terror behind me, I recognized in JJ that same fear I had as a child. He was sobbing just as I once did, helpless against an unknown threat. I couldn't let this happen; I *wouldn't* let it happen!

My flashback lasted only a few seconds, but it was long enough for the creature to creep closer. Its blackness now loomed above us, much larger than a man. This thing wasn't like anything I'd ever come across. It was something malicious and dreadfully evil, something supernatural.

Its stabbing glare reached through the cloak of darkness, like a baleful claw, probing, taunting me with its approach, invoking a sense of predestined certainty. Something formidable and life changing, possibly even life ending, was about to occur. No matter the outcome, one thing was certain: I couldn't possibly meet this thing sitting down.

I shot up on my feet. JJ still clung to my shoulder, and I forced his hands free. I needed to be sure where he was, so I transferred his grip to my leg. I worked to find my balance, to come to terms with what was happening, or what was about to happen. I had to shake off the disbelief and see this thing for what it was: something beyond reason, something else. All the while, the nightmarish manipulations continued: the cave walls appeared to be missing and the darkness had transformed into a vast and ominous hollow—a dark pit that mysteriously echoed the sound of distant screams and malicious whisperings. I struggled to feel the earth beneath my feet. Completely foreign emotions, displaced and incoherent, crashed erratically through my every defense, urging me to run or act irrationally.

I needed something, something more—something I hadn't yet understood. Listening to my breath helped a little. Then stepping back from my thoughts came next. Finally, watching from that silent retreat behind the world of thoughts was the most helpful, allowing me to sort out some of what was mine and to cast aside much of what wasn't.

It was working. In a matter of seconds only two thoughts remained: *It is now completely up to me how this night will end* and *I have to protect JJ*. It was the second thought that gave me strength. I decided to hold on to that thought above all else.

As if to challenge my determination, another low throaty growl thundered in the darkness, crashing against my chest like an icy wave. It was a bone-chilling sound—promising an attack at any moment. It was close now! I took a step back, pushing JJ back with me.

The more I worked to witness my thoughts, to observe them, the more my senses returned, amplified with the flood of adrenaline that was now surging through my veins. I could feel exactly where this creature was. I wondered if it was aware that I was breaking free from its mysterious hold.

I sensed its attention moving to JJ, and JJ felt it too. He recoiled and then positioned himself to burst into a run. I hurriedly reached down to hold him back. There was nowhere to run! This creature was between the cave entrance and us, and I was all that stood between JJ and it. For JJ to run now could only end in disaster. I needed to keep him under control. His breathing was erratic. His fear was pushing him to the edge. JJ's best chance of coming through this unhurt was for him to stay behind me, as far out of harm's reach as possible. My toes spread wide, pushing through the sand to the rock floor. A flood of determination surged into my muscles and bones.

"JJ!" I commanded. "Stay put! Stay behind me!"

Recognizing JJ's vulnerability gave me an unyielding stream of fortitude. My own fear of harm had fallen aside. I made up my mind: I would do whatever I had to!

5

BEYOND THE SHADOW

I understood it now.
Coming here was necessary. The masters had clearly
intended it so!
They knew that providence had chosen to put JJ
and me together.
He and I were destined catalysts for each other.

Beyond the world we imagine as real rests a mysterious sea of endless possibility, a transcendental deep that acts as the womb for all manner of possibilities. These waters are the essential underside of our consciousness, our limitless resource, positioned to offer us our rightful bearing in life. But that bearing can only be realized when we genuinely agree to sacrifice our desires, abandon our guardedness, and capitulate to our natural inborn authenticity. In humility and with acceptance of what comes—rather than what is trained into us by some misguided design that promises us our place and belonging—our higher course and purpose can come to life. But we must first be willing to sacrifice all we have borrowed from life that we use to limit ourselves.

Brushing against danger and possible death wasn't altogether new to me. I had survived a storm at sea in nothing more than a small kayak, escaped the erupting path of a volcano, endured a serious car accident, and more. But each time a sobering moment arrived to inform me that my time hadn't yet come. Each time I came through the danger unscathed. And while this encounter now was so different—dark, surreal, defying all reason—that sobering moment had once again come. I knew without a doubt that my future was still ahead of me. But to make it real I needed something I hadn't yet come to—something more.

I searched my mind for a clue, for anything that might help me solve what was happening. What was this thing? Why was it threatening us? And how could I defend JJ and me in this blinding darkness?

I sensed that a physical attack was coming any second. But why did this creature first choose to assault me in a paranormal way? Again and again, in the midst of this consuming intensity, the master's message surfaced through my memory: *what those dark forces are after can never be taken from you.* But what couldn't be taken, and what hadn't I understood? Those words, repeating themselves over and over—they had to be the key! That memory had to mean something.

My thoughts shot back to my early life. As is true for most children, I struggled to adapt to surrounding social demands and conventions. For me, it was an ongoing battle between what was deemed socially normal and my unconventional ways of feeling and seeing. And, like all children, I very much wanted to fit in. So I did the logical thing: I hid from the world what occurred most naturally for me, in particular those visual and auditory experiences that others around me didn't seem to be aware of. But in the end, I surrendered too much of what made me unique. I wanted love and not to stand out, and bland acceptance was as close as I could come to it. I learned to adapt to the world's censures under the pretense of being someone I wasn't. In search of approval, and too naive to know better, I cast aside my given way of being and created a more suitable cover—a dubious decision that went on to shadow me for a long time thereafter.

That incongruity—that had to be it. I'd persistently overlooked it. I had succumbed to the self-repudiation of my innate nature! Unwittingly I had reacted to those early demands made on me by choosing to live at the edge of nonconformity. But that was a reaction, not a genuine resolution, and that wasn't enough. I hadn't fully reclaimed myself; traces of that adaptation were still with me.

Like a fog parting, I slowly came to realize that the solution to the dark riddle I now faced depended upon my willingness to step into myself more fully. When we are where we are supposed to be in life, we're on firm ground—on the foundation of who we're truly meant to be. Without that foundation we have no real strength; we're not in sync with our destined path or our innate power. After all these years the master's words finally made sense: what the darkness always wants, always hungers for but can never truly have, is the light of our divinely intended legitimacy, our right to be who we are born to be!

I understood it now. Coming here was necessary. The masters had clearly intended it so! They knew that providence had chosen to put JJ and me together. He and I were destined catalysts for each other. Unbeknownst to JJ, his innocence had awoken exactly what I needed to break through my last confines. His natural beauty had so touched my heart that he became the perfect inspiration to compel me forward, moving me to sacrifice an old mask and make room for the possible. The denials that had held me bound to my believed vulnerability had fallen away. I had found my advantage. It was clear—neither JJ nor I would perish here.

The darkness was no longer darkness. In essence, it never was. It had been necessary, a hidden grace that I needed for this all to come to a head.

I could feel the creature now in a way I couldn't before. The menace had lost its grip of control. My mind was sharper and my perceptions more focused. I could now feel and understand it, but the presence could no longer feel me. It had relied on the darkness and my missing sense of self and power. This thing, whatever it was, could still use brute force, but now the darkness had betrayed it and rendered it less sure! This confrontation was psychological now, and I had the advantage.

As I worked to calm my mind and steady my body, my intuitive sense was growing increasingly more perceptive. This loathsome being was the personification of fear itself, embodying the kind of obscuring gloom that preys on innocents everywhere. Like most bullies who would do harm to others, its motivations were related more to fear than a search for power. Consumed with fright and self-hatred, it loathed anyone who crossed its path. This was a specter, a phenomenon of misery that was neither fully in nor out of this world. Somehow it must have cultured the ability to move between the lighter and darker worlds at will.

I reached back and placed my hand firmly on JJ's shoulder. "Listen to me!" I said resolutely. "Pay very close attention! I want you to repeat these words!"

Trembling, JJ wept a whisper, "S-s-sir?"

"Repeat after me!" I said. "Try to repeat the words I'm going to say as closely as possible! Can you do that? Do you understand?"

"Yes, sir. Yes, sir. Say what you say."

"There's one more thing, JJ. If you understand what these words mean, believe that they're true! Trust their meaning! But first you have to stop crying! You have to reach inside yourself and find your strength. Can you do that?"

JJ mustered up and bravely swallowed back his fear. "Now, repeat my words!" I commanded.

The words hadn't fully formed yet, but I sensed them coming. To hear them well enough to say them out loud, I had to let every other thought fall silent. Under closed eyelids, the darkness turned to light. I heard what sounded very much like the faint ringing of a large bell—its droning tone fragmenting into a melodic cascade of secondary sounds that quickly formed into words. The words came to me in the language of the old rishis:

> *"Main Atmatattva ki Prakash men pratistha hoon"*
> I stand firm in the light of true Self-knowledge.
> *"Main Ekatvacaksu seh ikse hoon"*
> I see through the eye of oneness.
> *"Aham Vitamoha"*
> I am freed from the power of illusion.
> *"Aham Apahatapapman"*
> I am freed from the power of evil.
> *"Aham Vitabhi asmi—Soham"*
> I am fearless—I am that.
> *"Aham Shradhavitta—Soham"*

For I am possessed with faith—I am that.
"Tathaiva astu"
So it is!

Although time seemed of the essence, I repeated the words again. JJ's faith in his task was faultless. In his natural, humble, and uncomplicated innocence, he echoed back each word perfectly.

"Say them again," I said affirmatively, "and continue to repeat them!"

JJ's trembling had stopped; his fear had been replaced with something he could believe in. The verses were effective. His mind was focused, breaking him free from the creature's terror-inducing aggression. JJ's words, forming so pure and innocent, reverberated off the walls like an ancient memory of a long-forgotten time. With JJ managing his own efforts, I could now face this being with the same level of conviction.

Many years earlier, an attendee at one of my lectures asked me if angels were real. I told him that I trusted they were but added, "Maybe not in the modern biblical sense." While I had long believed we all have invisible helpers, to gain more clarity on the matter I decided to use my saumedhika drishti skills to find a more exacting answer. What I discovered in the process was the tonal mantra of an ageless angelic invocation, seemingly Egyptian in its origin. I felt strongly compelled to apply this invocation now. First I chanted it mentally, and then I let it arise fully in the silence. It then seemed to rise up by itself to stream audibly over JJ's words.

"Aumon-ahu-Rapha'yea,
Aumon-ahu-Rapha'yea,
Aumon-ahu-Rapha'yea."

After three rounds of chanting, something I hadn't anticipated came about: a distinctive high-pitched tone started to fill the space beneath our chants—choir-like, though not so anthropic.

A pained shriek leapt out of the creature, betraying an excruciating air of revulsion and anger. A moment later, farther back in the cave, a scraping sound moved over the sandy gravel—a clear sign that the creature had pulled back. Through the corner of my left eye I glimpsed a vaguely luminous flicker. To the right, a second shimmer appeared. Simultaneously three similar lights sparkled in and out above our heads. Within the span of seconds, these mysterious glimmers became considerably brighter and then grew to be nearly human in size. Their shine became less subtle with each repeated invocation. Delicate red and gold particles glistened like dancing stars throughout the forms. JJ stopped chanting and rose to his knees.

I've seen similar apparitions before but never so bright or as distinct. They had always appeared vaguer and far more etheric, almost too subtle to see for more than a few seconds at a time. It was extremely rare to find anyone else who could also see them. JJ obviously could. The subtle self-luminosity of this sort of phenomenon rarely lent itself to the common eye. JJ's hand had found mine; he'd become more confident, believing that something powerful and wondrous had finally come to our aid.

Frustrated and unsure, the creature seemed to be slithering farther back across the entry side of the cave. The tide had turned. The icy cold had relinquished its hold and the air became more bearable. For the first time, I was able to sense the being's wretched and lonely battle. At some point in the distant past, it had escaped its ghostly world and manifested a physical form. As a result, it became an unwitting casualty of its own lust. Deep inside it, there had to be a glimmer of a lost soul. I felt its torment driven by a burning desire to find an end. Soon the full extent of this creature's pathetic existence became apparent. In place of fear, my heart moved to compassion.

There was no longer any doubt that it could sense my ability to see it. A cold, blood-curdling scream fractured the dark, a sound so dreadful it literally caused the boulders of our cave to vibrate. The shimmering presence of the five light forms, the chanting, and my ability to see the creature—combined with its own deepening sense of uncertainty—had crushed its resolve. It had succumbed to its fear rather than actualizing its physical strength. The being had lost its conviction and was now confronted with its own misery and self-hatred.

Barely a moment later, a gruff hiss gave way to a sudden whoosh of the last cold air rushing out of the cave.

The lights vanished almost instantly. All that remained was the reassuring sound of two people breathing and the natural peace that rests in a tranquil night. JJ rose to his feet and wrapped his arms around my waist. We listened in silence as the fright faded into the past. It was over.

6

THE AZARA

My mouth had gone dry and my browned skin
was turning red.
The heat beat down mercilessly.
Billy labored his way up a last scorched,
sage-covered hillside.
Cresting its summit, JJ impulsively yanked back on the reins.
For the moment, we sat in silence. There it was!

The night had left me physically bushed, but I was too stimulated to sleep. JJ fell asleep right away just inside the cave entrance. I chose to settle into a small, wind-carved hollow outside of the entrance that faced into the desert and open sky, an ideal vantage from where I could watch over JJ and consider carefully what had happened. My senses were clearer, freed of the drawn-out burden from my child-hood adaptations. I had shed a worn-out skin, allowing me to awaken a long-absent part of me. What had previously been separated into inner and outer realms now seemed to overlap as one.

At the first sign of dawn, the evening wind settled into a gentler breeze. An occasional drift of sand would sigh softly between the rocks. Pen in hand, I considered what to record in my journal. I heard something stir and spotted JJ standing motionless and sleepy-eyed in the cave entrance. Stepping from inside its dusky shadow, he plodded over to toss his gangly thin arms around my neck and then hold on, just long enough to make his point. We were now the best of friends. He darted off to check on Billy, who was tethered in a small stone alcove less than ten meters away.

Earlier, when I checked on Billy, he was missing from where we'd tied him to a bramble of thick roots. I found him a short distance away, resting contentedly on his belly. He had pulled free the fractured stump he was fastened to, plowing a groove into the sand, apparently spooked by the night's events. No need to tell JJ; I decided to let him find Billy returned to the alcove, with only the stump missing.

The morning sun surfaced through the distance like a gossamer-feathered angel. A thin spread of clouds had transformed the skyline into rose-colored wings. JJ had a befuddled look on his face when he returned but said nothing about Billy's new location. While JJ quietly watched the sun and wind turn the dune-topped sands into a sea of ghostly waves, I just as quietly studied his youthful profile. The night was there in his face; it had changed him, no doubt maturing him a bit.

"JJ," I asked, "have you thought about it, which way we should go?"

With a boyish shrug of his shoulders, he pointed reservedly. "I think maybe that way." Just then our eyes were drawn skyward to the soft swoosh of wings. A pair of white egrets flew overhead, followed by a third straggler.

"Finally, a sign!" I declared. "Where do you think they're headed?"

"To azara!" he exclaimed.

However, with each passing hour JJ looked more and more disheartened. He was quietly coming to terms with the inevitable: our water had dwindled and our food was gone. We were near the point where we'd have to turn around. Except I wasn't convinced. There was yet a glimmer of something in the air.

"Let's give it a little longer, another hour," I suggested. "At least then we'll know we've given it our best."

The expression on JJ's face told me he was beginning to feel he'd failed me. To lift his mood I sang an altered version of that old Dewey Bunnell tune: "I've been to the desert on a camel named Billy; it was good to get out of the rain. Lah, lah, lah . . . " Having forgotten most of the lyrics, I hummed the greater part, giving JJ his chance to jump in, which he did with a zestfully animated Bollywood version. He had taken the bait. For the time being, everything was fine.

It wasn't long before the sun was straight up and too hot. I was melting in the saddle, while JJ the musical desert boy rocked on. My mouth had gone dry and my browned skin was turning red. The heat beat down mercilessly. Billy labored his way up a last scorched, sage-covered hillside. Cresting its summit, JJ impulsively yanked back on the reins. For the moment, we sat in silence. There it was! A hundred meters below, on the shady side of a rocky knoll, a whitewashed bat-and-board house surrounded on either side with a pair of rustic brown shacks.

Billy burst into a downhill run. Maybe it was the smell of water or the sight of two camels lounging in the shade. Whatever it was, flying downhill at that speed was unsettling. Struggling to reclaim our balance, JJ and I heaved back hard on the reins. We came to an awkwardly clumsy stop just inside the compound's front entry.

A group of three men came rushing out of the main house, all looking a bit alarmed. Even from afar I recognized the character and spirit of the man in the middle. It had to be him. Too charged up to wait, I hastily slid down the saddle, igniting a prickly surge up my legs the moment my feet hit the ground. I pushed it aside and yelled out, "Krishnalila!"

For a moment the man hesitated and then transformed his look of surprise into a welcoming smile. "Yes, yes! Welcome, welcome," he answered. "We've been awaiting your arrival!"

The burden of years weighed in his stride. He looked much older than I had envisioned. I cupped his frail thin hands in mine. "It's really you!" I said. "You were expecting us?"

"Yes!" he answered. "Does that surprise you?"

"A little. I wasn't sure you would even recognize me, or even if I—"

"If you would find me?" he interjected. "Well, yes, that did cross my mind." Krishnalila burst into laughter, smile lines spreading out from the corners of his eyes. "Here we have plenty of room to hear."

"To hear?" I asked.

"The winds. They are the desert's voice. One merely needs to learn how to listen."

A lavender gauze stole draped over the sun-parched skin of his lean shoulders. His thinning silver hair boasted a few surviving curls that arched fancifully back behind his elongated ears. Thick white eyebrows and a short well-groomed beard, darker around his lips, framed his aging face.

A small hand slipped into mine—JJ's. "And who are you?" Krishnalila asked.

I was surprised when JJ just stared back, unsure and puppyish, so unlike how I'd come to see him. *Maybe,* I thought, *a holy man presents a different kind of challenge.*

"JJ, this is Krishnalila," I said. I turned to Krishnalila. "And this young fellow is my guide, JJ."

"Forgive me," Krishnalila interjected. "To avoid any future confusion, you should know that while Krishnalila may once have been my name in another time, it's likely that you and I are the last to remember that name. My friends and devotees now know me as Maha Vishram."

"That explains it!" I said. "Earlier, before I found JJ, the name Baba Vishram kept running through my mind. Maha Vishram—Baba Vishram—it's pretty similar." But then I flashed on something else. I turned to JJ.

"JJ, when I asked you at your home if you knew a holy man named Krishnalila, you said yes. How did you . . ."

But JJ dodged my scrutiny, stepping out of my shadow with a sudden but modest bow. Krishnalila reached for his hand. "Come along now!" he said. "Let us escape this dreadful heat."

Following a short tour of the ashram's facilities, I washed up in a small spring-fed creek that pushed to the surface through a split in the rock in the underside of a cliff wall. Cooled off and much cleaner, I headed back to the main grounds where the sound of laughter drew me to a table set for three. JJ and Krishnalila were attending to their developing friendship, chatting up a storm under a saffron-colored canopy that flapped like a glowing wing beneath the sapphire sky.

Krishnalila waved me over with a relaxed gesture of his hand. "Come along, Aaravindha! Come join us. You must be hungry."

The air was filled with the aroma of potatoes, rice, and curried okra heaped high on a cluttered mismatch of thick white plates. Frail in his movement, Krishnalila picked up a large, daisy-printed teapot and with an unsteady hand poured me a chai. Perched on his knees, JJ had barely noticed my arrival, yet he somehow managed to hover attentive as a hawk over the okra. Giving the potatoes a nudge, Krishnalila asserted, "Eat, please eat!" Though instead of joining in, he laid his fork squarely down beside his plate.

While I piled some okra and rice on my plate, I felt Krishnalila's eyes quietly studying me. "JJ has told me a great deal about your experience, about the incident in the cave. It must have been quite an ordeal."

"He did?" I asked. JJ opted to give up his fork and started scooping up mouthfuls of rice with his hand.

"From what I have gathered, I believe this may have been a clash with the shadow world—the darker realm. Perhaps what you encountered was an *apadev* or a *pishaacha*? In your country, a—"

"A demon," I replied.

Unsure if he'd said too much, JJ pulled sheepishly back from his food and looked up to me for my response. "Don't worry," I said reassuringly. "Try some more okra."

Krishnalila leaned closer, his request for more information expressed firmly in his expression.

"It happened quite fast," I said. "And in total darkness, like a nightmare."

"But this wasn't a dream," he replied.

"No," I said, "it wasn't." I paused, searching for where to start.

"Aaravindha, please go on," he urged.

I hesitated. "Following the setup of our camp," I began, "in a cave not far from here, we spent the evening talking, relaxing, and telling a few stories. But once the fire died out, something entered our cave, something not human."

He said, "This demon, it wasn't merely an apparition or ghostlike. JJ told me it was physical and large, no doubt quite dangerous. I believe this was no ordinary demon. It may have been a *maantrik*, a very powerful devil. Yet you and JJ survived!"

I wanted to change the subject, to ask him more about his life, but Krishnalila insisted on learning more. Finally, after I had answered every question conceivable, Krishnalila fell silent. Meanwhile, JJ had found his own challenge: Should he reach for a second helping of food or should he wait for a sign that it was okay? I passed him the potatoes.

After a contemplative sip of chai, Krishnalila patted his lips with his napkin and then folded it into a precise square. "Aaravindha," he said. "I've heard a few stories; some told to me by my early teachers and some I learned through my university studies in Calcutta. A few involved the diabolical, and a few were nearly—"

"Unbelievable, like what we encountered," I added.

"Yes. But to me, your experience is believable. After all, this is India, a land filled with mysteries. I am inclined to believe that a maantrik must have come from a lower world. Such things cannot stay long in this realm. I sense it may also have fought with you in another time, perhaps long ago. Its previous defeat might have provoked it to seek revenge, causing it to cross over specifically to do you harm or hinder your path."

He looked down in thought, and then peered up pensively through his bushy eyebrows. "From what you have described, I might deduce that it came to do more than some harm; it had come to kill you. And yet it must also have feared you, particularly if you had defeated it once before. You see, my dear, something so formidable must be very powerful, and yet in the end it fled."

Recognizing my hesitation to talk about it, he extended his hand to my forearm. "Please forgive my directness. Perhaps I can share my thoughts more suitably."

"It's fine," I said. "I had come to that conclusion myself. I was just reflecting back through my life. I *had* sensed this thing once before, or something very much like it, as a child."

"As a child?" He cleared his throat in surprise. "We have many names for these creatures in India. Maantrik is the most notable, but more specifically it would be an *anupalala maantrik*, an especially sinister creature that hungers for the hearts of innocent children. Especially if that child has something important to offer the world."

"I would imagine that would be just about every child," I replied.

"Yes, but not every child threatens the authority that darkness has over much of this world. You are a teacher of knowledge that brightens the soul. Aaravindha, an anupalala maantrik is a very dangerous demon, indeed—very dangerous! You are truly fortunate to have escaped unharmed. This is not a forgiving beast, and it does not give up easily. Most likely when it could not pull you from this world as a child, it was drawn through its resentment to take vengeance. I cannot yet say why, but I sense you are protected. Perhaps you have a *sharmavarutha* shielding you."

"I'm not familiar with that term."

"It is an uncommon word that is no longer used. A term from ancient myths, a reference to a protective blessing often bestowed by a guardian. A safeguard you can call on when times are dire. This is also quite rare, quite rare. For such a thing to last, it would have to be imparted by a truly gifted master."

A spray of sand whipped across our legs and then swirled back, causing the canopy to flutter like a trapped bird. JJ darted off after his napkin and then returned to fasten it under the weight of his plate. No longer hungry, he ran off to explore. I nodded to Krishnalila.

"There's a great deal more to this world than meets the eye," I said. "We live out our lives between shadow and light. I believe we're constantly being tested, whether we know it or not."

Krishnalila added, "I agree completely, and most often these testing moments flurry by unseen. There is more at work around us that is invisible than visible. Considerably more!"

"These invisible influences for good or bad," I continued, "they seem to have an important role to play. And those creatures from the darker realms, they might also have a value, in a tempering way, if we survive them. The dark is more or less a natural polarity. The dark challenges us to grow, to discriminate for the right way. In effect, it forces us to our path."

"Aaravindha, as far as conventional humanity believes, these forces no longer exist."

"That's true. But certainly there will be a time when everyone will be pressed to remember, to listen again, and to step past their learned boundaries and reclaim what has been forgotten. I see light and dark playing themselves out all the time through people's lives. There are those who are waking up to it, who see it too; and there are some who are ready to go beyond the mainstream way of seeing, to reach past their programmed limits."

"But not many," he said. "Overall, our world has forgotten the old ways. For many, to remember is too difficult, particularly when it's so very convenient to explain the old ways away."

"But that comes at a steep price." I answered. "What was once considered necessary is now assigned to myth, restricted almost entirely to the sterile limits of our matter-of-fact sciences. There's no denying the good in our sciences, but our more personal sense of reality is too often reduced to a distinct or defended territory and then gated for the sake of our make-believe security."

Krishnalila added, "In my life, I've heard only a few stories of demons so powerful they could span the gap between the spirit world and our material world. People don't survive such encounters. You're quite fortunate, old friend—a heaven-sent blessing has kept you safe!"

Two words most caught my attention. "It's been a very long time since you've called me your old friend."

His face brimmed with gladness, "Yes, indeed. That we are! I do remember you, Aaravindha. We truly are old friends, I am sure of it! I believe we were predestined to meet again in this life. Perhaps there was an old promise."

7

DESCENDANTS OF THE SUN

"Aaravindha!" he said delightedly.
"You must realize that you are on a journey
into a very mysterious and highly sacred tradition.
Their legend reaches beyond our most ancient historical records
to the Devayuga, the most sacred of ages,
the epoch of the gods."

Krishnalila had repeatedly used the word *punyabhu* to refer to his azara. Punyabhu refers to holy ground where the sacred offers life its blessings through the earth. An ascetic siddha named Shri'Kantha Vasistha had been living in a small cave on the far end of the grounds when Krishnalila first arrived. A siddha is a highly advanced spiritual being of accomplished purity. Although many call themselves siddhas, a true one is quite rare. Krishnalila assured me that Shri'Kantha was one of those rarities. He had selected the cave for the same reason Krishnalila had chosen this area—its air of sacredness and its seclusion. The old siddha had planned to alchemically extend his lifespan here, hoping to win the extra time he needed to master eight mystical *vibhutis*—esoteric powers—that he believed would help him ascend into a higher astral world known as the *bhuvar loka*. His goal was to join the eighty thousand immortal siddhas that he believed presently inhabit the ethereal realms located between our sun and the seven-star constellation of Ursa Major.

Sensing my curiosity, Krishnalila asked me if I wished to visit the old siddha. He said he believed it was possible, but warned me that Shri'Kantha's many years as a recluse had made him oddly asocial.

Two of Krishnalila's students had once gone to visit the siddha unannounced and the old man responded by throwing rocks and chasing them off with his cane. Krishnalila told me that Shri'Kantha was especially protective of his alchemical secrets and advised me that if I chose to visit him I should be careful not to appear too interested.

Halfway out of his chair, Krishnalila paused in a faltering glance and then sat back down. "Please," he said, "before I go speak with the old man, may I ask you something personal about your journey? It's obvious your visit here isn't your final destination."

Every step on this journey—befriending JJ, our encounter in the cave, and now finding Krishnalila—had served some kind of purpose. While I now understood the purpose and meaning in meeting JJ, as well as our ordeal in the cave, I was still piecing together the possible motives the masters may have had in wanting me to find Krishnalila. Surely it had to be for more than just rekindling an old friendship.

I decided to share it all—to tell Krishnalila everything I knew or could remember about the Himalayan masters. I began with my childhood and past-life connections and then filled in as many details as possible. After a lengthy narrative, I told him about my two invitations: the one in the Delhi market so many years ago and the more recent one that had brought me back to India. I then told him I had lived in their hidden valley in a former time. When I shared my reasons for leaving the valley, which also led me to meet Krishnalila in that life, a glow of recognition spread across of his face.

"Aaravindha!" He broke in excitedly. "In that life I believe you were more than a friend; I believe you were also my teacher. Is that true?"

He lifted his hand haltingly. "No need to answer that!" he asserted. "I know it's true. I knew it the instant you touched my hands when you arrived here."

He nudged his chair a few centimeters closer. "You may find this of particular interest," he said. "When I was quite young, doing research in Orissa, I came across an especially intriguing shastra."

"A scripture?" I asked.

"Yes, quite an old one, dated to the early part of the twelfth century. I came across it entirely by chance. I found it sleeping in the dust amid a few other writings buried in a medieval monastery, from a time prior to the Mughal Empire. It had been penned under the hand of a *mahapandita*, a great spiritual scholar. It contained a rare description of an ancient lineage of masters. If my memory serves me correctly, I believe the mahapandita's name was Svarupacarya. Yes, yes that was it, Svarupacarya. I believe it may be one of the only accounts still in existence that points directly to this ageless tradition. This shastra was of particular interest to me because it echoed a story that my father's guru had once told me as a child, a story about a mystical Sampradya of Amartya."

I cut in. "Amartya?" This was the first time I had heard the term *Amartya* mentioned.

"Yes, Sampradya of Amartya—the Amartya tradition! One could also say *Amara* in place of *Amartya*. Classic Sanskrit, my dear. *Amara* can be translated as "imperishable." It is a term used to represent the enduring life of a mountain, or in this case a great master who has overcome the decay that leads to death. This text described these beings, identical in every way, to how my family guru had spoken of them. It named them as the ageless 'Descendants of the Sun: The Suryaparavara.'" He added, "A master of this tradition is an *amara'manushya*, an immortal being! Their mystique, the elusive enigma that sets them apart from other traditions, is that these great beings have overcome the greatest of all barriers—death itself!"

"Amara'manushya." I carefully repeated the words, savoring the sound of each letter. "So *Amartya* is plural for Amara?" I asked.

"Yes, Amartya relates to their combined tradition, but this can also be a bit misleading because when naming one, all are inferred. It would be correct to see Amartya as all rooted in one Being, one Supreme Being. It may be more suitable to refer to an amara'manushya as *amaravasu*, an illustrious master who has attained Supreme Being."

Krishnalila took a slow, measured sip of tea while looking up to the sky in search of a thought.

"Aaravindha!" he said delightedly. "You must realize that you are on a journey into a very mysterious and highly sacred tradition. Their legend reaches beyond our most ancient historical records to the Devayuga, the most sacred of ages, the epoch of the gods. For thousands of years the devout have searched for them. But rarely has anyone found them. To be invited has proven to be the only sure way. You are truly blessed, my friend! No, no, Aaravindha, we are both blessed! You see, my dear, my lifelong beliefs are now confirmed—these great masters do still exist!"

"Thank you, my dear, you have made an old man very happy." His dampened eyes glistened like stars. "This affirms the life path I had chosen for this life. In my youth I often dreamed of making a journey like this but couldn't find the means. Knowledge of these ancient masters is simply too rare and elusive; little knowledge of them exists—hard to find, even for an old scholar like me. When I tried to share my findings with my past gurus, they all offered me the same sad anecdote: 'Finding them is simply not possible!' But now you have reawakened what has always been in my heart. This is wonderful news, Aaravindha! No . . . it's fantastic, simply magnificent!"

A childlike expression suddenly claimed his face. "Do you believe one day that they will also call me?" he asked. His look then shifted to a look of sadness. "Ah, but I fear I am far too old to undertake such a journey. My years here are nearing their end. I can feel death calling me in my bones. No, for me it is too late; I can no longer make such a journey. Too late."

I wrapped my hands around his. "Krishnalila," I said, "I understand now why the masters wished for me to come this way. They know the sincerity in your heart! Despite your old age or whenever you might pass from this world, I know now as surely as I am sitting here that they *will* call you—if not in body, then in spirit. My coming here wasn't only meant that I should reconnect with you; it is also that I should pass this message on to you! To confirm your beliefs and to tell you to hold true to your faith. Krishnalila, they have been with you all along!"

Krishnalila pulled a hand free and wrapped it firmly around the back of my neck, then leaned in to kiss me on the cheek. A warm tear fell from his eyes.

In a whisper, he revealed, "I truly am blessed. I do believe when I have finished this life, they *will* come for me. They will guide me home!"

8

THE OLD SIDDHA

A few minutes later, in an age-cracked voice,
Shri'Kantha began a chant—a hauntingly melodic sound
strung together in a long sequence of esoteric mantras.
In the quiet, and with my eyes closed, I saw his words
turn to light
as they showered over me like a stream of liquid gold.

Krishnalila placed his hand on my shoulder, steadied himself, and then pushed to his feet. A short while after leaving to speak with Shri'Kantha, he returned bearing a telling smile. The old siddha had granted me a visit.

At the summit of a steep winding dirt path, I found Shri'Kantha sitting cross-legged atop a flat boulder, facing the desert landscape below. He wore nothing more than a tattered loincloth and a red rudraksha seed mala. He was small, petite like a child, loose-skinned and sinewy-thin. A wide, flat smile stretched from ear to ear. His eyes were dark, his face leathery-brown, and his thin, gray hair fell like a weighted cloud on his bone-thin shoulders.

He turned only a little, stiff-necked, to study my approach. The stare of his narrow, wrinkle-wrapped eyes came across stern and emotionless.

"Namaste!" I said.

He remained silent with no discernable change in his expression.

He turned back to his view of the desert. Five minutes passed in silence; he just kept staring, his steely-eyed focus reserved and unflinching.

Krishnalila was right; he definitely lacked social skills. I sat down beside him and then turned my gaze to share in his view. I could feel him staring at me through the corner of his eye, tracking my every move. I searched my thoughts for an alternative approach, something that might help ease the tension.

I decided to introduce myself. *"Meera naam Aaravindha hai,"* I said slowly.

He said nothing.

Then suddenly, without warning, he frog-leaped off his rock, scampered over to a small hole in a nearby stone wall, and crawled out of sight. I was about to leave when his head unexpectedly reemerged. With a slight wave of his hand he signaled for me to follow, then disappeared backward through the hole.

At the end of a short crawl, I entered a hollowed-out sandstone cavern. The cooler interior walls felt like sandpaper beneath my touch and smelled mildly of incense, sulfur, and damp earth. A ray of sunlight streamed in through a spatter of small cracks from above, creating just enough of a muted amber glow to keep me from tripping over a granite boulder. A few strides farther on, a single focused beam of light pierced the ceiling to strike the surface of a shallow pool of water, its reflection causing a bright reflected web to flicker across the low-hanging boulder above. A cool breeze filled the air with a hushed sigh. There was a deeper opening somewhere farther back in the dark.

The sudden touch of Shri'Kantha's long fingernails against the back of my arm gave me a jolt. But before I had a chance to say anything, he had already plunged up to his neck in the pool. The cave's dome dropped low over the water, allowing just enough room for his head to stay above it as he passed beneath the stone. Throwing aside my shirt and sandals, I followed like a child on a treasure hunt. The water felt instantly fresh and cool against my sunburned skin. A few steps over the sandy bottom, past the overhead squeeze, a second, larger cave opened up. The beam of sunlight that reflected ripples in the first cave now glowed turquoise in this side of the pool. The only other light in this part of the cave came from a thick, brown candle resting precariously on a rickety, wax-coated table.

Inviting me into his private inner chamber was an unexpected honor, especially considering Krishnalila's warning regarding the siddha's alchemical secrets. Mindful not to show too much curiosity, I waited at the edge of the pool for my eyes to adjust. The air smelled heavily of burnt sandalwood. Though dimly lit, I was still able to make out a series of glass jars filled with dried herbs stacked from small to large on a wooden shelf. Below the jars stood a long row of rusty silver canisters methodically arranged behind a large, burn-stained crucible that held a stone pestle.

Shri'Kantha was sitting across the cave, enveloped in a velvety stratum of incense smoke. The moment my eyes met his, he broke into his first real smile. His eyes sparkled with candlelight; his elfin grin saying, *Welcome to my secret world.* He pointed for me to sit on a reddish fabric he had laid over a small stone shelf. Still wordless, he closed his eyes and positioned his hands in a prayerlike mudra.

After a short wait, I decided to join him in his meditation and instantly sensed a strong pull into stillness.

A few minutes later, in an age-cracked voice, Shri'Kantha began a chant—a hauntingly melodic sound strung together in a long sequence of esoteric mantras. In the quiet, and with my eyes closed, I saw his words turn to light as they showered over me like a stream of liquid gold. Three-quarters of an hour passed before his chant came to an end.

I felt the touch of his hands on my feet. I popped open my eyes. He was kneeling directly in front of me. He carefully moved his touch to my knees and then my hands and then to my eyes, each touch accompanied with a different mantra. He tapped my hand, signaling me to extend my wrist, and then tied around it a three-colored string bracelet. He reached over to a small silver dish, dabbed a finger in a yellow paste and then a red powder, and pressed the colors to my forehead. After an unexpected and scratchy kiss higher on my forehead, he stood up and bowed, and then with a smile gestured for me to leave. He had given me what he'd intended. I thanked him for his gift and left in silence.

The chant continued to run through my mind as I walked back to the compound. The mantras he used suggested he had performed a *kavach*.

A kavach creates an energetic armor around the body that's meant to repel negative influences. I noticed that my previous exhaustion from lack of sleep had completely vanished.

In the morning, Krishnalila performed another kind of ceremony—a special sunrise puja intended to bless me with good fortune. He told me it would inspire good health and prosperity for my friends, family, and me.

Shortly after our departure, JJ timidly asked, "You ever come back to visit me?" With a worrisome look he added, "My family soon move to Jodhpur. Very big city—how you find me there?"

"One day we'll see each other again," I affirmed. "I found you before—I'll find you again!" Billy sprinted most of the way back to the village, cutting our riding time in half. My driver, Atmaraj, was waiting.

After sharing my heartfelt appreciation with JJ, I paid him three times his rental fee and said, "Maybe this will buy you your cell phone."

Leaving JJ behind was one of the most difficult goodbyes I've experienced. Looking back at him standing with his sister by his side, holding his little brother's hand, and with a solitary tear rolling down his cheek, tore at my heart.

But soon something else started to dominate my thoughts. I was now on my way to face my most demanding task—one I believed would surely push me to my limits! I was headed toward the Himalayan foothills, from where I would somehow have to find my way to the valley of the masters, a place so elusive it has stayed buried in a cloak of mystery for thousands of years. My only hope was that a guide would come to meet me. But I had no idea how that might happen.

9

A FORMIDABLE TASK

In this place where death and renewal merge in
sacred ceremony,
I opted to emulate what the devout around me were doing,
to raise my eyes to a higher purpose
and let the conditions that held me bound give way
to the present.

Atmaraj headed north through Jodhpur and then drove us on to the Taj Mahal in Agra. After spending a slow day touring its white marble halls, we headed northeast through the state of Madhya Pradesh until we arrived in Khajuraho, a city famous for its erotic Kama Sutra temples. In Khajuraho, I bid my driver farewell and booked a short flight to my route's final destination, Varanasi.

For the duration of my travels, my thoughts were repeatedly drawn to an imminent circumstance. I had begun to sense the inevitable—that meeting up with a guide might not occur. But to be sure, I chose to stay where I was for a few more days, to not make any hasty moves or leave prematurely.

I had originally intended to travel overnight by train from Varanasi to Darjeeling, and then up to the Himalayan borderlands by jeep. Once the roads came to an end, I hoped to trek by foot—surreptiously, if at all possible—into the lower eastern range. With the exception of slipping off into the mountains, traveling through Sikkim was fairly well arranged; I had my use permit and gear in hand. But during my flight to Varanasi, a bright-minded English woman who managed an Asian travel agency told me that this year's monsoons had washed away most of the roads north of Darjeeling, rendering my plans moot.

In Varanasi, the city's unexpected filth and stench gave me an ongoing low-grade headache and recurring waves of nausea. After a few days, I broke away from the city's main districts to discover Varanasi's better side: the Muslim silk district; the golden Vishwanath Temple; Sarnath, a hamlet in ruin where the Buddha delivered his first sermon after attaining enlightenment; and Varanasi's sunset fire pujas, performed on the steps of the Ganges. I kept myself active but was all the same troubled by a growing sense that I was being left to find my own way.

The task ahead was daunting—trekking without a defined destination through a mountain range that averaged six thousand meters in elevation and stretched over twenty-four hundred kilometers across India, Pakistan, Afghanistan, China, Bhutan, and Nepal. After three days of meditating, studying possible routes, and wishing a guide or another letter might come, I had worn my hope and maps to a wrinkled mess. But in the end I was drawn to a small section of my maps so intensely that I suspected that something out of my usual range of perception was affecting my search—possibly a less obvious message. On my fourth day, I decided to begin my journey.

I spent my last night in Varanasi on the Ganges. I hoped to avoid the riverbank Brahmins selling their blessings, the beggars searching for coin, or any other form of distraction. I wanted to be left alone to mull over the coming days and ponder my route and a possible entry into the mountains, and hopefully to tone down any lingering doubts. I couldn't afford to doubt myself now. I dressed as much as possible like a local to make myself as invisible as possible. I found my seat close to the river's shore and concealed myself inside a crowd of religious devotees—orange-shawled pandits and chanting sadhus. The marble steps of the Dashashwamedh Ghat felt cool and polished smooth beneath my bare feet. As the last trace of daylight slipped into darkness through the smoggy orange horizon, the tolling temple bells that neighbored the ghats echoed their ritual praises. Hundreds of flickering candle boats carrying secret prayers had been launched into the river's currents, setting off a shimmering ghostly glow inside the low drifts of funeral pyre smoke.

Five priests clad in red and gold silk swayed in unison to praise Siva, Surya, Agni, and Ganga, the river goddess. As they lifted their oblations of flowers, camphor, and burning *aarti* lamps toward the night's sky, I remembered Krishnalila's words: "For thousands of years, the devout have searched for them. But very rarely has anyone found them." Without a physical guide to show me the way, I'd face the same challenge. However, I wasn't searching for them out of ambition as so many had—I had been invited. Surely the masters would still help me in some way. I had spent a large part of my life learning to listen for my path. Now I would have to listen more deeply.

The route the masters had plotted out for me in the letter had brought me to Varanasi and, in a way, to this holy ghat. For thousands of years, the devout have come to the ghats in Varanasi to die. Or they have come here to find their way in life. Many believe the sacred undercurrent of this ghat inspires a new beginning, whether for the dying or the seeker. With no further word from the masters, I chose to believe that the means to this journey must already be in my hands. This is where they had sent me: the place one comes to find a new path—an appropriate end to my stay here.

In this place where death and renewal merge in sacred ceremony, I opted to emulate what the devout around me were doing, to raise my eyes to a higher purpose and let the conditions that held me bound give way to the present. Once, long ago, I had left the Himalayas behind. Something told me I still knew the way back. I had long believed that whether we are aware of it or not, we all know the way of our destiny, and its path becomes clearer when we're willing to listen humbly. I stretched my thoughts out to the mountains that I had been studying. Their charm felt so familiar.

I could see it now. The other influence that had called my eyes to that section of the map was a distant memory—a freer, more enduring part of my self. Images of snow-capped mountains, flowering meadows, and glacial brooks streamed through my mind. Yes, I was remembering.

I was so utterly engrossed in my inner world that I hadn't noticed the two chanting Brahmins who had taken it upon themselves to wash my feet with the holy water of the Ganges. As my eyes came back into focus, I was met with innocent smiles and glistening brown eyes. Both were young and notably pure of heart. Once they finished with their blessing, I impulsively reached back for my wallet to give them a small tithing, as is customary at these ghats. But as I made my offer, my hand was instantly turned back. One of the two young priests laid his hand on my arm and said, "No, sir, please no money. Not you, sir. No, sir." He then quietly withdrew backward with his companion, their heads bowing and hands taking the form of the prayer mudra. Whatever their reason for not accepting the tithing, I chose to see it as a positive sign, as an affirmation of my intentions.

The next morning I booked a flight that would bring me as near to my destination as possible. Within a few hours of landing, I hired a driver and began a long, bumpy jeep ride. Two days later, we came to an impasse. We had driven as far as the backcountry mountain roads would allow. The peaks that obstructed our progress were simply too high and dangerous to cross, even on foot. After an exhaustive search through our maps, and a long discussion about alternatives, I came to a conclusion: I needed a new plan.

I spent the next hour and a half sitting alone in the cool mountain drafts, searching through my maps and studying every possible way around or over this defiant stretch of peaks that loomed before me. In the end, I asked my driver to take me to the nearest climbable pass. He told me that it was a long distance off and was likely guarded by border patrols. Entry there would be prohibited. I argued that there had to be some way. He then confessed that there might be another option; he had a friend—a pilot—only a day's drive away. This friend had wanted to start a charter business, but for lack of funding his efforts failed to develop. He was penniless now, but for the right price he might be willing to help me out. As incredulous as it sounded, it had become my only conceivable option.

The pilot was a gruff and unkempt man and, as the driver had said, clearly down on his luck. He had a look to him that told me he wasn't the most scrupulous. I informed him of my intentions and offered him $300 to fly me over the border as far as possible in the direction that I hoped to go. Right away he came off stubbornly impervious to my request—a ploy to raise the ante. Once I doubled my offer, he snapped it up with a controlled grin, but his acceptance came with a warning. He told me that we'd be flying through restricted airspace, so I must never tell anyone of our arrangement.

To remain undetected, we flew perilously low over a number of lush green valleys and came hair-raisingly close to a few craggy peaks. After informing me we'd be landing on an abandoned British military airstrip, I asked if it was truly the farthest we could go.

He turned to me with a scowl. "No airports here!" he said. "You must be crazy, man! How you get back? No tourists here; no one to call if you get lost! You crazy!"

His reaction wasn't surprising. By any reasonable standard I must have come off as utterly reckless. There weren't any roads this far into the bush and no sure way back over the mountains we'd just crossed. His analysis of the situation was dead-on. If I were to become injured or lost, who would know? I'd simply disappear, alone and unseen. Barely out of the cockpit, the pilot throttled his plane back in the direction of legal airspace and disappeared.

I headed toward a small collection of pastures bordered with a cluster of shacks that I had spotted from the air just prior to landing. The fields looked planted and there was smoke coming from a couple of small rooftops; someone was living there. I found an overgrown path that pointed me in the right direction. After a mile, I found a larger trail that led directly to a small community—smaller than it looked from the air, with only a few sun-grayed and worn shacks. An old stalky woman and a young adolescent man watched me arrive, both showing an unmistakable expression of suspicion—outsiders rarely came here.

An elderly man sitting on a narrow porch rose out of a wooden rocking chair, paused for a moment, and then meandered over to greet me. Deeply carved wrinkles circumscribed his wind-worn face. A charcoal wool cap crowned his coarsely braided matte-gray hair.

His first effort to greet me came off unintelligible—probably a localized Tibetan dialect. I tried to tell him I couldn't understand him. The look on his face told me he didn't understand me either.

After a few efforts at using hand gestures, with an occasional English word thrown into his dialect, he and I both started to laugh. After sorting out our efforts, he managed to get across that a number of years ago his wife had either left or died. He chose to leave Lhasa and come to this remote outback, leaving behind his only trade as a Sherpa. That small bit of information was the best news I'd heard all day. With a little persuasion and the flash of a few rupees, he agreed to be my guide. He owned two ponies and a small donkey that we could ride and use to carry our supplies. Within a few short hours we were off, tracking a charcoal line I had scrawled down my map.

After a few days of travel, our communication developed into a kind of unspoken body language. But with each day farther into the bush, he seemed a bit more anxious. It wasn't long, barely a week of riding, before he refused to go any farther. He had traveled beyond his knowledge of the land and was growing increasingly concerned for our safety. Offering him more money proved fruitless. He was simply too fearful to go on, most likely because he saw the real dangers of trekking into a region this far removed from any village. He tried his best to turn me back, even going so far as to throw a small, indecipherable tantrum. He kept repeating the words, "*Nieyen kha tsha poh*," which I assumed represented some kind of warning. In the end, he had no other choice but to accept that I was going on with or without him.

10

A MESSENGER IN RED

In quiet resistance, a subtle nausea had gripped my gut.
But to not heed the council of someone who knew
these mountains
would be a reckless mistake.

The only people I had come across were now days behind: a family of nomadic goat herders who had laid claim to a ramshackle military outpost, likely a remnant of the 1962 border conflicts. On occasion I would come across some yaks or would spot flocks of blue sheep clinging to the higher, rocky crags. I traveled lighter and much faster than I had with the old Sherpa. I brought only a small amount of food. Mountain streams were plentiful, providing me with ample water. I supplemented my meals with a few edible herbs the Sherpa had shown me and a few others that were useful for making tea.

I had often trekked alone, even for weeks at a time. But this time around was wholly unique. Here in these remote mountains, nature's undisturbed harmony bestowed a kind of healing solace for the soul. The untouched beauty satisfied my heart with the slow serenity we've all but lost in our human-made worlds of concrete and steel. Its vestal charm and unflawed scenes, and the unfettered drift of uncounted hours, became a purifying balm.

Time had turned to a blur, a unified stream of unrestricted sovereignty. Some nights I sauntered along under the light of the moon. Other times I catnapped under the warming sun, arms and legs spread wide like a bird in flight. I shifted my familiar rhythms. When to sleep or when to wander no longer demarcated the end or beginning of a day. Daylight simply morphed into nightlight. Blue skies merely darkened to expose hidden moonbeams and star-studded imaginings. I moved in tempo to a broader natural order. When I had energy, I walked on. When I grew tired, I stopped to rest. Setting a goal of how many miles or how many hours seemed foreign here, as foreign as I likely appeared in my red jacket and shiny sunglasses to the occasional yak or musk deer.

I did my best to avoid trudging through the forests. Trekking without the benefit of a trail, I followed shallow, tumbled-stone streambeds, strolled through blooming knee-high meadows, and climbed over boulders and pebble-blanketed hillsides. Whenever a doubt would threaten to steal away my resolve or I found myself caught in a moment of uncertainty, I made it my discipline to stop. With closed eyes, I'd wait, sometimes for hours, until my inner sense of direction returned. I couldn't afford to be careless, not even a little. There was no deviating from the subtle urge that secretly called me on. It was all I had to rely on.

I had lost nearly twenty pounds since leaving Rajasthan, most of which had converted to air or muscle over the last week. The days were mostly sun-kissed, warm and golden. But higher up, the clear nights were chilling. My lungs grew a bit sore, but I hadn't yet shown any signs of altitude sickness. I set up my camp in lower elevations, in small valleys and meadows close to a water source. At higher altitudes, where every breath became an effort, I trekked slowly and carefully. My food was nearly gone; only a few wrinkled apples and a pair of protein bars remained. I rationed what there was and purified the stream water with my ultraviolet pen before drinking it. My legs were showing the worst wear. My feet and ankles ached nonstop. A slow, searing burn had taken hold of my hips and lower back, but my spirits stayed high.

I had been ascending steadily for the better part of the day. The cold was coming on; I had little reserve left in my stomach to keep me warm. With nightfall arriving, my only option was to hunker down and wait for the promise of a new day. Under the full white moon, the mountain breezes blew so cold they flushed my skin an icy pale. I pressed my body back into a small surround of split boulders where I fed a wind-sheltered fire one small piece of wood at a time until all I had left to burn were the last few pages of my maps.

Despite the cold, the beauty was mesmeric. At dusk the frosty surge of evening air had settled over the day's sun-warmed rocks to wet the landscape with a coat of dew. As the twilight faded and the moon rose into the sky, the dew crystallized into jagged ice blossoms that carpeted the otherwise bleak stone hillside with millions of tiny moonlit rainbows.

Too cold to sleep, I passed the time sending honeyed messages home to my beloved via angel mail. When the dawn finally arrived, my shivers started to give way. Under the starry sky, the mountains had looked like a horde of sleeping, indigo-hooded giants pressed shoulder to shoulder. But now the solar god had roused them into form, shaping them into flaming gold-gilded masterpieces. Ghostly blue mists lifted in oceanic waves at their base and then curled away in slow motion through a sinking cascade of shallow ravines. It was here, for the first time since I had entered these mountains, that my heart truly swelled with recognition. It was undeniable—I had once long ago sat in this exact spot.

The next stretch of passes proved especially challenging. The thin, cold air tested the limits of my every breath. Loose rock repeatedly gave way beneath my feet to challenge my strength and balance. My ankles were abraded and severely bruised. I transferred more weight to my arms and shoulders using two walking sticks, but it was now certain: I needed to rest. I needed some time and shelter to mend.

After laboring my way through a long series of boulder fields, I stumbled across a broader-than-usual trail. Not just another goat trail—there were human footprints mixed in. I followed it over a steep rise to an upward sweeping plateau. A few slanted rooftops stood out above the distant ridgeline. It appeared as if four people were standing on the plateau's forward rim. I decided to stay where I was, to catch my breath and gauge my prospects. By law I had no right to be here. I pondered the possibility of an official being this far removed in the mountains. The people had soon tripled in number, confirming my suspicion that they were aware of my approach.

I meandered in their direction but paused again a hundred meters out. For a few minutes no one moved. Then four men broke away from the group and started trudging down the hill. Once I was able to see their faces, I saw their smiles. Any tension I had previously sensed vanished in that instant.

The men were all dressed in short, hair-felted robes trimmed with tattered silk hems, cuffs, and collars. A banded white shirt collar stood out brightly against the burgundy robe of the leading man. A woven belt cinched each robe high around the waist. Cloth boots were laced into place over their pants. The men all had long black hair tied back in different ways. The youngest-looking man, thinner than the rest, wore a fur-felted hat with flaps drooping over the front and sides.

I called out, "Namaste!"

The two older men responded in kind, while the others hailed me with "*Tashi dalek!*" Everything else they said was beyond my understanding, lost in an unrecognizable dialect. The two youngest men, likely in their late teens, took an immediate interest in my hair and clothing. The oldest was marked with a small scar on his upper lip, bushy eyebrows, and a salted, black beard. He arrived a few steps behind the others and turned with a smile to signal those still waiting above. A few seconds later the chorused sound of young, high-pitched voices called my attention to a flurry of five children—three girls and two boys—tearing down the hill at full speed. In a blink I was surrounded on all sides with a rally of robust young faces, each ogling with astonished interest.

None of the men spoke English, but they understood a strong handshake with hands gripped tightly around the wrists rather than palm to palm. Within minutes the group decided it was time to head up to the village. On the way, the children all vied for his or her turn to hold my hand.

The village was a blessed and unexpected boon. I assumed I hadn't seen it on my maps because of its remoteness and small size. At its entry, aside from the children, twelve adults had gathered around in interest.

Everything was handmade: their clothes, the wooden buckets, stone-stacked hut walls, braided rope, split wooden boards. Even their few timber structures were built using wooden pegs instead of nails.

I pantomimed most of what I wanted to say, invoking an occasional round of laughter. Everyone seemed in good spirits until a short, muscular man with a single thick black braid and strong, squared-off features joined the crowd. He wielded an authoritarian influence over the others. He gestured for the group to disperse and they obeyed without question. He studied me with a scowl but said nothing. Using his ornately carved walking cane, he motioned for me to follow. A short distance over a narrow rope bridge, a hardy, full-bodied woman—approximately fifty years old, with large clear brown eyes—opened her hut's door. Peering out curiously from inside the shadow of her doorway, she too considered me. She and the man argued for a moment. Then, plainly frustrated, the man huffed off, grimacing a rude glower.

The woman, notably relieved by his departure, waited for the man to slip out of sight before turning to welcome me, surprisingly in English. Her usage was rough, but she managed to make it clear that I was right about my original impression, that the people here had never seen a traveler like me before. She let me know that the man who had just blustered off was her brother. He was highly suspicious of my arrival, but she failed to tell me why.

My body needed care: broken water blisters bit unmercifully into my toes and heels, and my lungs were fatigued and raw. I was hungry to the point of nausea. I tried my best not to let it override the moment, but she understood. Without a word, she slipped away into her hut, returning a few seconds later with two flour biscuits and a handful of rock-hard kernels of yak cheese.

"Eat!" she commanded and then pointed up the path. "Good place for you. We go there. You rest!"

The hut was a tiny, stacked-stone shanty with a low, slate-layered roof. Forcing the door open with the brunt of her shoulder, she grumbled, "Door no good. You want open, you push hard! Okay?"

Ducking into the undersized doorway, I worked to adjust my eyes to the dim light. The plain single room smelled abandoned and of old rock and dust. But its split-board floor and whitewashed interior seemed well maintained. An old hemp rope mattress was tied to the rim of a sturdy wooden bed frame. A cracked sepia photograph, frayed around the edges and pinned into place with a rusty tack, hung like a fading memory above the headboard. A pair of bleached-white silhouettes lent the impression of two people sitting beside each other. A few others seemed to be standing around them. Likely a family photo.

As I considered the photo, she told me the hut had once housed a teacher for the children who lived here. The teacher's death had left it vacant for years. A stone's throw from the door stood a small Buddhist stupa, an outdoor shrine. The teacher had probably been a monk.

I was tired and needed rest, but I was driven to ask, "Do you know if there is a valley somewhere nearby in these mountains? It would be home to a reclusive community, a group of spiritual masters?"

Her blank stare offered me little hope. I added, "Amara, maybe Amartya?"

Staring through the hut's only small window, she pressed two fingers to her lips. A flash of recognition crossed her face. "Amara?" she repeated.

"That's right! Amara."

Another short pause. Then she said, "Yes, I know Amara!"

A rush of adrenaline shot through my veins.

"Yes, but here we say Xain—how old fathers know Amara!"

"Xain . . ." I repeated. "I don't know that word. Old fathers . . . are the old fathers your elders?"

"Yes, yes, old fathers are elders. They call Amara Xain. I believe Xain same meaning." She paused again to look into the space beyond me. "You talk Indian? Hindi, Sanskrit?"

"I speak a little Hindi and Sanskrit, not much though," I answered. "I've only just come to know the name Amara."

She told me that her community's elders had on occasion shared stories about the Xain masters. They were once a celebrated part of their ancient folklore. She pointed through the window to a pair of distant mountain peaks. "Long ago, fathers say Xain live that way."

"May I speak with your fathers?"

"Old fathers? No. No more living. Maybe Xain still live there, maybe not," she offered in an uncertain tone.

I was elated. Of course they were there—they had to be!

Shrugging her shoulders, she turned her eyes back to the horizon. "If they still living, they be that way."

"Can you tell me anything more?" I asked. "How far that way, or how many days to go there?"

Her expression turned suddenly stern. She pursed her lip and centered her weight. "Those mountains, my people not go! Too much danger. You not go. Bad people live that way!"

"What kind of people?" I followed. A warning wasn't what I wanted to hear.

She sensed my apprehension and snapped. "You not go that way! No people go that way, never go that way! Go that way, never come back. Too dangerous."

In quiet resistance, a subtle nausea had gripped my gut. But to not heed the council of someone who knew these mountains would be a reckless mistake.

"I understand," I said hesitantly. My answer seemed to give her some peace.

She went on to explain that for generations her people lived and interacted solely in the opposite direction. She said she knew another small village existed somewhere beyond those mountains, but communication with its people had ended a few generations back. The bad people she had warned me about were a clan of nomadic bandits. The clan occasionally sent small raids down through the passes to loot her village, stealing animals and food, which explained why her brother had acted so suspiciously upon my arrival.

I asked where I might wash up. She suggested a spot just outside the village where a stream snaked down from the nearby hills. I found a small sandy beach that gave me the means to wade up to my knees in the stream before encountering any slick rocks. While hurriedly splashing the icy water over my face and arms, I spotted someone watching me through the corner of my eye. I stepped back out of the water to relieve the painful chill on my feet and clear the blur from my eyes. A man was standing across the stream on a stony, flat-topped knoll, a bit too far for me to make out the finer details of his face but close enough to see he had his gaze focused entirely on me. He wore a peculiar style of bright red clothing, a fashioned combination that was curiously out of place. His head was capped with a pointed, bulbous red hat stretching a good hand's width above his crown. Waist-long snow-white hair fell thick and bright over his narrow shoulders. A maroon-red kurta stretched down to his knees and his pants narrowed into tied cuffs at his ankles.

He nodded to signal that he knew he had my attention. He slowly raised his left arm to point. I strained to see what he was pointing at but couldn't see anything unusual—just the distant pass in the mountains the woman had warned me about.

"Hello!" I called, my voice muffled under the rushing sound of the stream.

No response.

I tried again, louder: "Namaste!"

Again, no response.

"Can you hear me?" I yelled. "Tashi dalek!" I strained to see if he was showing any reaction at all.

He dropped his arm, nodded again, and lifted his hand to point in the same direction as before. Had I missed something? I scanned the distance: blue sky with a small, white cloud hanging between two peaks and a V-shaped pass. Nothing else stood out as unusual.

The moment I started wading across the stream he abruptly turned and ducked out of sight over the backside of the knoll. I splashed across as quickly as possible without losing my balance. Stumbling across the rocks barefoot, it nonetheless took me two minutes until I stood exactly where he'd been. He was nowhere in sight. Bewildered, I ran up to the highest point on the knoll. Not a trace, not even so much as a footprint. A barren, half-mile basin of slate and small fieldstones stretched out below with nowhere to hide.

Something new and mysterious was afoot. I looked back to where I'd been washing up. At the edge of the village, the woman was watching me through a small open window in the back wall of her hut.

I worked my way back across the stream and called out, "Did you see him?"

She looked at me questioningly.

I pointed, "Over there. Did you see the man in red, just a minute ago?"

She stretched her neck out for a better look. "Man in red?"

"Yes, over there where I was standing."

A perplexed look claimed her face. She shrugged her shoulders and rocked her head no.

I was about to explain what had just transpired when I felt a sudden compulsion to hold it back. The experience wasn't mild. It came across as a strong, intuitive, say nothing kind of hold-it-back.

Mulling it over, I realized that this man, dressed in red, and his uncanny ability to disappear like that reminded me of something I'd nearly forgotten. A few years earlier a similar but less real appearance had come into a few of my saumedhika drishti visions. Whenever I had taken notice of him, he would instantly vanish, as if teasing me. His ability to appear and disappear like that had intrigued me to no end. Was this the same man? I now faced a conundrum: Whom should I trust? The woman or this elusive trickster?

That evening I slept like a rock, waking only once to the wind whistling through the outer layers of the roof. I had planned to begin my morning early, at first light. But when the dawn arrived, my aching muscles fought back. I gave in, slumping into a half-sleep against the bed's headboard.

From somewhere inside the half-lit whispers of my partially formed thoughts, I heard the unmistakable sound of my name. It roused me just enough to pull me out of sleep and into a more typical stream of meditation. Soon the vision of the mysterious man in red appeared, just as it had years earlier in previous visions. I watched a reddish glow form into an aura around his slender body. A purple belt fastened his red kurta at his waist. His aged, brown hands appeared slightly protracted, revealing curly fingernails that extended a good inch beyond the reach of his bone-thin fingertips. The red hat over his long white hair shimmered like sunlit silk. A small, feathery goatee narrowed to a point below his angled chin. The lyrical combination of his white hair and oddly misplaced style made him look like a cross between a Buddhist monk, a Catholic bishop, and a Chinese kung fu master.

As had happened before, the moment I narrowed in on his eyes the man shut them and disappeared. His extraordinary ability to vanish seemed to defy all reason. Saumedhika drishti sight, being above the sensory mind, isn't subject to manipulation. The senses can be fooled, but pure awareness is simply pure awareness. His image reappeared a few more times; each time I came close to seeing his eyes, he vanished in another reddish flash. I was determined to win this game, but the sound of my name being called again sidetracked my focus. My name sounded more musical than before, as if chorused by a celestial choir. And then it rang out once more, still subtle but now it seemed to bounce off the inner walls of my hut. Startled by the idea of someone being inside the room, I forced my eyes open, rubbing my eyelids to clear away the haze of sleep. A delicate shine in the shape of a tall oval appeared to be resting beside my window, nearly as close as arm's reach. Its extreme transparency made it impossible to bring into focus. It hovered soundlessly a few inches above the floor, more than half of it washed out to a point of invisibility in the morning light. For a fleeting instant, the ghostly image of a face and then a human figure flickered at its center.

When it slipped out of sight, passing directly through the aged glass window, I wrenched the door open with a loud scraping sound on the wood floor. I caught sight of it again, framed in a soft silhouette of light against blue sky. It glistened like an angel's dream, trailing behind a misty gossamer wisp that faded into rainbow hues at its end. A moment later, all that remained was the bluish morning mist that cloaked the distant pass.

It had vanished exactly where the woman had warned me not to go and the man in red had pointed. I felt a sudden surge of urgency. A driving compulsion took hold of me. In order to travel through those mountains, I would have to leave immediately.

11

THE CALL OF THE FLUTE

The wind was calmer here, allowing me to hear
 the faint cry
of a hawk, or maybe it was the wail of a distant gust
 singing out
between the ebbs and tides of the breathing mountains.
Once I gave it my full attention, I began to realize
this was neither a bird nor the wind—
it was the call of a distant flute!

Leaving Varanasi behind, my sense of direction had grown increasingly stronger and more focused. But now that I was here in this small hamlet, whenever I attempted to divine my way forward, a confusing mental blur would cloud over my thoughts. The haze had become so disorienting that had it not been for the woman's story of the Xain, I would have been at a complete loss of where to go next. My initial impulse was to head straight into the pass, but I couldn't ignore the woman's warnings. *Jin*—forbidden. I lost my certainty. And then, on cue, the mysterious man in red, followed by the phenomenon that pulled me from my sleep, had set me back on track.

When I left the village, the old woman's look of fear stayed with me—a fear reiterated in the eyes of the few locals who had come to see me off. It was hard to push aside: they saw my choice to go this way as my probable end.

It was still early when I left. I crossed the stony flat just beyond the village and then waded through a few shallow creeks, moving at a better-than-average pace. But my progress slowed substantially when I began my ascent. I was soon trudging along at an elevation where the slightest slip or stumble would cause my pulse to surge and my head to pound. In the thin air, my lungs burned icy hot, every breath straining for oxygen.

Earlier, and eight hundred meters below, I had altered my course. It would have been easier to follow the more established path, but I chose to follow an intuitive feeling, one that told me if I continued to track the path I'd been following I'd risk encountering the outlaws the woman had warned me about. As an alternative, I chose to climb up the rim of a much steeper, cloud-cloaked crag, an ascent even a seasoned mountain climber might have thought twice about. Under any other circumstances I wouldn't have given it a second thought. Lacking the gear, I would have seen it as far too dangerous. But every fiber in my being told me that the lower road would lead to disaster.

In this harsh and barren corridor of high-altitude rock and ice, I faced a new threat—the body-numbing cold. I was wrapped from head to toe with my hood pulled tight and my nose and mouth masked beneath a scarf, but the howling glacial gusts chilled me to the bone. Every advance was compromised amid the continual threat of loose rock and ice that on occasion broke into small rockslides. The slightest slipup here could cost me dearly.

Looking back through the thin veil of clouds at the hamlet's huts—now just black specks—I understood I'd come to a point of no return. Once I made it over the upper summit, there would be little chance of making it back. My strength was worn too thin from exposure, and I had all but depleted my last reserves. Only a single apple and a few crumbs remained from biscuits that were still warm when I took them from the old woman's cracked, dry hands. She must have gotten up before dawn to bake them. It might have been better to first gather a few more supplies, but I had opted for a quick departure, driven by an indomitable sense that I only had a small window of time.

The higher I climbed, the more my surroundings morphed into a desolate world of frozen ghosts and shadows. The towering rock walls facing both sides of my ascent ensured that I'd never see the sun rise or set here. Occasional flutters of something dark would flash here and there, but never long enough for me to say for sure. The aggressive cold and extra labor caused my gut to ache. But what I had left to eat would have to wait. There was no telling how long this final stretch of my journey might last or when I'd find more food.

After scaling a sheer thirty-meter cliff, the worst of my climb was over. I found a gradual upward winding trail. No doubt only mountain goats roamed this high. The trail guided me through a thin layer of clouds and a final stinging bluster of icy spray. Like waking from a gloom, the summit emerged. With only the sound of my pulse whooshing in my ears and the hollow rush of wind brushing the snow-capped crests, I surrendered my last effort into the thawing light of the sun. Here I waited in stillness for its warmth to return some small measure of what the cold had stolen.

Unbelievably, my watch showed only a little more than five hours had passed; the climb had seemed to take days. I forced back the burn in my legs and slogged my way down the steep, snakelike spine of a winding ridge. With the air warming and my descent leveling, I paused to rest against the sunny side of a large, black boulder. I let it warm me while indulging in a sumptuous bite of my last apple. The wind was calmer here, allowing me to hear the faint cry of a hawk, or maybe it was the wail of a distant gust singing out between the ebbs and tides of the breathing mountains. Once I gave it my full attention, I began to realize this was neither a bird nor the wind—it was the call of a distant flute!

Remembering the woman's warnings, my muscles tensed. I turned my ears to the wind, working to find the source of the sound. It was coming from somewhere lower, farther along the stretch I was following. Had I miscalculated, taken the wrong turn, brought myself closer to the danger I'd hoped to avoid? But I couldn't help but wonder: Could a flute-playing bandit really be so bad?

I descended the mountain inside the cover of a narrow gully, and then another, until I came to a long row of streaming watercourses. Glass-like jets cascaded down an overhanging ledge into a small creek, the sound creating a perfect mask for the constant crunch of rocks beneath my feet.

I followed the creek's course until the sound of the flute was merely a stone's throw away. A small outcropping of boulders still stood between the mystery flutist and me. I calculated my last few steps, doing my utmost not to disturb any rocks or gravel. Inching my way to the outside edge of the boulders, I leaned my head forward for a quick look. A white mountain pony with some supplies tied to its back came into view. Chewing idly on a mouthful of weeds on the bank of the creek, it seemed completely oblivious to my presence. Then unpredictably it swung its head around, snorted, shook its head, and pawed the ground. I ducked back out of sight but too late. The flute fell silent.

My initial instinct was to run and hide, but a deeper logic told me to stay put. If the flutist had heard something, running off and crunching rocks like a spooked deer would only affirm my presence. I stayed put.

Within the span of a few minutes my decision paid off. A new song filled the air. I waited a couple of minutes and leaned in for a second look. I was in luck; the pony glanced over briefly, but not unnaturally so, and then reached for another bite of greens. The flutist was farther out of sight. With not so much as a hint of sound, I edged my way forward. Then, unbelievably, the music stopped again. For some unexplainable reason I had been discovered. So I did the only rational thing that came to mind: I summoned my resolve and stepped into the open.

A man dressed in blue sat cross-legged and peaceful a few meters ahead on the split trunk of a fallen tree. I scanned the surrounding landscape—he was alone. Under the filtered shade of a large mountain cypress, his body was dappled with a gentle play of soft shadows and light. The image of him sitting there in blue—so tranquil and undisturbed—seemed serenely surreal. Rather than reacting to my sudden appearance with a start, he offered me a peaceful, disarming smile so obviously welcoming that it instantly lessened my concerns.

I noticed there was something remarkable about him. Wherever his olive skin fell bare, it was as if a vague trace of light brightened it from within. Clearly this was no bandit! He was simply too resplendent, like an epic master in an old Eastern folktale. This was one of the Xain—an Amartya master!

A sudden rush of relief fell over me. My initial feelings had been true. I had been in their care all along. How else would he have known to be here? I nearly started to laugh. I now saw how I had wavered, tottering on the edge of doubt. And I had let the fears of others haze my judgment and certainty. But now it all seemed just as it had to be. If I had dismissed the woman's warnings, I wouldn't have come this way and I wouldn't have heard the call of his flute. The coyote had played his tricks the way life so often does, if for no other reason than to affirm the mystical ways of the Divine.

The moment of our meeting had come. I searched for the right words, but before I could utter a sound he had already slipped his flute into a crimson sheath and spread his arms in greeting.

"Aaravindha. Welcome, my dear friend. Aware that you were near," he continued, "I set my flute to song. With the help of the wind its call found your ears, and now you are here. Well done!"

He formed the character of each vowel and consonant in a way that clearly spoke of a cultured flair for English. But there was something else, something hauntingly familiar in his voice. Hearing its sure and calming tenor invoked a memory, one I had held in secret for the greater part of my life. Countless times the feel of this voice, *his voice*, had come to me during times of need.

"I know you!" I declared in a manner that sounded awkwardly too bold. "What I mean is, I recognize your voice."

"That's to be expected," he said, gesturing for me to come and sit near him.

I unbuckled my pack and lowered it to the ground, sat down, shut my eyes, and surrendered the whole of my exhaustion into a lingering exhalation. I was startled when I felt the soft touch of his hand on my arm, not so much by his touch itself but by the surge of energy coming through it. It wasn't an openly visible force, but it was nonetheless palpable and so generously nourishing that the strain and pain of my journey were clearly being relieved.

He smiled reminiscently, the way an old friend might after a long absence, and then said, "Aaravindha, even from afar, whenever you have laid open your heart or turned your eye to the friend above, we were in company."

I nodded in acknowledgment. I had only seen him once in this life. When I was only six years old, our friendship had begun in that ethereal realm that lives untouched by the limits of our worldly senses. Back then he had appeared as tall as life itself, but now he stood my equal in height and by no reasonable measure did he look any older. Except every so often, half-hidden in the delicate folds of his skin, a subtle whisper of something else was there, something ageless.

Providence had cast our meeting in a heavenly setting. The sky was passionate with blue, the peaks eternal and hushed. Here the stark gray of the barren altitudes yielded to the lush embrace of nature's green. In this virginal streamside flat, mottled with sleepy shadows painted purple beneath a gently lifting mist, I sensed nature's embracing calm. The sun resting on the florally embossed folds of his long, cobalt-blue coat caused it to emit a whisper of sapphire light. Thick braids, glossy and black and woven with coils of blue, fell like silky garlands across his shoulders. A small tilak, an ornamental blue-gray dot painted with ash between his obsidian eyebrows, drew attention to the rare color of his eyes. Unlike the dark brown so common in this land, his Persian blue irises were ringed in a trace of amethyst and glistened like precious gems, so mysterious and clear one might easily imagine he had come from another world.

I wanted to tell him how often and how grateful I had been for his lifelong support, but how does one convey the immeasurable? No, he had already said it well: "When the heart is laid open, or when the eye is turned to the friend above, we are in company." That was enough; I couldn't say anything its equal. So in place of words I offered him my undefended heart and paused in a silent salutation.

He stretched his saintly gaze, fearless and pure, beyond the cover of my eyes. A slow flowing response rose through my thoughts: *Without knowing how or from where, in this soundless chamber beyond my form where there is no you and me, in that silent land where the one Self rests forever undefended and free, I offer you my gratitude!*

The unfathomable depth that dwelt beneath his eyes—the absolute, unsullied eyes of this true Amartya master—pulled me into a kind of unexpected aesthetic arrest. The boundless wild I touched in that passing moment stretched beyond the stars. Not in this life have I beheld its equal. The old dream had fallen away as if I had never left here. In his presence alone I was home.

I thanked him for his flute song and then arbitrarily began to highlight the key details of my journey, my gratitude for the letter in Delhi, and my reuniting with Krishnalila. I shared just about anything worthy that came to mind. He just listened, his smile suspended in his flawless presence, and watched like I had sensed him watching me so many times before.

"I believe it's a good time to ask," I said. "I don't have any idea—"

"What my name is?"

With a subtle bow of his head, he said, "It is Amir. Amir Re'maat Kalarohan!"

"Amir Re'maat Kalarohan," I repeated, careful not to make any mistakes. "A beautiful name! It has a royal ring to it and a strong presence."

"That would be my presence!" he said jokingly.

He reached across the space between us for my hands. His clean hands contrasted with mine, stained brown with the dust of the mountains.

"And your name, Aaravindha!" he said. "It means lotus light!"

"Yes, I believe that's right!" I replied.

"It's Master Rambala's preferred name for you."

"Master Rambala?" I asked. "That has a familiar ring to it."

"It should! Rambala Saundra Himadra. You'll be meeting him before nightfall. He's quite pleased that you're here, young master, Lotus Light."

"Himadra is the last part of his name too?" I asked. "Like mine?"

My birth name was Yanis. In a powerful vision I had accepted the name Aaravindha Himadra as a blessing from one of the Amartya masters. A little research revealed that Himadra was an ancient name for the Himalayas.

Amir stayed silent as if to think it over.

"I'm assuming Master Rambala gave that name to me?"

"Yes," he said. "But that story can wait. I'm certain he would prefer to share it with you himself."

Secretly my mind was already piecing it together. If he had given me that name, then was he the Amartya who was once my father?

Master Amir turned his gaze in the direction from where I'd just come. "That climb," he said, "it spared you at least two days of walking and an encounter fortunately missed. That way is the Tamachaya Davra, a place of gloom where no shadow is cast."

"I believe there's a somber spirit living up there," I added. "Maybe that's the reason for that name."

"You've done well to find your way. Very well indeed! We are within a day's journey."

I told him that I had believed I was close, but once I found the small hamlet I couldn't sense where to go next. I was about to ask about the man in red and the morning phenomenon when he interrupted.

"That's understandable. Precisely why I chose to meet you here."

"Oh?"

"Yes! The route ahead is forbidden, protected by a *sthagmudra*."

"A *sthag* is some kind of veil, isn't it? And *mudra* means a lock or seal?"

"Yes, you're right on both counts. As a barrier it is quite formidable. The way beyond here cannot be found unless we will it so, not by any power or ability!"

"Is a sthagmudra called a *varita* in Sanskrit?" I asked.

"Yes," he answered. "The word *sthagmudra* is also Sanskrit."

"A varita is some kind of paranormal defense, like a *nisiddhi*, a supernatural blockade that negates attempted entry."

"And it has protected our valley sanctuary from uninvited intruders for thousands of years," Master Amir continued.

He picked up my pack and walked over to the pony to secure it. Slipping his hand into a small cloth sack on the pony's back, he pulled out a handful of treats. A faint aroma of mountain sage drifted up from the hills below. Soft smile lines fanned up alongside the outer corners of Master Amir's eyes as he turned his face into the breeze and took a deep breath. Impatient for the treat, the pony pressed his nose to his shoulder and gave him a nudge.

"This is Dhak," he announced. "Dhak has come to ease your burden."

"Very generous of you, Dhak." I walked over to massage the curly forelock between his ears. Dhak was shorter, though notably sturdier in build, than the other wild ponies I'd seen wandering these mountains.

His shiny gray mane, overly large for his body, fluttered lightly in the breeze. Small locks frizzed up and back like tiny wings behind his hoofs. An apple-sized *grivaghanta*, a pony bell, dangled around his thick neck. It was knotted in place with a tattered red and blue braid.

Master Amir whispered something into Dhak's ear. The pony straightaway rambled off over the rise. Master Amir turned to me and said, "He knows the way home!" He then asked, "Aaravindha, do you remember when we first met, perhaps some of the details?"

"Some," I replied. "I also remember a few times after that, in particular when I heard your voice during my meditations. When I just now saw you, I recognized your eyes. I've only seen eyes like those once."

He asked, "From the time of our earliest meeting, do you remember your little Ganesh?"

He burst into laughter, so contagious it became all but impossible not to join in, even though I had no idea what we were laughing about.

"My Ganesh?" I asked. "The Hindu elephant god?"

"Yes! With the red ears!"

"With red ears?" I answered, puzzled. I searched my memory. What could he be referring to? Then it came to me. "Ah yes! You mean my sleeping buddy, the stuffed gray elephant with red flannel ears I had as a child!" I recalled, half laughing.

~

It was well past midnight when an unsettling sense of someone standing in my bedroom disturbed my sleep. Bright moonlight streaming through the floral lace of my curtains fell luminous and ghostly over his body, silhouetting it in a spectral shimmer of silver. Even in those half-muted tones the haunting color of his eyes was evident. I struggled between feelings of fascination and fear. I curled up into a ball beneath my blue flannel sheets—only a single, uncertain eye continued to peer through the ruffled folds.

I had told the world that I had outgrown my stuffed toy. I was six years old—too old for a toy like that. Secretly I was too fond of it to just cast it aside. One day I had been careless and left it lying in our backyard. It had been missing for days until my father, kindling an autumn fire of fallen leaves and branches, found it sleeping limp and wet in the tall grass and mistook it for a discarded toy.

Peering through our kitchen window, I saw my little friend fly from my father's hand into the fire. A panic overtook me. Forcing all former pretenses aside, I raced at breakneck speed to his rescue and saved my steaming, fire-singed friend from the flames.

On the night of that mysterious man's visit in my bedroom I did the unspeakable: I sacrificed my little red-eared friend, hoping he might suffice as an appeasement to whoever it was watching me. I pushed him out from under my blanket and whispered, "Take him." And though I had secretly clenched my fist around the elephant's frayed little tail hoping he wouldn't be taken, I still remember it as a harrowing betrayal.

~

The delight in Master Amir's eyes reflected just how funny that must have appeared.

"That's why you're laughing," I said.

Still amused, he reached behind me to untie a small black bag from the branch of the fallen tree and poured an aromatic mixture of seeds, powder, and dried fruit into my hands.

"For the journey ahead," he said. I picked through the blend, sorting out a few odd-looking seeds. "Krishna Tulsi," he said.

"And this?" I pointed to a sampling of gray powder.

"*Aranyani atichattra*—goddess mushroom!"

"Goddess mushroom?" I muttered as I ineptly forced down the taste.

"While you enjoy your meal," he said, "I can answer some questions, possibly concerning your struggles when you were a child."

I was still adjusting to having just found him while he seemed perfectly comfortable talking about things that had affected me very deeply for a large part of my life, as if it was all quite normal to do so.

"The attacks?" I asked. He nodded.

"I don't really have many questions. Most of what concerned me about my childhood struggles was answered in Rajasthan, in a cave."

A trace of recognition spread through his eyes. He knew about the cave. Of course he did.

I added, "I was too young to understand what was going on. I remember feeling hopelessly vulnerable and almost always exhausted. I scarcely ever slept for fear of closing my eyes. When I did manage to sleep, I quite often woke up in a puddle of blood—frequent nosebleeds."

I continued, "I tried praying but didn't really know who or what I was praying to. I was skeptical—praying felt strange to me. Still does. I learned to pray through watching others. I preferred listening to prayer; listening revealed things, prayer never told me much. I wanted to know what caused things like that to happen. Those attacks came nearly every night and I was willing to try almost anything."

"It's not uncommon for one's strengths to begin in a state of vulnerability," he said. "That was a particularly susceptible time for you. Your sensitivities, alongside your youthful naiveté, had compromised your safety. Master Rambala and Nil'Amma Tara recognized the threat. They asked me to come to your aid. It was through their concern for you that I first came to know you."

The herbal mix was taking hold. A gentle surge of vitality coursed through my body; new warmth spread into my muscles.

"Nil'Amma Tara? You said she and Master Rambala were watching over me. So I must know her from another time?"

I watched his face light up in the sort of delight that's obvious in the face of someone experiencing a heartening moment.

"Nil'Amma Tara is the splendor in love; she is the glory of the illumined," he said. "She is Devayana, the guide and the path. To merely speak her name, one is blessed."

For a brief moment I felt a grander pair of eyes watching us—a feeling so strong it made the fine hairs on my neck and arms stand on end.

"So I did know her, in the past?"

"Yes, you have known her. She has blessed and safeguarded your journey through a number of lives."

"Maybe that has to do with why I so often felt a mysterious feminine presence around me as a child. My imagination wasn't so far off. I always believed a secret mother was watching me, a divine mystery mother whom I imagined living in the earth, sky, and even in the moon. I tended to believe God was a Her."

He offered me a deliberate smile.

I paused momentarily, unsure if I should ask. But then again, we had some time on our hands while I rested up, and he seemed comfortable with talking openly about anything I might want to ask him.

"I do have one question," I said. "You came all that way from your valley to my bedroom in the middle of the night. If it hadn't happened as it had, it would have been hard to believe that anyone could actually do that. But you were there. It was undeniably real! Not a vision. How did you accomplish that?"

He raised an eyebrow. "You know how!" he answered. "Forgotten in part, but you know! The method is called *yatrakama vasaya*! Now that you've come back to us, much of what you have forgotten from former times will return to you." He waited for my response.

"Well, okay!" I exclaimed. He said nothing. "I'm guessing that yatrakama vasaya is some kind of bilocation siddhi?"

"You see, it's already coming back to you," he smiled.

"Well, if that's true then it's definitely not a projected thought. Bilocation isn't actually the transportation of one's body to another place, is it? It must be a manifestation of a projected perception."

"Very good! Yatrakama does involve manifesting a second perception, which is possible—"

"Because the Self isn't bound to a single locality," I interjected. "It's omnipresent, which means rather than being solely local, the Self is already where the perception will occur."

"*Sarvavyapin,*" he affirmed.

I was starting to enjoy the challenge, getting into the possibility of actually solving the mystery.

I said, "That would mean bilocation can't be performed in the thinking mind. Our mental awareness is bound to a single location. It's wired to the body. But beyond our mental limits, above our thinking mind, our awareness is forever free. Like you said, the Self is sarvavyapin, which I assume means omnipresent."

He said nothing, so I continued. "As individuals, we typically only use a small part of our larger consciousness, due to our dependence on our physicality. So bilocation has to be performed outside the restrictive boundaries of the thinking mind—or at least at its transcendental edge. Yes, that's it: bilocation is definitely performed transcendentally. It's initiated within the unbound part of our consciousness, beyond any limiting conditions or mental interference."

The pleased look on Master Amir's face told me I was definitely on track.

He added, "This world is under the rule of Maya. When the eye of the mind relies entirely on that rule, the observer is reduced to live in a defined moment and place. But if the eye returns to its natural home, to its essential freedom, the observer can attain a power that is not bound to Maya."

I said, "To truly be free? True freedom is a controversial concept. At least among most philosophers, even here in the East. I have had this conversation countless times. Most people theorize that free will isn't really possible because of the relenting sequence of karma."

I paused to see if he would respond. He tilted his head slightly.

I added, "It's classically believed that one act leads to the next and that the ongoing succession of those acts brings about every future act that might follow. But that's only the case if our awareness is bound to Maya's dream, isn't it? That would all change if we would transcend the dream and realize ourselves to be the dreamer."

"It is the providence of every being to wake from Maya's grip, to experience eventual illumination," he answered. "In ignorance, the mind's eye sees and believes only in the dream. When the dream of life comes to its end, Maya falls away, then there is only darkness."

"In death?" I interjected.

"Yes! Lost in the dream, the ignorant trust solely in Maya. As their reward, she offers them their illusions. But as payment she demands that the soul should live and die within her confines, subject to her progressions of karma. In truth, we are not her subjects. She is ours!"

I said, "Maya doesn't dream us; we dream her. Maybe it would be better if I had said that we're not her creation. She is merely the rule of the created."

"*Aikatmaya!*" he said.

"I believe I know that word, at least in part," I said.

He answered, "It is when the eye of Oneness is at home in the light of Supreme Self. Then the initiate touches upon the means to perform any siddhi. When the observer renounces the demands of Maya and comes to rest in the high Self, the dream is realized for what it is. When the dream falls away, what remains is illumination: *samyaksambodhi.* Then there is no darkness, not even in death. The Self is forever free! In freedom, all is possible."

I added, "So pertaining to bilocation, our true nature is ubiquitous like an ocean, whereas our individuated awareness is always localized, like a drop in the ocean. Bilocation can't be accomplished without first attaining the larger consciousness of the 'ocean.' Then the observer can initiate and sustain an intention to uphold a second perception in a second location, in that transcendental state of awareness. Because in Oneness there isn't *really* a second location. There the boundaries of time and space are erased." I continued, "But there's more to it than that. There's more involved than just knowing *how* to do it. The person bilocating would have to be capable of sustaining the intent to uphold the perception while remaining on the edge between that transcendental expanse of freedom and the human psyche. And that takes time to learn!"

"In truth, freedom *is*—always. But first we attain knowledge," he said, "then comes technique, and then we realize freedom. That is the way!"

"I understand," I said.

He said, "Knowledge, technique, fortitude, and commitment—mastery involves time." He affirmed, "Aaravindha, you do know; a deeper measure of your memory is returning even now. Yatrakama is based upon the exact principles by which you apply saumedhika drishti."

This was the first time I had actually heard the word *saumedhika*. "You said saumedhika drishti. You mean an ability to retrieve knowledge beyond the usual limits of the mind?"

He answered, "It too is a siddhi, a power. It is the means by which the ancient oracles within our tradition drew forth the supernal knowledge. Drishti is to the spiritual seeker what water is to the earth. But to attain drishti, to gain true spiritual knowledge, there must first be a heroic act."

"I don't understand what you mean."

He replied, "It requires a fearless willingness to listen. True knowledge is often fierce and uncompromising. To attain it, one must find the strength and be willing to sacrifice any interfering attachments, aversions, or old beliefs."

"Like an impeccable innocence and a core surrender—a sacrifice of one's ingrained ways for a renewed listening?"

He answered, "Yes, innocence! And a sublime humility. Humility opens the door to freedom and potential. To present one's mind and body as a living sacrifice is the only path that is holy and suitable to attain a true siddhi. Sacrifice is the sole means to freedom."

He continued, "Aaravindha, only when we pass through the time of our sacrifice are the holy powers accessible. This is why you have returned to the *varman* of our tradition: to fully restore and reclaim the light of your true nature. You are here to remember. This is your hour."

"Varman . . . do you mean a sanctuary or a shelter?"

"Yes—I am a sanctuary. In my presence, the rules that reign over the ignorant are burnt to ashes. What the masses accept as their unyielding law is mere dust beneath my feet. I am the one free Self of every being; I am everywhere. I am divine authority! But so too I am the friend, the balm, and the goal."

Time seemed to stop. The conviction and power revealed in Master Amir's face wasn't that of a mere intellectual, a religious believer, or a philosopher. It was the mark of a true master who had conquered the great knowledge. His words wielded palpable authority, his amethyst eyes revealing the puissance of a mighty utopian mysticism, illimitable and pure.

While we had been talking, my senses had reclaimed much of their sharpness. The cloud that had previously settled over me due to fatigue had lessened substantially. I now realized exactly why he had called me to remember. He was calling for me to let the illusory world fall away and to walk beside him, shoulder to shoulder in his realm, in his world of unyielding truth.

Starting our trek, he said, "The well-beaten path is always the fashion. But those who follow it do so at a great cost. It is not for the righteous to abide life in an obedience forged in blindness. Worldly life is a dream of tests in which the disciple of truth must learn to discern the Will of God and actualize what is virtuous, flawless, and real."

He tapped his forefinger on the bridge between my eyebrows. "Aaravindha, my dear, you understood this path long before this life. It is how you attained drishti, the basis for all sight. Had it not been for the sthagmudra, you would have found your way without my help. That talent, as you have often thought of it, is a rishi's *atisiddhi*, an advanced vibhuti. You had it available when you left our home long ago. It is still there after all those lives! Young master, now use it to remember. From here on this is your only task.

12

KUBITHA

Nervously fondling an amber and coral mala,
the young woman stepped forward, immediately
*   surrendering*
her body to her knees. Looking up at Amir, she seemed
*   tiny and frail—*
her gown spread on the ground like a small bird's wings
supplicated to the mercy of a greater power.

Trekking with Master Amir, time seemed to pass more quickly than before. We descended through an altitude where the temperature varied dramatically between shifting microclimates, on occasion fluctuating eight to ten degrees in just minutes. Above us the white peaks were nearly lost in a thick coat of clouds. We passed a few feathery waterfalls that plummeted long distances with a soft thunder into misty pools and dropped again, sometimes hundreds of feet below us. Passing through a thickly wooded area, Amir pointed out a small, catlike animal resting with its legs dangling on a mossy branch of a broadleaf tree. It reminded me of a small raccoon but with Irish red fur, black legs and belly, and a candy-striped tail. Master Amir called it a *wahdonka*.

The air was easier to breathe, but the hammering stress of our constant downhill plod had brought the ache back to my knees and ankles. Now and then Amir would come to a stop and close his eyes. Possibly he was just being thoughtful, slowing to accommodate my slackening pace. But I suspected there might have been more to it; he seemed to be listening for something.

I was about to request a mercy stop when we came across a pair of wheel ruts worn into our trail. The furrows were narrow, pressed into the earth by a pushcart or a small wagon. More than a mile back, Dhak's hoofprints had led off into a different direction. Amir must have sensed me thinking about the pony's wandering away from our direction of travel. He noted that we'd catch up to Dhak later, adding that we would first stop in a small community. He didn't explain why.

He told me the people living there had migrated into this part of the mountains thousands of years ago. They followed an ancient shamanic tradition he referred to as *Mundhum*, a lineage rich with songs and stories. It wasn't long before a small herd of yaks came into view grazing on a distant hill within the boundaries of a broad stone fence. Farther ahead a few newborn goats frolicked about in a game of tag. A longhaired ram and a group of smaller nanny goats stared at us warily inside a field of tall, thick grass. After rounding a bend that ran over a flat-topped butte, we came to a pair of stone-stacked huts, their small yards enclosed in a weather-beaten, split-board fence. The hut's grounds were covered end to end with orange, yellow, and black kernels of corn spread out to cure under the sun on frayed, brown blankets. A pleasant but faint smell of roasting grains, possibly baking bread, was adrift in the air. My stomach reacted with a growl.

Two lanky-limbed girls in their early teens, both with long braided hair, came into view. The moment they saw us they scrambled away over the crest of a small hill. The hill offered us our first view of the village. It was small, holding only a few more huts similar to the first two. Higher up, a larger, whitewashed brickwork building was built directly into a looming cliff that provided an overlook of the valleys below. The village looked notably time worn, as if it had been resting there for an eternity.

The high-pitched hollers of the two girls called several men out of the largest hut at the head of the little village. Barely a minute later, a woman, roughly twenty-five years old, ran down to join them from a smaller hut farther up the main walk. All but the two girls rushed down to greet us.

The people here had an altogether unique appearance I hadn't seen before. All had similar facial features, the most pronounced being their striking almond-shaped, gold-brown eyes. Their cheeks were set high in their faces and their black hair was especially dense and silky. The style of their clothing was completely dissimilar to what the residents in the former small village had worn. The garb here was more lavishly embroidered and woven into multiple layers of brown, red, and white fabric. None of it showed any visible signs of Western or other Eastern influence.

Within seconds we were surrounded. Their hands were pressed together above their heads as they bowed in greeting. Evidently they already knew and revered Master Amir. But then upon seeing me walking a few steps behind, they presented me with the same salutations, likely an overflow of their respect for Amir. The only response I thought to say was, "*Kadrin chey*," words of thanks I'd learned from the old Sherpa guide, although I suspected they didn't understand his Tibetan dialect here.

One after another they began ranting so raucously it was nearly impossible for me to sift out any meaning. With a downward wave of his hands, Master Amir said, "*Ga-nang*," which I assumed meant stop or quiet down because they instantly hushed to silence. A husky, muscular man came forward to address Amir more calmly. After a short statement, Master Amir motioned for him to step aside and then gestured for the young woman to come closer. She wore a brightly textured red dress over a pair of loose, woolen white pants tucked loosely into calf-high, cloth boots. Her face was small with delicately petite features—lovely by any standard. Her hair was long and lissome, laced back with a weave of thin, beaded braids. Her face was blushed and wetted with tears. A striking man who had been standing directly behind her seemed to be shadowing her every move—conceivably her father. He was older but fit. He emanated ostensibly more confidence than the others. His eyes were steady and his face held strong chiseled features that spoke of conviction and also clearly of concern. His hair fell straight and long over his shoulders; tufts of it were weighed down at its ends by a woven blend of colored stone and silver metal beads.

Nervously fondling an amber and coral mala, the young woman stepped forward, immediately surrendering her body to her knees. Looking up at Amir, she seemed tiny and frail—her gown spread on the ground like a small bird's wings supplicated to the mercy of a greater power. Master Amir joined her, dropping down to one knee on the ground, and wrapped his hands around her wrists and drew her back to her feet. Pleading and gasping tears, she pointed worriedly toward the hut she'd come from.

Searching for a clue to what was going on, I could see an unexpected loveliness in the faces around us, filled with the uncompromised and exquisite beauty of a true faith and inimitable piety one might expect of a deeply spiritual people. We all walked a few steps behind as she and Amir led the way up the hill. We trod up an age-worn, smooth slate path. We came to a halt at the foot of a smaller path that led to the hut's door.

Standing next to a small clay fireplace, an old woman, white-haired and bent with age, had quietly eyed our approach. She lifted her hands above her head and nodded toward Master Amir and then me. Amir paused to nod in acknowledgment with an air that told me they were familiars.

The young woman took a few steps up the path, but once she realized Amir had stayed put, she turned back with a look of desperation. She started to plead with him to come along. Instead of following her, he took two steps back and said something in a muted tone. He then gestured for her to come to where he stood. Shoulders wilting and looking clearly distressed, she did what he asked.

Master Amir used a small white cloth wrapped around his palm to wipe away her tears and then calmly folded her hands together over her heart, her mala still dangling in a clasped loop between her fingers. A few breaths passed in silence as he peered into her wistfully tear-filled eyes, as if searching or waiting. He leaned in to her left ear to blow in a breathy whisper. Whatever he said, it instantly subdued her weeping. I watched in wonder as her face transformed from a look of anguish into the innocent loveliness of a child's hope.

His quick glance to those watching had an instant effect—everyone stepped back to give Amir and the woman more room. The old woman had quietly shuffled over to join us, one small step at a time. Now that she was closer, I noticed a discernible difference in her clothing: small ethnic patterns were expertly woven into her layered sleeves. A thick, red wool vest was laced up around her torso over a tattered gray blouse. A plain brown and gray layered skirt hung to her ankles, its rough-cut hem frayed with wear. A necklace of amber and ceramic beads with symbolic markings hung in a long, double loop around her neck. She smelled strongly of sage and amber. *Likely the village healer,* I thought. It seemed that we were standing in front of her hut. She was the first to settle onto her knees, close her eyes, and begin a soft murmur of chants. One after another, the others followed suit, their combined whispers sibilated like the rustle of leaves in the wind.

Master Amir's left hand remained folded around both the young woman's hands; his right moved to pillow the back of her head. Drawing her closer, his lips pressed another whisper into her ear. Then everything seemed to change. An extraordinarily mesmeric tranquility fell over us all. Everyone could feel it. Their faces pushed skyward, their eyes closed, and muted tears streamed down a few cheeks, as if somewhere in their inner visions they were witnessing a beauty too grand to contain. In unison, their chants fell suddenly silent. Everything went silent. Even the wind fell unbelievably still.

Only one thing now stood out in the quiet—the beguiling after-effect of Master Amir's words, "*Me-je ashi, me-je,*" which I trusted meant, "Don't be afraid." Her body wavered back and forth and then started trembling, its weight suddenly giving way almost entirely to the support of Amir's arms. Her eyes rolled up and back, her eyelids fluttered briefly and closed. In that moment the expression on her face conveyed such a depth of stillness and became so patently white that one could easily imagine she had died. The wash of peacefulness that had claimed her was spellbinding, so much so that for a moment I nearly forgot where I was.

A scarcely visible glow had formed around her and Master Amir's heads. I wondered if anyone else could see it. The surroundings, the village, the people, everything appeared hauntingly different, dream-like. I intuitively closed my eyes too. I felt a strong urge to release myself entirely to the consuming stillness. Whatever was happening, it quickly advanced into a numinous and irresistible attraction to something indefinable.

Suddenly there was only light! Astonishingly blissful, timeless, white light. Then, like being startled out of a dream, it was over. My eyes flew open just as a gentle rush of warm wind washed over us. Time had flown by, but there was no way to tell how long it had been. The woman was standing on her own; the tears and the redness in her eyes were transformed into an expression of luminous gratitude.

A rushed exchange of glances and whispers blew through the group as they rose from their knees. Master Amir said something that compelled first the woman's head and then her body to swing around toward the hut. But before she could take a step, Amir caught hold of her arm.

I heard her take a deep breath and then call out, "Kubitha . . . Kubitha!"

Silence hung in the air like an unsung note. The only other sound was that of another sand-sprinkling gust of wind. No one uttered a word, except the old woman who quietly started to croon another chant beneath her breath. Just as the young mother was about to call out again, the door to the hut creaked open. An old man standing beside me started to cry. Tears rolled down his weather-wrinkled cheeks. The man I had envisioned was her father took a step toward her but then held himself back. A young, wispy-thin girl, pretty like her mother, staggered drowsy-eyed through the hut's shaded entry. Rubbing her eyes with her fists, she gawked at us, astonished.

"*Ama, ama eh?*" she called, reaching for her mother with outstretched arms.

Overflowing with joy, the mother ran to embrace her, calling out a reassuring, "Kubitha, Kubitha, *ngey* Kubitha!"

The villagers rushed up to join them, clamoring in excitement while airing a tuneful blend of cries and laughter. Only the old woman held herself back. She was gazing at Master Amir in an obvious reverence. He nodded, his face radiant with satisfaction. The old woman pressed her eyes closed and nodded in kind, as if to humbly offer thanks.

While I tried piecing together the details of what had just happened, Master Amir slipped his arm through mine and prodded me to slip away. "Aaravindha," he murmured, "our time to leave is now. To wait any longer, the villagers will attempt to fill our pockets with their gratitude. Better for us to be on our way."

Just fifty meters out of the village, the group caught on, one after another they hollered their blessings, "*Thu che cho! Iha thu che cho!*" Everyone but the mother and daughter were waving. They were too absorbed in each other.

Just as Amir had predicted, we found Dhak waiting for us on the crest of a grass-covered knoll. Once he spotted us coming he plodded on, leaving behind only a brief kick of dust.

Master Amir sensed I wanted to ask him what had happened. He offered, "The young girl had torn the flesh of her arm. Her wound had infected her bloodstream and the poison had entered her heart."

"Septicemia blood poisoning?" I asked. "Once the toxins reach the heart it's fatal, isn't it?"

"Death was imminent," he affirmed. "She had passed beyond the reach of the healer's medicines. Her life was in its final moments. Her senses had fallen into death's darkness and this world was no more."

"Was she in a coma?" I asked.

"Beyond that," he answered. "She was standing at death's door! But even there the darkness is only a shadow. Her path back to life was not yet closed."

"The old woman, the healer. Was it she who asked you to come, to help?"

"No! As a healer she had no more to offer, only a prayer for the dying. It was the young mother who had called me. It was *her* faith and love that made the healing possible."

I turned to face Amir directly and said, "I could feel the healing as it happened; the others felt it too. Might I ask what it was that you said to her?"

He didn't answer right away. Instead we walked on in silence. A few minutes passed and then he stopped to say, "Aaravindha, I did very little. All beings possess a sovereign right! In our true existence, we are not the subjects of fate. We are its creators. In our true existence, we have the final say over the arrival of death."

"What you just said, that we have the final word—that's not commonly believed. Few imagine that they might actually choose the hour of their death."

He answered, "Tied to a body of imperfect perceptions, the common thinker becomes an ignorant dealer of beliefs. These beliefs are always limited in their reach. Yes, it is rare. For most, the face of the high Self is guarded by a clever defender that reinvents its existence under a cunning sleight of hand, turning one's sense of that Self into a becoming, creating a loss of presence that conceals the truth from view. In a becoming, there is always an ending—both are equally elusive."

I said, "In becoming—in ignorance—the immortal sight is narrowed to serve incomplete beliefs, so a lesser sight forms to serve our faulted views of life and death."

"A sight," he said, "that still bears in it a measure of the greater knowledge—glimmers of the truth are yet there. But it isn't within the nature of the formed or forming thoughts that we come to know the truth of our existence. The mental person knows only the law of forms and forming. At best, this law might provide us with a clue or a sign that might help us surmise the truth, but it is not enough to give us that truth. Self-knowledge is the realized truth of an existence that is no longer defined or limited by any gauge of time or appearance."

I stopped to think over what he had said and replied, "So it was the mother's realization of the truth that exists beyond the form that healed her daughter!" I then asked, "When we met, did you already know this would happen?"

He nodded. "The time had arrived for the mother to awaken. It was necessary for her to abandon her last attachment to her dream, to realize the Supreme Self."

I affirmed, "So her awakening and her daughter's healing were intimately interwoven. Her daughter's slip toward death was the catalyst."

"There is a necessary order," he said.

"Do you mean *dharman*?" I asked

"Yes, dharman!" he affirmed. "Although the path lives unseen in the heart, it is the sacred Self that calls into life the waking powers from the truth-light above. It instills a divine order into the feeling nature of mind and body, which is what guided the mother to ready herself and to make possible the realization of her greater Being. She had come to her time, to which all beings must one day come—to establish in life the holy Self's own manifestation."

"When I first saw her," I said, "she was shining like a star. She was clearly distressed but was all the same radiant. Beneath her tears her purity was unmistakable. So although her virtue was true and her dream was thin and her time had come, her tears seemed to indicate that she was still held back. She was still attached to her daughter?"

"Her waking was only possible once she let her daughter go," he replied. "In her surrender she could finally hear. Then I merely whispered her way."

I searched for what he meant by whispering her way. "So you told her—"

He interjected, "My words were simple and true: 'Kubitha is with God!' This was always true, but it was only then that she could truly realize it."

"So she found her faith; her faith allowed her to let Kubitha go. And so her last attachment to her dream fell away!"

"Aaravindha, when the last obstruction to the truth of our existence falls, there is but one power that remains—the power of Supreme Love. There is, in and beyond all the fictions of our corporeal mind and its methods, a grace that prepares the living through its unfolding. Inevitably that grace will bring forth the birth of truth. There is—in and beyond all our faults, offenses, and foolishness—a secret power that compels us homeward to love and order. That power is a beauty that compels the wanderer to go where he or she must. It shows us the error of our mistakes and prepares our path before us. Again and again it shows us the ways of dharman. The emergence of this power—this *shobha*—is the indispensable qualification for attaining immortality."

I said, "You wanted the others and me to see this today. That's why you held her back from the door, why you initially didn't let her go into the hut."

"Yes, for you to remember," he said.

"And for the others, the villagers?"

"To deepen their faith! Life here in these mountains is stitched together by the acts of all who share in the holy path. That power the mother realized is sleeping in them all. It waits for an auspicious moment. That moment must arise for everyone; life innately requires it. The outcome you witnessed in her awakening came about once she acquiesced. She realized Supreme Being in her surrender. This healing was not merely the child returning from the call of death; it was the call of Supreme Being and a promise of eternal life for all!"

What he wanted me to see, to understand, had found its mark. Life and death may be common occurrences, but Self-realization occurs only once. The mother had woken to her true Self under the guidance of her master. And she had found a power greater than her belief in the dream of death. Her faith became her medium for her final sacrifice—her attachment—giving her the means. I reflected back to what Amir had said when we first met: "To present one's mind and body as a living sacrifice is the only path that is holy and suitable to attain a true siddhi."

Master Amir continued, "The Supreme Mother gives life. Kubitha had no other choice in the moment of her helplessness than to answer that call. All else was darkness. The Supreme Mother's call is more powerful than the darkness of death. Her power has no equal in this world or beyond."

"So in her release her conditional human love bridged that gap to become her unconditional divine love—the Supreme Mother's love," I said.

He added, "Human love is merely a disguise for a greater power."

A soft wind spiraled up around us, calling up the scent of the earth as we walked. Amir placed his palm over my heart and said, "You know this! Whether love is found in the human heart or the heart of the Supreme, it is really the same. Its only limitation is the resistance used to veil our true nature—the resistance borne of our misguided attachments and aversions. The love of the mother for the child *is* the love of God for the holy son or daughter. Nothing can defeat it, not even death. And if death does come, it is of no lasting consequence. In the end, death *must* yield to life. Death is only the blink of an eye. The eye must open again. Death is the mask of ignorance, but that darkness cannot withstand the true light of our existence."

I said, "So that divine love—we feel it as the rush, the breath of the sacred flowing into realization through our lives."

He replied, "It is divine will that carries the soul to life. Faith is the means by which we surrender the mental limitations and our imagined identity into the sacred heart of the one Great Mother. Awaken her offer through an undefended presence and death means nothing."

I said, "The Atman, the soul, it can't die. It lives on forever, one way or another. Life is God's bride; death can't still that."

Amir said, "In silence and listening, and without affirming the need to limit, faith isn't merely a belief, nor is it one's trust in a hope. It is the power of the Knower! That power is resolute. Our path must include our willingness to be present to the light of the Knower. Aaravindha, it is easy. So very easy."

I placed my hand on the back of Master Amir's shoulder and thanked him for the sweetness of his words and his generosity. He quietly nodded in a gesture of equitable acknowledgment. For the next hour we didn't speak, but walked silently side by side.

13

LAST STRETCH TO THE HIDDEN VALLEY

Love is seldom understood.
Most believe it's an emotion when, in fact,
emotions arise when love is lost.
Love is a state of limitless presence,
a free availability to the high Will.

A few miles from the village, our trail faded to a narrow goat path and then disappeared altogether. After splashing through a series of small streams, we passed through a forest abounding with rhododendrons and melodic birdsong. On occasion we came across sets of split-hoof tracks indicative of wild boar. A family of blue-black ravens had taken to following us—cackling, laughing, and scolding each other. We stopped for a rest on a jutting rock shelf that offered us a view of a rolling meadow a few hundred meters below, its tall green grasses speckled with a collage of red, white, and yellow wildflowers. Dhak had waited for us there, having busied himself with the task of separating out the tender grasses from the less friendly brambles.

Leaning back against the green cover of a moss-coated rock, I stretched out my legs and closed my eyes. The time that passed while we had walked together in silence had given me the pause I needed to fully appreciate what had occurred back in the village. Over the length of my life, I had persistently applied my efforts to the retrieval of a class of knowledge that might shed light on living a true and authentic life, founded in direct experience rather than a cultured or prescribed conformity. I had sought to avoid the eristic disputes of religious rights and wrongs that are too often the driving subject of modern metaphysicians and spiritual pundits. My search was for a knowledge that stood above human opinion or the manufactured morals of differing societies. And while I understood that an uncorrupted knowledge might serve as a great purifier and a means to infer the truth of our existence, I intuitively knew that knowledge alone couldn't give a truth seeker what he or she is ultimately seeking. Amir had coined it perfectly: "The mental person knows only the law of forms. And there is—in and beyond all our faults, offenses, and foolishness—a secret power, a power that compels us to come home to love and order."

Amir was a master of that power. His love was not merely a human love conditioned by sympathy or any other emotion but a love that belongs to something greater. I couldn't remember in my life having even once felt its equal. It was in his every move—ever attentive, graceful, and free of effort. He reminded me of an eagle soaring weightless in an unseen current. And while some might call that *being in tune with nature*, that alone doesn't describe it. Amir wasn't merely in tune with nature. His nature was in tune with the truth of existence.

He had held the young mother back at the hut's door for the others to witness. He said, "It was to deepen their faith." But his words, "And for you to remember," affected me profoundly. I was certain that task couldn't be fulfilled through calling up my stored memory; it was too narrow—the result of only one life. What he wanted me to remember ran much deeper, beyond any knowledge I might have gathered through one life's effort and beyond remembering the life I had once lived among these masters or, for that matter, any other past life.

Amir's assertion that our path must include our willingness to be present to the light of the Knower was the key, the criterion I was now mulling over. The light of the Knower may live in fragments within memory and thought, but remembered knowledge is only a partial shine of something greater, something that lives beyond the thinker's reach. If we align ourselves to an inward surrender, transcend to and release ourselves into the invisible currents of its alluring bliss, and allow that bliss to inspire and entice us closer, we might awaken that power through our lives. The order it supports is the glow of an omnipresent sea to which we all belong—the glow that rights us with our intended destiny. But to own it, we must first learn how to let go of the attachments that bind us until that moment arrives, like it had for Kubitha's mother. Amir had demonstrated its secret and had said, "It is easy, so very easy." It was that ease, that way of effort-free being, that he wanted me to remember and what I saw exampled in his way of being.

Whenever an attachment falls, possibility arrives to replace it. The deeper the attachment, the greater the possibility. The greatest possibility is the discovery of our unconditioned love, for that kind of love is the closest to divine love. But love is not a power in itself; it is its medium. Nor is love limited by the arranged conditions of a mind that knows only the law of forms. It is a medium that brings through it a potential divine manifestation through those laws. When we awaken to this kind of love in our hearts, we only need to listen to the call life brings us and then sacrifice our resistance to allow our bodies and minds to become instruments for doing, not mere mechanisms for control. This is what I was being asked to remember: to let the light of the Knower fill my wings as it had Master Amir's. Our stop in the village had given me a rare glimpse into the sacred ways of the Amartya masters, and an invitation to return to them.

Master Amir fastened a bridle over Dhak's head and cautioned me that our upcoming trek would require a bit more care. But after visually tracking the nearest goat trail down through the meadow and beyond, I really couldn't see why: the way appeared to be rather simple and straightforward. Upon taking my first few steps, Amir surprised me by calling me back to tell me I was heading in the wrong direction. There was only forward or back; two seemingly impassable cliffs rose on either side of us. All the same, he started climbing up the steeper of the two slopes, pulling Dhak along by his tether.

Our climb was steep but manageable. We filtered our way through a small border of trees, which from below had obscured the base of the cliff we were nearing. Once we cleared the trees it started to make more sense. Amir was leading us around a cluster of tall, craggy pillars. From the trail they had looked like common outcroppings pressed against the cliff walls, but up close their hidden side came into view. To the rear of the pillars a large, vertical fissure widened from top to bottom to form a small passageway that opened into a narrow ravine. Amir explained that this ravine was our most viable way to reach our destination.

Inside the passage, a splash of narrow sunbeams spilled in from above to light our way. Their warming touch falling on wet stone conjured up a steamy drift of ghostly mists, which spiraled into skyward-reaching forms. Descending a series of slippery black steps, we entered a chilling rush of cold air that was arriving through the mouth of an even darker and tighter tunnel. Dhak cleared the ceiling easily, but Amir and I both had to walk hunched over for a good twenty meters before the tunnel descended into a dusky cavern. A faint light found its way in from the cavern's opposite end, just enough to instill a pale, eerie glow into an enormous set of dripping stalactites clinging to the frost-covered dome. The dark—as well as the echo of ice cracking beneath our feet—affirmed Master Amir's words of caution. Entering a second tunnel, we waded the length of a shallow, ice-lined creek. The flow of water echoed melodiously as it tumbled down and disappeared through a black crevice in the ground. Just ahead, the afternoon sun found its way in, landing with brilliant intensity on sections of the wind-sculpted walls.

As the sky above opened into strips of blue, we stepped onto a broader, human-made path where a series of small caves was carved into its bordering walls. Amir told me that more than a thousand years had passed since these caves were last used. They had once served as a sheltering sanctuary for a group of fugitive Buddhists who had fled persecution after the assassination of the Tibetan emperor Langdarma. A clan of sympathetic hermits had provided the Buddhists a secret refuge here. The assassination of the emperor had set off the first decline of Buddhism, propelling its primary factions into a chaotic period of turmoil and rivalry.

Small footholds were carved beside a few of the caves in ascending vertical rows, providing access to more caves that rested above a crumbling sandstone shelf. The sunlight spread diffusely into some of the caves, exposing an occasional relief, mostly of unrecognizable deities carved into their inner walls. Rounding a narrow turn, we were met by a large, stone figure carved menacingly into the center of our path. Its ominous appearance suggested a wrathful presence, though it probably wasn't Buddhist. Oversized eyes bulged forward like those of an irate cartoon character. Its wide, downward-curled tongue jutted out insultingly between two fractured fangs. Three of its four arms held carvings of primitively forged weapons. The fourth arm, broken at the wrist, was missing its hand. Just beyond, the passage widened farther into a flat, stone vestibule—a stone yard that stood before the last and largest of the caves.

Amir agreed to a short break and led Dhak to a patch of spindly, lemon-green grass. Too alluring to ignore, my curiosity pulled me into the cave entrance. Inside the air was damp and cold and smelled musty and stale. Through a small, star-shaped opening on its far end, a dust-speckled ray of sunlight pierced the darkness, spotlighting a table-sized block of granite, a stone perhaps once used as an altar. At its center, an egg-shaped object stood on end, about half of my overall height. It resembled a Siva lingam but stood broader and more oval. Most likely it was an older symbol of the ethereal cosmos, a *bhuvanandaka*—the symbolic world-egg. A thick crust of hardened dust cloaked its surface. With a few taps and some scraping with my fingernails, pieces began to crack and fall away, revealing a smooth, polished piece of black stone and quartz below, with an opaque white vein spiraling up around its body to its crown. It must have once carried great value. I couldn't help wonder why its owners had left it behind.

The cave walls were blanketed end to end with an elaborate combination of carved reliefs. Most were in ruin. A wealth of nude figures was still recognizable on the entry-side wall. A few larger and more prominent deities rose above them. The deities seemed strangely incongruous to this part of the world. All were crowned with symbolic sun headdresses that bore a mild resemblance to the solar discs worn by ancient Egyptian gods. Two fierce-looking, human-sized statues guarded both sides of the cave's exit, each with one hand holding a spear, the other hand reaching up to symbolically support the ceiling. A collection of stone urns, fragmented clay pots, and an assortment of small, badly corroded pieces of metal were sleeping half-buried along the cave perimeter.

A growing sense of having trespassed on a sleeping sacredness urged me back outside. I walked over to the sunny side of the yard to find my place to rest and detected through the corner of my eye that Amir was quietly assessing my physical condition. I undoubtedly looked much the worse for wear. I had been walking well over twelve hours at a pace that had called up the deepest of my reserves—reserves I didn't know I had. I knew he could see my struggle beneath my mask of tolerance. My face was hot with the burn of too much sun and wind, my lips were cracked, and my ankle joints were swollen. An ongoing throb of pain was afflicting my knees, causing a growing uncertainty in every step. I was feigning a strength I no longer had, and I fought back a mental fatigue that had advanced into lightheadedness. I knew if I relaxed too much now the effort to start again would be much harder. So I sat with my legs dangling free over a small rock shelf, with my back propped up straight against a textured wall of sandstone.

Pushing my tiredness aside, I turned to Amir and said, "Leaving the village, you said that there is, in and beyond our humanness, a power that compels us to come home to love and order."

He nodded.

"That reminded me of a difficult time when I was young."

"You still are," he said, grinning.

"I mean when I was a child. There was a time when it seemed there was little else going on in the world around me that wasn't in some way dominated by people's pain or the friction caused through their relationships. I think I was just too sensitive, so sensitive that I felt the suffering and misery from miles around."

"Your sensitivity had no defense," he said. "It was acutely tender."

"I think that's true," I said. "It was difficult, particularly the noise of my parents' conflicts. Their dislike for each other made their relationship strained and volatile. The leftovers of their fighting upset me the most. Not the noise of their constant arguments—their bickering wasn't nearly as loud as the unspoken overflow of their ongoing blame. I heard and felt their every emotion. Their conflicts seemed to trigger my sensitivity to more distant ones, and the noise just got louder and louder. I remember one day curling up in our backyard under an old willow tree and pressing my knees in over my ears, hoping to block it out. But the opposite happened; the more I tried, the worse it became."

"The duty of youth is to accept life's challenge. Having tried, you may have failed to achieve what you had wanted, but you found something more valuable—your way," Amir replied.

"I believe you're right," I continued. "Once I stopped fighting it, I first discovered an alternative way of listening. When I let go—truly let go—I was able to hear their deeper needs reaching out from behind their struggles. That may have been my first connection to what you said earlier: 'Behind our faults, offenses, and foolishness, there's a power that compels us to come home to love and order.' I believe I found that love, though only in part. It wasn't until I was older, and I learned to answer the need, that I found it more fully. Over time, answering the need became a core motivator in my life; it provided me with the order that inherently lives inside the love. So now, during my lectures, whenever someone asks if I can help them discover their dharma, I nearly always offer them the same answer: 'We don't need to search for it, we just need to learn to listen, let go of ourselves, and be willing to answer.'"

Master Amir came closer to sit directly in front of me. He said, "Listening for the cause of one's suffering opens the path to healing. But to truly hear—that is rare! The deafening influence is the presence of too many emotions that rise up in defense of the right or wrong."

"I think that must be the foolishness you spoke of," I said.

"Believing that emotions are some kind of justification rather than a symptom of an attachment or defense. Or that they're just mechanized reactions that show up when someone's views are threatened. I've often noticed that whether they're aware of it or not, people primarily tend to argue or resist rather than really listen. Even with the best of intentions, they often do more harm than good. Returning to love as a foundation for hearing is rare."

Amir added, "Love is seldom understood. Most believe it's an emotion when, in fact, emotions arise when love is lost. Love is a state of limitless presence, a free availability to the high Will. It's a common mistake to define love as kindness or as caring for others. While those may be benevolent intentions, love is not an act. Love achieves nothing in itself. It is a medium, a sacred passage through which the high and pure creative intellect takes birth. Back at the village, when the woman let go, when her attachment fell away, her emotions also fell away. She found her love not through mental reflection and not as an act but through her resulting presence."

Amir paused. The subtle tilt of his head told me he awaited my response.

"I believe that's the heart of it," I said. "When we're not defending a past notion or a possible future outcome we're completely in the present. When we've truly given up our attachments and are genuinely standing in the glow of an undefended heart, our love becomes the medium for our actions, which would then be a direct expression of the sacred Self. In other words, we then honor the light of the Knower."

Amir sat back against the stone and smiled at me with an unexpected look of sweetness reflected in his eyes. He added, "In love, right knowledge and action are the same. A person who believes his or her individuation is law is bound to endless uncertainty and the haunting darkness of death. Such a heart is perpetually guarded; the mind is then faulted by the consequence of those laws. Thinking this way, the person tends to obey only the rules of his or her personal knowledge. He or she is then governed by desire, established habits, and mental predispositions. The person lives in a whirlpool of emotion—a whirling eddy—fully unaware of the global tide of our greater existence. Thoughts become dark and quarrelsome. Those whose hearts are sleeping seldom recognize the spreading effect of those thoughts."

"Those thoughts don't just vanish!" I said.

He answered, "The thoughts may change, but their effects remain. To every act—even the act of a thought—there are always consequences.

Those effects are recorded in the *jagadakash*, where they are bound to a divine edict that demands their resolution. Truth is the light and sword of the divine Self. It has no tolerance for illusion. It is the *devaheti*, the *sudarshan*, the might of the Knower. It does not allow illusion to rule enduringly."

"The jagadakash?" I asked. "That's the astral expanse that encircles our physical world?"

"Yes, it is the storehouse of *vasana*, shadowed perceptions. They may seem to be hidden away, but they are merely masked in other forms or expressions through which they persistently seek their liberation."

"So the jagadakash is our world's unconscious!" I exclaimed. "Where our collective illusions are stored."

"Yes, the *samtanomaya*, the shared unconscious. *Akash* is its vessel. All life is embedded in akash. Everyone is to some measure affected by what it bears. This is what you felt affecting you in your environment as a child."

"The samtanomaya? Are you saying I felt the world's unresolved issues, its karma, floating in the ethers of the collective unconscious?"

"Yes, Aaravindha, I believe so."

"You said the effects of quarrelsome thoughts don't vanish. Those effects are stored in the collective field, in the jagadakash. I know that the unconscious is the repository of denied perceptions. And negative or quarrelsome thoughts are always the result of denied perceptions, some truth not seen."

"That's it exactly, Aaravindha. They are the seeds of *apunya*, unresolved karma. These seeds wait for their moment to break free, bewildering the mind and igniting human emotions in the background of the world's collective dream. A single drop of water generates very little influence on our skies. Just as a sole negative thought has very little effect on our shared unconscious. But when they have amassed in great numbers, a potential storm emerges. They join with other seeds to form a *mayanabhas*, storm clouds built of humanity's denied perceptions, which are ready to rain down a torrent of emotion and discord upon its creators."

I added, "In other words, the collective unconscious seeks a release through some kind of liberating event or even a possible disaster. Like a pressure cooker that's reached its limit."

Amir patted me on the shoulder and began walking. It was time for me to put my feet back on the ground. After a sharp descent we exited the ravine and entered a tall bamboo forest where segmented green shafts swayed in unison under the gentle sigh of rustling leaves. Here and there a few smaller vine maples, lanky and crooked, broke through to give contrast to the otherwise parallel rising lines. On one occasion we came across a grove of poinsettia trees bursting with bright pink blossoms. We waded through an open meadow where cannabis plants grew to the size of small trees, their dark green leaves sprinkled sticky-white with resin. Passing beneath a grove of large vine-enmeshed trees, black-faced monkeys, some with their young clinging to their bellies, prattled and screeched above. We entered a small clearing that held in its midst a half-buried ruin, which was barely visible beneath a tight bramble of gray serpentine vines. The sound of insects, birdsong, and whistling beetles filled the air. Master Amir pointed up toward a large, cloud-covered mountain.

He said, "Tigers are the lords there."

Responding to the surprise on my face, he added, "There is no reason for alarm. The tiger knows its prey; we are not that. I know these creatures and they know me."

Amir told me we were nearing our destination, but I was at a point where my legs were giving out. My calves were twitching and my hamstrings were trembling persistently. A ten-centimeter-wide ring of blue bruises had formed around both of my ankles. It was taking every bit of my willpower to override the pain.

I splashed the heat from my face in a slow, flowing brook. I was about to take my boots off to immerse my ankles when Amir tapped me on the shoulder and asked me to sit by him. Once seated, he quietly knelt down and wrapped both his hands around my left knee. The gentle pressure created an immediate soothing balm for the surging pain. He asked me to let go of any protection around it and to relax into the pain. A moment later, a pleasant tingle coursed up and down my leg, followed by an involuntary series of sporadic contractions in my calf. I flinched when a popping sensation suddenly burst through the center of my knee. An instant later the pain was gone!

"It's fine now!" he said. "Feel free to move it."

And it was. The pain was completely gone. And so too was the trembling—my muscles seemed certain and sturdy. The bruising was still visible, but the swelling had disappeared. Before I could say anything he started with my right leg. A moment later I stood up, completely pain free!

"It's time for us to move on," he said. "They're awaiting our arrival."

14

THE ARRIVAL

Level to the final courtyard, our path
led to a large, pointed archway with wide, open doors.
An elusive sound of voices echoed through its threshold.
A few seconds later, two men and a woman
emerged from its shadow. The diffused afternoon light
caused a thin, turquoise-white aura to lift off their bodies,
endowing their silhouettes with a faint glow
against the dark doorway.

We entered a forest clearing that connected to a well-defined dirt footpath, which led us into a tall, walled-in canyon flanked on both sides with large, overhanging trees. A warm breeze blew to our backs as we gradually ascended into an enchanting view of an emerald green valley. It was unmistakable—we had arrived!

Pointing with the sweep of his hand, Master Amir said, "What you see before you is Devodyana, the forest of the early spirits, home to the progeny of the sun. The ground you are standing on is where Mahattara Amamriprabhu, the oldest of our tradition, first looked down upon these lands and envisioned here Amarpura, our home."

"Mahattara Amamriprabhu?" I asked.

"Yes, Mahashaya Pitamah—Grandfather!"

As a child, I was fascinated when I first saw a black-and-white movie called *The Razor's Edge*, an adaptation from W. Somerset Maugham's 1944 novel. The post–World War II story was about a man's search for meaning and enlightenment that took him to a mysterious Shangri-la sanctuary hidden deep in the Himalayas. Later, during one of my research studies, I learned about another hidden realm that the Tibetan Buddhists refer to as Shambhala. Shambhala is a vital part of the Kalachakra tradition, wherein it is presented as a luminous ethereal city that one can visit under special circumstances. But unlike many contemporary interpretations, it shouldn't be mistaken for a physical location. I also learned of the Tibetan Bönpo record of the hidden lands of Olmo Lungring, which is sometimes mistaken for Shambhala. However, Olmo Lungring is believed to be a physical realm that has existed in secret from the time of our human beginnings. Olmo Lungring is described as the land where the heavenly clear-light gods descended from the upper worlds to incarnate as human luminaries. But long before I learned of these places, I already knew there was another realm.

Due to Master Amir's mysterious appearance in my life when I was still too young to understand or disbelieve, I nurtured the secret belief that I would one day visit the world he had come from. Now, after a lifetime of waiting, I was standing not above the etheric Shambhala, Olmo Lungring, or the fabled Shangri-la but at the edge of the equally mysterious home of the legendary Amartya masters—the Amarpura valley. Unlike the descriptions of Shambhala or Olmo Lungring, what I saw stretching out below was not a grand city made of elaborate streets and corridors filled with royal palaces and temples but a natural green world surrounded on all sides by high mountain peaks, distant waterfalls, and extraordinary beauty.

As we descended into the valley's lush undergrowth, Master Amir told me that the Amartya *Parampara* is the oldest spiritual tradition of its kind, and that it existed well before the Great Deluge that took place around twelve thousand years ago. It was a time he referred to as the *Jalaplavana Kalpa*, which I assumed meant the time of the great flood. He explained in an air of recognizable admiration that our lineage has remained both original and pure in knowledge because it has never been unnaturally corrupted by outside influences nor has its core teachings ever been indoctrinated into any form of dogma or religion.

We passed by a bubbling spring that filled a human-made surface well and then emptied into a narrow stone culvert that distributed the water farther on into other offshoot channels. A diversity of colored wildflowers lined our trail in long, intermingling patches. Above us, dozens of yellow butterflies fluttered between shades of light and dark inside the canopy of tall trees. All around in the air, tiny seed parasols were adrift, each reflecting a glimmer of gold from the setting sun. The place was a utopic dream.

But beneath all the natural beauty and hum there was yet something more, something less visible. There was a remarkable feel of expansiveness. Coming to this valley, I had inadvertently left behind a persistent mental white-sound. My mind was now freed of a heaviness I hadn't previously recognized. Here, the background static that I was so accustomed to was completely gone, opening my awareness to a salient depth that made my thoughts feel more like mere glimpses of something much grander.

It wasn't long before I heard the recognizable clatter of people laughing, between the erratic blows of wood being chopped. The first to come into view was a small boy tossing fruit down from the branches of a wild plum tree. Two young girls were gathering the fruit into a large double-handled basket. Three adults, all men, stood hip-high farther back in the underbrush, hacking down large fern branches with machetes. A fourth man, who had been balancing a tightly packed bundle of ferns on his head, let it fall to the ground the moment he saw us walking by. The girls whispered and giggled and the men all turned, first smiling and then bowing with their hands in the prayer mudra, referred to in the East as *ghasso*.

I asked Amir if these people were born here or if they came from somewhere beyond. He said almost everyone who lives here is native; only a few had been invited. He then affirmed what I already knew: only the invited could find this place.

"To be invited here," he said, "is the result of very good karma."

Crossing a small bridge, Amir paused to close his eyes, as if to drink in a pleasure. "This wind you feel blowing across your skin, it is *atmasani*, fertile with life force. This water flowing beneath us is holy.

It is *tiryodaka*, a blessing to all who touch or drink it. Amarpura is an unblemished land; no form of violence has ever occurred here. A sacred natural order has been guarded and preserved in this land by our lineage for millennia." He pointed onward with a gentle gesture of his head. "They are expecting us."

"So we've finally arrived?" I asked.

"Yes, three are there to greet you."

"So four masters live here?"

"Five live in Amarpura. And one more—the old one—resides there at the foot of that mountain." He pointed upstream to a thinly misted view of a soaring, white-capped peak.

I asked, "Are you always aware of each other, of what you are doing?"

He said nothing. But I saw my answer in his expression.

We entered a series of interconnected courtyards, each one ringed with a snug row of broadleaf trees. We then passed through a tall, florally carved stone arch. A stone stairway led us out from under a sheltering weave of branches, exposing a sheer cliff wall ahead. The wall was bordered on both sides by two spike-toothed crags that guarded the base of a steep mountain slope. The mountain rose for a few hundred meters before vanishing inside a sunlit, amber mist. The air was sweet, flavored with a delicious scent of earth and forest. Thick, leafy verdure blanketed the wall. A few dozen red-blossoming vines rambled down its face. Judging by the occasional arm and leg that protruded through the leaves, I could see that a carved relief was hidden beneath the cover. In the central uppermost part of the wall, a stone-embossed symbol looked down on us like an enormous rotund eye. The carving was symbolic of a large sun that encircled an embossed triangle and had a second sun engraved in its center. Ten meters below it, three ornate stone balconies with weathered, rust-red doors were cut directly into the wall. Level to the final courtyard, our path led to a large, pointed archway with wide, open doors. An elusive sound of voices echoed through its threshold. A few seconds later, two men and a woman emerged from its shadow. The diffused afternoon light caused a thin, turquoise-white aura to lift off their bodies, endowing their silhouettes with a faint glow against the dark doorway.

I felt unexpectedly apprehensive, experiencing a sensation I hadn't suffered since the first time I kissed a girl. My breath drew shallow and my heart began to race. I stopped for a few seconds to close my eyes and take in a full breath, but even so, as we drew nearer my pulse continued to race.

My eyes were immediately drawn to the woman. For an instant I thought it was the tree-filtered sunlight glistening off her long, silvery-white hair that had so caught my attention. But it wasn't that. There was something far more gripping about her—her amazing celestial beauty. I was awestruck at how otherworldly she appeared, like a heavenly Tara incarnate.

Her smile was both amiable and warm, while at the same time her eyes were unusually deep and incredibly penetrating. I felt utterly transparent beneath her gaze. She wore what looked like an Indian Ghagra choli dress. A delicate shawl, silky and ashen, swept down over her left shoulder to wrap around her narrow waist. A braided, soft, blue-and-white sash garlanded her abdomen, fastened in place with a cast silver brooch. An amber necklace, augmented with a few light-catching pieces of green jade, adorned her neck. White-pearl bracelets stood out brightly around her copper-skin ankles. Her mystical allure was so entrancing, her gaze so halting, it wasn't until the man in the center stepped forward that my eyes were finally able to break free.

The moment I looked him in the face I knew I had seen him before, though never more than briefly during my meditation practices. Seeing him here and now seemed weirdly like having a reunion with someone I hadn't yet met. His gaze was straightforward and certain, like that of a principled being, and also calmly assuring, like that of a caring confidante. His silvery-white hair rippled to his shoulders in layered, silky waves. A loop-knitted purple stole crossed casually over his shoulders. His eyebrows were thick, his face chiseled and handsome, and his skin amber-brown and flawless. Beneath his short, groomed white beard, a dazzling turquoise-and-red coral necklace looped down in three successive layers over his mossy-green, banded-collar jacket, which dropped down to just above his knees.

In a clear, Eastern-flavored English he said, "My dear Aaravindha, this is a glad moment, and long awaited. I am entirely delighted that you are finally here."

"Master Rambala?" I said, uncertain.

He hesitated to answer, instead examining me with a distinct look of approval. "Could it be that you still recognize my face?" he asked.

"I do!" I said. "I'm sure of that! But it was Master Amir who told me your name."

"There was a time when you knew it well, but this may be the first time you have used it—rather than *pitaji*—to address me." He added, "I have followed your travels through three births, and with great interest. You have now brought your promise to completion."

"My promise?"

"You long ago promised me you would return. A difficult task and a rare achievement. Many have searched, but few have found us."

"To be fair," I said, "I'm not so convinced I found you. Had it not been for Master Amir coming to meet me, I'd probably still be searching."

"That would not have been due to any lack of yours," he replied.

The idea of three lifetimes was once again bringing home to me who these beings truly are. I tried to imagine living so long; what it might be like to see generations pass and to see loved ones die and be born again with new faces. And yet he looked no older than a young sixty.

He stepped closer and placed his hands squarely on my shoulders. His touch immediately set loose a curious rush of sensations throughout my body. He focused with a deliberate stare into my eyes. The moment I met his gaze, a pleasantly golden feeling washed over my thoughts. One after another, bits and pieces of what I had once known about this valley began flashing through my mind. It seemed as if all else faded away. What emerged was my past life as a young man standing here in this exact place. Master Rambala's face looked a bit younger but not by much. I heard myself asking him to accept my reasons for leaving while trying to assure him that one day I'd return. Three deaths and three births—a full circle had been completed!

I remembered Master Amir's words: "In the end, death must yield to life. Death is only the blink of an eye; the eye must open again." The love that Master Rambala and I once shared now owned my heart; its splendor, its unconditional purity, was returning. I quietly surrendered a few joy-filled tears. Miraculously, through his touch, he had opened me to a broader awareness of myself, one that transcended any residual sense of being confined solely to this time or to the love of just one life. And then the vision shifted. I felt surprisingly weightless, free-floating in a celestial hall of mirrors, surrounded on all sides by a limitless number of distantly familiar reflections, all different but all me. Then in a single breath, the sound of his words called me back to the present.

Clearly pleased, he said, "Any confining perceptions, all traces of them, will come to a conclusion here. Your time is now! Together we will burn away any lingering hold. Here you will recover the knowledge of eternal life, a knowledge that will remain with you throughout time. But the world will not in itself alter its demands. You must yet prepare the ground and be forbearing. Here one learns to wait until the soil is fertile and to plant the sacred seed only when it will survive the limitations of individuation. This will unquestionably change your actions in the world: to reveal the secret ways only to those who are ready, and to let all others believe what they will."

I was about to respond when I noticed his demeanor shift into an even more serious stance. He asserted, "My dear, listen carefully to what I will now tell you and know that my words are indisputable! Any future offer of your teachings must from now on be a free choice! The vow you set out to fulfill in once leaving here can no longer bind you—it is finished! Were it not so, you would not have found your way back to us. Know that its completion rests in your return. Do not doubt my words. What you choose to do henceforth must be solely an act of your love—nothing less!"

He continued, "And this choice will be challenged. The true path is narrow; any act bórne of love will nearly always be challenged by the negations of conformity or interpretation. During those times, there will be no need to answer. *Prem tattva'vit*: only through the purity of love can one hold true to the light of the Knower."

I knew he was referring to the vow I had hoped to fulfill when I left the valley so very long ago. I truly could feel its age-old hold had fallen away. I could feel the truth in his words—answering a vow, or any need, cannot be bound to a duty borne of a promise! Giving is pure only when it remains an honorable and truthful response of the heart.

He said, "Your journey here has been long and strenuous. You must be quite tired. A place has been prepared for you. It is humble but should suffice. He turned his gaze to the man standing next to him and said, "This is Master Janjuran." But before I could greet him, Master Rambala turned again to the woman. "But first," he added, "I would like you to meet our beloved Nil'Amma Tara."

The moment Nil'Amma Tara stepped forward, a pure aroma of spiced-rose filled the air. I had grown accustomed to the namaste palm mudra as a way of greeting another, but instead she offered me her hand with her palm facing down. Awkwardly, I hesitated to take it, hoping first to brush the dirt from my hands. All the same, she reached out for me. The moment she touched my hand, a mild tingling sensation ran up my arm followed by a spreading sense of peace.

"*Swagata*, young master," she said, "Your arrival is a truly welcome sight. It has been a very long time since we have seen each other in this way."

I thanked her for coming to greet me. I wanted to ask her a thousand questions, but I was so completely rapt in her aura of sacredness that I was at a complete loss for words. She seemed to sense my awkwardness and reached out for my other hand. Then she paused to look at me from a deeper place, a place I instantly knew I had once cherished. Her face was hauntingly beautiful but somehow also fierce. And it was delicately pure while also strikingly powerful. Her dark brown eyes drew me into them so completely I nearly lost my balance. For an instant, I envisioned her sitting in a lotus meditation in an ancient shrine, her body silhouetted in gold against a background covered in iconic symbols and shining hieroglyphs. Although the vision was only an instant, I was left with a vivid imprint that she had once been my teacher.

She said, "Young master, while you are here your first task will be to let fall the conditions that Maya may have demanded of you, to let go of any limits and no longer restrain your beliefs of what is yet possible." Her English was smooth, steady, and relaxed.

She added, "Here you will realize that what you have sought in coming here is already with you. In truth, it has always been. Amarpura is this world's true heart—the heart that is forever free of the mistaken drives and pretenses found in the self-limiting realms. You already understand. To know the human heart you must make yourself defenseless to love. Now realize, to know Amarpura's heart you must make yourself defenseless to your boundless nature. There is no obstacle here that will separate you from mountain, stream, or sky. There is only one Self of things, one Presence in innumerable forms. In body and mind, you and I may continue to appear divided through our outward differences, but beyond this simple work of light we are the same Self of all things. You have already come to experience a peace here that is unaffected by the turbulence of the world. So too you will discover here a bridge to a power that far exceeds the dreams of the common world."

I acknowledged what she said with a nod but said nothing. I was filled with a sense of gratefulness.

"On your journey here," she said, "you were confronted with many difficulties, and yet you prevailed."

"There were times when I thought I had lost my way," I answered. "There's no denying it—there were some real life-altering challenges."

"*Pariksha!*" she said. "Before the splendor of recognition there is always a trial by ordeal!"

"Pariksha?" I asked.

"It is the challenge between the knower and the thinker. Consider the *tanpura*," she said.

"The gourd instrument, the one that looks like a sitar but has only four strings like a vina?"

"Yes," she said, "but the tanpura, unlike the vina or sitar, is not used to play a song. It is used to establish an understanding, a harmonic realization that other instruments will rely on. The tanpura is used to set a single divining tone, a unifying resonance that gives the music its bearing. A master musician knows that before he can play it, he must first adjust its strings to produce the exact tone, the one that will carry the actions of the other instruments to perfection. Some strings must be loosened, others tightened. It is a complex work that takes time and sensitivity to master. To accomplish this, the musician must first learn to listen to the greater need. Only then can it be correctly tuned."

"So when I started my journey here, when I entered the mountains, that's why you left me to find my own way—to listen for my greater need?"

"My dear, your journey here began long before then. It began the instant you left this valley. Your path here was not lost when your plans ran astray. You found it again the instant you renounced the effort and humbled your listening. There are four conditions in which the way to this valley can be found: *shraddhaya*, faith in your highest nature; *pratibhaya*, adhering to the direction to which your heart and intellect are in agreement; *anandabhajin*, following the stream of your bliss; and *atmasampradha*, surrendering all mental effort to the greater Will."

"Faith, divination, bliss, and sacrifice. Those are the four strings. Together they created the unifying resonance," I said.

Nil'Amma Tara responded, "If the Supreme calls, even while it creates a shadow to obscure the way, one must persevere. To recognize the reward in answering the challenge is indispensable." I felt her words striking the heart of my mind, rousing in me a deep knowing that I had been working to uncover in myself for a very long time.

"You were not alone. Our support, and the support of your guiding messengers, was not the only directing force." She affirmed in a steady tone, "To have found this path, it was only necessary that you appreciated the trials of darkness. That is pariksha!"

"I'm grateful that it was just as it was. And I'm grateful it's over and that I'm now here. But no doubt, I look a bit worse for wear."

She folded her hands into a prayer mudra over her heart and then lifted them to her lips. She separated her hands to shoulder width and slowly brought them back together, while exhaling slowly and softly. A fruity, sweet floral aroma burst into the air. Separating her hands again, she revealed a perfectly formed white lotus between her palms. It was both delicate and brilliant. She then lifted the velvety cool blossom to my lips.

"For you to eat," she said softly. "To heal your body."

Once the flower was on my tongue, its petals immediately melted into ambrosial nectar. I closed my eyes to follow the flow of sweetness as it quickly spread through my entire body, creating an inner glow and instantly relieving every ache and pain on the way. When I opened my eyes, her face had become breathtakingly luminous.

She lowered her hand to touch my heart and said, "Aaravindha, you have already been told there is no other place like this in this world. And I tell you now: here the sweetness of Supreme Grace abounds in my *lila*, my delight."

The man Master Rambala had previously introduced stepped forward to say, "Before you go to your rest, I too would like to welcome you."

Master Rambala interjected, "Aaravindha, you will not remember Master Janjuran; he has come to live here just ninety years ago. But you will see in him a brother. You have a great deal in common. There will be much for you to share."

"Just ninety years ago?" I said half laughing.

His appearance conjured up a nearly forgotten memory of an old Latvian sea wizard, Vanemuine, who was fabled to be a part of the creation of the earth. As a child, I had come across his image in an old burgundy, clothbound encyclopedia. And now here he was again. He was small-boned and thin. He had a mildly Western appearance. Particularly, the color of his skin appeared more sun-bronzed than naturally dark. His long hair and beard fell lightly over his narrow shoulders in a mixture of white, dark silver, and a faint touch of blondish-red. The bones in his long, thin face created an elegant, elfin-like look that summoned up the mythic Baltic memory.

Welcoming me a second time with a gentle hug, Master Janjuran promptly suggested I should go rest. He told me that some fresh fruit awaited me in my hut. But only then did I realize that Master Amir had already slipped away. I had been entirely too immersed in meeting the other three masters to sense his departure. I felt a momentary pinch of not having thanked him for guiding me to this moment but then remembered his comment back at the village: "If we wait any longer, the villagers will attempt to fill our pockets with their gratitude—better for us to be on our way."

A small boy and two slightly older girls had come out of the forest. On Master Rambala's request, the two girls walked over to offer me their hands. He told me that they were to guide me to my hut. He said that although the children didn't speak English, they were very perceptive and I shouldn't hesitate to tell them if there is anything I might need.

Only a trace of sunlight still brushed over the surrounding peaks. The valley had fallen asleep in shadows. My hut looked like a fairytale cottage inside a spacious grove of large broadleaf trees. It was humble, as Master Rambala had said, but well crafted—built with a thatched roof and basketwoven walls that were attached to narrow pine posts. My cot was surrounded with a finely woven mosquito net that seemed redundant. I hadn't seen or heard a single sign of mosquitos. A white cotton blanket and smooth silk sheets were neatly wrapped around a thin, futon-like mattress. A glass urn filled with water stood next to a florally embossed ceramic basin. A mismatched stack of clean towels had been neatly placed on a small footstool. My pack was hung on a hook beside the cot. The only thing that prevented me from going directly to sleep was a basket filled with a variety of nuts and fragrant fresh fruits.

15

MYSTERIOUS BLUE

*The white light was so lustrous
that even the undersides of the surrounding branches
were delicately aglow.*

I awoke early to the sound of a distant prayer echoing through the hills. Now that I was alone, Amarpura's aura of serenity seemed significantly more apparent, offering me a calming sense of being bathed in sacredness. I pushed aside my blanket and sat up, pulled my legs into half-lotus, and let my thoughts fall to the pull of gravity. In seconds I found myself suffused in Amarpura's tranquil luminosity, its limitless touch converting my simple process of letting go into an effort-free and motionless observing. All sense of constraint or need for control gave way to a fluid expansiveness so immense that I was no longer able to sense myself in the world. Instead, I experienced the world inside me. My relationships, my journey here, the lifetimes that had passed since I had left this valley, the masters—all of it was there in a solitary sweeping perception. Then even that view seemed too small, vanishing into a preeminent goldenness, an absoluteness—lush, free, and immediate.

It may have been minutes, or possibly hours, but when my bodily awareness finally returned it was due almost entirely to the seductive pull of the warming daylight brushing over my eyelids. I would gladly have stayed there with eyes closed, floating in the sweet afterglow, but a peculiar scratching sound came from the opposite end of my hut. I opened my eyes sedately, slowly focusing through the blur only to catch sight of an enormous spider, nearly half the size of my shoe, creeping ominously along the base of the wall.

My awareness had been so broadly spacious that it took me a moment to reclaim my focus. By the time I did, I realized that my body was already standing. Rather than the spider turning out to be a sci-fi monster readying itself for an imminent attack, it rushed out through a small, frayed rip in the wall the instant it saw me move. Its mind-blowing size conjured up a salvo of potential future confrontations, making my first task of the day to repair the rip.

My hair and clothes were a muddle of disheveled conflicts. My skin was sticky to the touch and my face felt scratchy. Snapping up a razor, soap, and a small towel from the table, I set off toward the nearby sound of flowing water. The morning air was freshly moist, warm, and abounding with the scent of flowers and cinnamon. A gentle breeze rippled through the branches, spilling chutes of sparkling dew from leaf to leaf. By the time I found the stream's rocky bank, my clothes were soaked. There was something new and interesting in the air—an enticing sound of children singing. I followed a narrow footpath to a slightly arched, wooden bridge built of logs and expertly woven branches that led to a sunlit, green clearing. A group of children, possibly twelve in all, were gathered in a half-circle around a small-statured, white-haired man. All swayed with their hands above their heads in gentle rhythm to a charming, pentatonic folk song.

I tried to hide behind a small cluster of trees, hoping to watch their performance unseen, but the man conducting the song instantly motioned for the children to stop singing and then turned around to look directly at me. At first glance he appeared quite advanced in years, but his sprightly movements hinted at a much younger vitality. His especially long white hair, fluffy eyebrows, wispy mustache, and feathery beard stood out glowingly against the aged tan-brown of his skin. *Possibly Burmese or Thai,* I thought.

Barely loud enough for me to hear, he called out the words, "*Oh'loy.*" And then, "*Chapha nang!*"

I didn't know what those words meant, but I chose to believe they were intended as a greeting. A few seconds passed before he called out again, "Eh, Aaravindha! Chapha nang!"

I strolled to the end of the bridge and called back, "Oh'loy!" A few of the children waved and a few more giggled. After a short pause, the man's face lit up with a seemingly amused grin, and then he shifted his use of language into an irregular English. Pointing upstream, he said, "You *gau dak way! Jima yaiyong.*"

He either wanted me to move along or he knew I was looking for a place to wash up. Or maybe there was something else he wanted me to see upstream? "Gau dak way" was easy enough to understand. The rest, like the man himself, was a mystery.

I left the trail to wade into the cool, knee-high water. Pushing against the current, I traced the smooth feel of the riverbed's polished stones beneath my bare feet. The stream was brilliant with a mixed abundance of colorful stones. After sifting the streambed and bringing up handfuls of agates, quartz, and red and green jaspers, I came to an abrupt drop in the flow of water, where a succession of minor water-falls formed small pools. The lowest and largest formed a bubbly basin just deep enough for me to plunge in up to my neck.

Refreshed and smelling like peppermint soap, I decided to explore a bit farther upstream. The main trail eventually pulled away from the water to amble through a sleepy, upward-sloping meadow. On its higher side I reentered the forest. The trees were especially thick and full there. Once I was under their shade, an enticing mystery caught my interest. Just ahead, suspended in the air between the varying shades of green, I detected a pale glow so faint I wasn't entirely sure I was actually seeing it. My first reaction was to write it off as a blur in my eyes—a possible aftereffect of the peppermint soap. But after a few rubs and blinks I realized that as faint as it was, the colorless glow was undeniably real. I soon noticed that it transitioned from extremely pale into a soft, bluish luster a bit farther into the trees.

Initially I wondered if it was some sort of natural phenomenon, one I simply had no reference for. Kayaking in seawaters surrounding the San Juan Islands, I had on occasion come across microplankton tides that came aglow at night when disturbed. And I had heard stories involving electromagnetic sparks and fiery spheres that could appear in the atmosphere when pressure intensified or shifted inside the earth's crystalline crust. Or maybe it was in some way similar to the phenomenon known as Saint Elmo's fire, an uncommon weather marvel that creates a coronal blue-violet discharge around grounding objects such as lightning rods or ships' masts. Whatever this was, it clearly wasn't anything I had seen before.

The more I worked to see it, the more elusive it became, at times disappearing altogether. But when I let my eyes relax fully, I could see it again. More than curious, I opted to investigate the direction from where it seemed to be the strongest. But after just a few steps, another mystery entered the brew—a delightful tingling sensation started to ripple through my skin followed by an inexplicable feeling of weightlessness in my arms and legs.

I used my body as a compass, letting my feelings track the light through a tightly knit wall of dense underbrush. Here and there, broken fragments of an all-but-missing ruin jutted up through the earth. I paused to pull back the underbrush and soon realized I was standing over an area where, thousands of years ago, an extravagantly carved building once stood. A few more strides led me to a natural opening that led between two broad-based tree trunks. I was standing at the edge of a flat, circular courtyard, perhaps once belonging to the ruin. It was hemmed in by a group of banyan-like trees. The sun streaming through the dimming branches appeared ghostly, creating a supernatural dreamlike setting inside the soft, luminous blue ambiance.

But it wasn't the celestial feel, or the ruins, or the massive trees, that held my interest. It was the apparent source of the glow. On the farthest end from where I was, the soft blue brightened significantly around an even brighter white center. The white light was so lustrous that even the undersides of the surrounding branches were delicately aglow. After a few ardent attempts at focusing into its center, I was astonished to see an ethereal outline of someone there! Long ago I had heard of reclusive monks who had once lived in these mountains and knew how to generate an auric glow around their bodies through directing their pranic life force. That auric glow was described as being especially noticeable at night, but this glow utterly dominated the daylight.

Dear Sounds True friend,

Since 1985, Sounds True has been sharing spiritual wisdom and resources to help people live more genuine, loving, and fulfilling lives. We hope that our programs inspire and uplift you, enabling you to bring forth your unique voice and talents for the benefit of us all.

We would like to invite you to become part of our growing online community by giving you three downloadable programs—an introduction to the treasure of authors and artists available at Sounds True! To receive these gifts, just flip this card over for details, then visit us at **SoundsTrue.com/Free** and enter your email for instant access.

With love on the journey,

TAMI SIMON   Founder and Publisher, Sounds True

SOUNDS TRUE
many voices, one journey   800.333.9185

It suddenly dawned on me. I had literally been walking through the extended nimbus of a remarkable being. Desiring to see who could create such an astonishing phenomenon, I took a few steps closer. It was Nil'Amma Tara! I was completely taken aback. As if the light itself wasn't already remarkable enough, there was something even more fascinating going on: there wasn't anything beneath her but empty space. She was levitating cross-legged about a half meter above a blanketed stone-slab bench. Blended into her shine, a scarcely visible aureole of rainbow light formed a corona around her head, deepening into what looked like a tiny, ethereal blue flame dancing directly above her forehead.

I've been blessed with more than my share of truly extraordinary visions, on occasion witnessing specters of deities and possibly even angels. But this exquisite vision of Nil'Amma Tara, her body shining and suspended weightless in the air, was simply beyond words. I was rapt in awe, until it dawned on me that I had probably intruded. Just as I took my first retreating step, she opened her eyes. Incredibly, her gaze radiated the same blue luminosity; the outside corners of her eyes shimmered white. Her palms were turned up, holding something too transparent to distinguish, which vanished altogether the moment she raised her hands.

Without a word, she turned her right palm forward to face me, with her index finger and thumb touching to form a mudra. I instantly sensed a warm surge of energy pass into my chest and heart. I couldn't really say if it created pain or inspired bliss, or an abstract blend of both. I intuitively let go into it, knowing she was offering me some kind of blessing. As the warmth increased, a whooshing surge of energy shot up from my heart, through the associated part of my spine, and then moved up into the center of my forehead. I felt my back arcing involuntarily. My head felt suddenly blissful and dizzied. I abandoned all resistance and shut my eyes. Then in a sudden moment of intense bursting light, I completely lost my sense of where I was. I felt myself quickly spiraling into an ascending expanse. I was soon enveloped in an energetic storm, filled with waves of ecstatic bliss, every new wave followed by another burst of expanding light.

Before I knew it, I found myself crouched down on one knee, hiding behind two large, round boulders and ankle-deep in a slow flowing stream. I was somewhere I knew I wasn't supposed to be, somewhere up higher in the valley. I was someone else, an adolescent—a lean, fit boy with long, shiny black hair. My heart was racing and my breath was hurried. I was eavesdropping, viewing a scene through the entrance of an old crumbling temple. A striking young man, also with shiny black hair, was sitting cross-legged at the feet of Nil'Amma Tara, between two fractured stone pillars. The man was a younger version of Master Rambala.

Nil'Amma Tara chanted something while pouring small trickles of water from a golden urn into Master Rambala's upward cupped hands. Three times he lifted his hands to his lips to sip the liquid, and three times he sprinkled what remained of it over his head, sending clear flowing drops down over the taut muscles of his bare back. Now and then, Nil'Amma Tara would halt her movements to recite a few time-stopping mantras. Each time she did, my heart accelerated. And each time, Master Rambala would join in to echo the mantras exactly as she had chanted them. Standing on either side of her, two women dressed in white added their voices in an evenly paced monotone chant. They swung what looked like a pair of double-tiered, flaming gold puja lamps.

Master Rambala's body started to quiver and sway and then slowly settle back down. When his movements stilled completely, Nil'Amma Tara placed both of her hands directly above his head. With obvious care, she lifted her upturned palms as if she was drawing something invisible out of his crown. A faint, nearly transparent grayness formed into a small blur above his head. Then in a dramatic, unexpected burst, Nil'Amma Tara clapped her hands together exactly where the blur was. In sync with the clap, she called out the mantra: "*Hum Tham, Hum Phat!*" The grayness dissipated instantly.

I had completely forgotten that this had somehow been an induced experience. The events had been so undeniably real, I came to believe I was actually there. I had entirely forgotten my present-day body. The instant I began to question where I was and how I had come to be there Nil'Amma Tara looked up from her ceremony and fired her gaze directly at me. Who was she looking at—the boy or Aaravindha? I felt utterly confused. Was I looking into the future or looking back into the past? Before I could make any sense of it, I was spiraling again, uncontrollably, through expanding light waves.

Disoriented and somewhat nauseous, I struggled for my footing. Realizing my eyes were pressed closed, I forced them open only to see that I was Aaravindha again. I tried my best not to lose my balance. My thoughts were disjointed and fragmented, like waking a bit too fast from sleep. Nil'Amma Tara's unwavering gaze was still focused on me, exactly the way she had looked at me when she caught me peering out from behind the boulders. With the exception of a few subtle traces of blue quietly disguised in the shades of her face, the glow had completely disappeared. And though she was still cross-legged, she was now sitting firmly on the bench.

I struggled to understand what storm had just picked me up, spun me through time, and brought me back again. My mind was reeling. Sensing my confusion, Nil'Amma Tara gestured for me to come sit by her. And then I knew. She had somehow done that to me.

16

NIL'AMMA TARA'S BRILLIANCE

There were moments that I felt fully grounded,
and then in an instant my sense of time would drop away
into enormous spaces—silent expanses without form or end
that drew me into them with an irresistible allure.

In the contemporary West, levitation is primarily seen as a magician's trick or a staged illusion. In the esoteric East, the real possibility of weightless levitation has long been accepted, identified under a number of Sanskrit terms, among them: *uparipitri, udana gaman, dardura siddhi,* and most notably, *laghima.*

Uparipitri is the most commonly documented form of levitation in both Eastern and Western history. It appears as a consequence of intense devotion-inspired rapture, wherein spiritually devout men or women, having surrendered into a blissful state of worshipful ecstasy, suddenly find themselves floating through the air. One of the most prominent cases is that of Joseph of Cupertino, an Italian friar who lived during the first half of the seventeenth century. In his early life he was considered by his peers to be a badly tempered simpleton lacking in both intellectual and worldly skills. But that all changed once Joseph answered his calling to become a friar. His parish assigned him the unassuming task of caring for their stable horses. It was there, while caring for the animals, that he first learned to love and cherish life unconditionally, and as a result to calm his emotional restlessness. His intense devotion in performing his tasks, combined with his impeccable faith, led Joseph to become so enamored in his adoration for God that he regularly lost himself in unrestrained rapture that would at times lift him off the ground, sometimes for hours. After nearly seventy such levitations in which Joseph became so entranced that he no longer responded to the demands of his Catholic Church superiors, he was categorized as unmanageable and therein deemed a threat to their authority. Shortly thereafter he was hidden away in secret seclusion far from public view but was all the same canonized a saint a century later.

Other documented cases in the West include Padre Pio of Pietrelcina, Teresa of Ávila, and Francis of Assisi. Religious historians claim that hundreds of similar cases have been chronicled throughout Europe's past. In the Far East, recorded examples of levitation are more prominent and numerous, most likely due to fewer religious prejudices ascribed to the phenomenon than in the West. While uparipitri is the most common form of levitation, it's rarely noted as the principal means for accomplishing it. Reliable knowledge on the practice of levitation is difficult to attain. In the few isolated places where it's still taught, it's most often practiced in secret as a systematized discipline that acts as a progression toward furthering the greater goal of attaining an overall mastery. Levitation, or any other siddhi, is never taught as a goal in itself but as a partial means toward Self-liberation.

Udana gaman, at times referred to as *vayu gaman*, is a rare breath control technique that requires a high degree of caution and discipline, as do most advanced pranayama-induced techniques. Its preparation involves a rigorous rarefication of the body's vital life-force currents, in particular the *udana vayu*—one of the five divisions of pranic life force (the other four being *prana*, *apana*, *samana*, and *vyana*). These vayus reign alternately over the various regions of the body and its extensive range of life-sustaining actions. Through the use of specific pranayama techniques, the body's life-force meridians are rarefied and saturated with pranic life force in the region of the throat, where udana vayu flows from the heart to the brain. If a state of transcendental samadhi is sustained while a complete capitulation of body awareness is offered into the natural ascent of the udana vayu, the body can be induced to take on the quality of the ascending life force, and then levitation is achieved.

Dardura siddhi is the most practiced levitation technique and also the most accessible form, although among masters it's rarely thought of as a genuine siddhi. The dardura technique can cause energetic surges of Shakti to burst through the body's subtle meridians, triggering it to leap like a frog through the air but with little or no noticeable muscular involvement. Though it doesn't fully qualify as a true levitation, it typically acts as a transitional phase in the development of the more advanced practice of laghima. However, to accomplish a full expression of laghima, a number of extenuating mental obstacles must first be overcome.

Both dardura and laghima rely on identical principles. Both depend on an ability to meditatively transcend into a state of clear-light awareness. Clear-light awareness is rooted in a sustained samadhi wherein the perception-illumining power that acts as the quintessence of the psyche is no longer altered by any unconscious tendencies, patterned habits, or beliefs. Laghima requires a systematic process of constant, inwardly directed letting go while also consciously releasing one's awareness into the resulting subtle flow of bliss. This leads to deeper and more expanded states of consciousness to where the psyche's mental clutter no longer interferes with the inception to be weightless.

Earlier in my life I had an opportunity to witness the successful performance of laghima levitation by two devout young monks living in a cloistered hermitage in northern India. Later, using what I learned, and after lengthy periods of study and practice, I personally experienced the direct potency of laghima a number of times. However, never in my life had I beheld the beauty and grace of this siddhi made so magnificent as I had this morning. It was beyond anything I imagined it could be—so free, so heavenly, so luminous and awe-inspiring.

My thoughts were still sifting through the aftereffect of having discovered Nil'Amma Tara levitating here in this forest setting, and then having so effusively and convincingly been transported into the past. I did my best to piece together the events that had transpired. But even more so, I was trying to understand what this moment was meant to be. I was aware that an accomplished master never uses a siddhi to exhibit this level of skill without having a very good reason. But at present, that reason was a mystery.

It was evident that the old man conducting the children in song had pointed this way because he knew Nil'Amma Tara was here. This meeting wasn't coincidental; little in this journey had been. Every event or step had revealed some kind of purpose. But I was beginning to suspect that seeing Nil'Amma Tara floating on air wasn't one of those purposes. As I sat on a small stone bench in front of her, she confirmed my suspicions. She said, "It was essential to first provide a setting wherein the improbable was made probable."

I asked, "You let me see you levitating as a means to an end?"

She told me it was necessary to slacken my hold on the familiar, which is precisely what it did. I reflected on what she had said when we first met: "Young master, while you are here your first task will be to let fall the conditions that Maya may have demanded of you, let go of your limits, and no longer restrain your beliefs of what is yet possible."

I was still fluttering back and forth between worlds, between the known and an incredible new view of what that "possible" might be. There were moments that I felt fully grounded, and then in an instant my sense of time would drop away into enormous spaces—silent expanses without form or end that drew me into them with an irresistible allure. The sensual, physical world now seemed more unsolidified and evanescent than real—still linear, but commingled with moments of nonlinear discontinuities.

On my day of arrival, I was physically and mentally bushed and largely overwhelmed with the prospect of finally being here. I had already sensed the incredible difference in my perception of my surroundings, but now it was unmistakable. I truly was in an altogether different reality. I was in a place where the finite and infinite merge to avail an aura of potential unlike anywhere else in this world. She had told me in our meeting, "You will discover here a bridge to a power that far exceeds the dreams of this common world." I had no idea it would be on my first morning.

To be somehow transported through time like that gave me a new level of respect and reverence for Nil'Amma Tara's genius. She knew exactly what would break my hold on my limits, and then she applied her masterful expertise to lead me back through time. I was still grappling with the results, let alone the odds of something like that even being possible.

As a child, I hadn't fully bought into the idea that death was a final statement to life, but its sway still had an obtrusive effect on me. That grip had now been obliterated. A seeming side effect was how the physical now appeared so much more illusory than before. The passing of hundreds of years and my multiple incarnations was no longer a half-lit memory; it was crystal clear. The dominant rule of death was irrevocably wrecked. I had crossed over and returned. And this wasn't just another vision. What had altered my sense of time the most was that I had briefly experienced myself as being real in two places simultaneously. It was in one of those timeless gaps, one of those enormous spaces that I had fallen through, where I now sensed myself as more real in this transitional way than in my usual physical form.

Many years ago, exploring a historical district in New Delhi, I had come across a back-alley bookstore. Rifling through a mountain of tattered hardbacks, I uncovered an old, limited-edition book written in both Hindi and English. In its pages I found reference to a secret Indian society that had formed at the start of the first millennium with the intention to keep secret many of the ancient works of the great masters and to keep them out of the hands of the corrupt or undeserving. The book listed and described a number of rare siddhis. One was *kalapurvinavasa*—it gave its master a rare ability to transcend the limits of time in order to transport the practitioner's consciousness (or someone else's) into the past.

When I asked Nil'Amma Tara if she had done that, she paused to close her eyes and consider my question. A few seconds later, beaming a lustrous smile, she answered me indirectly.

"It was necessary to purge your consciousness of a past burden—a *manociri*—in order to liberate a karmic hindrance."

"*Mano* means mind or psyche?"

She replied, "And *ciri* refers to a subtle interference of one's lucidity, which shadows the inner depths like a thin mist over water. It affected a part of your sight in casting a shadow over a portion of your heart. In the days to come, when this transformation is complete, Master Janjuran will aid you in advancing your lucidity further."

"You said this ciri was a past burden. So is it a consequence of something that happened during that past lifetime?"

"It is! You might see it as a knot. It hindered a part of your ability to feel, which in turn influenced your sight. Our senses naturally progress toward comprehension. Hearing directs feeling, and feeling directs sight, in that order."

"So it's like a *hridyagrantha*, a heart-knot?" I replied. "I actually felt it loosening. It was remarkably tangible. It initially felt like an unanswered grief, and then it broke free."

She leaned in to emphasize, "When a part of the heart is eclipsed, an equivalent portion of one's intuitive nature is also eclipsed. The feeling nature of the heart is intimately bound to intuition."

"You said Master Janjuran would aid me. What a blessing. I felt unusually close to him the moment we met, like remembering a dear friend."

"He came to live here many years ago, arriving with talents similar to yours. His abilities are now fully developed."

I might have asked my next question earlier, but I was still landing. Now that I was integrating a bit, I noticed that my skin was tingling. And as my focus was narrowing to the moment, I could see that there was still a subtle trace of light around her body—barely there but noticeable.

"I'm struggling to understand something," I inquired. "It's about the technique. I was hoping you could tell me more about the siddhi you did?"

She exclaimed, "I have no use for techniques! A child grasping the hand of the mother, desiring to learn to walk—that is technique. The mother's hand reaching out to the child—that is siddhi."

She extended her right leg out of her lotus position and touched the ground lightly with her toes. "Young master, you experienced my *prasada*."

"Prasada?"

"When the sun peers into its own reflection, it grows brighter. That is the nature of what transpired."

Briefly I felt the touch of something coming from her to me, something quietly powerful that softly trembled through the earth beneath my feet. Everything was changing so very quickly. Standing in these ancient ruins at the edge of the world, a place once filled with animation and hope, now just rubble returning to its source . . . it was the perfect setting for a dream's end.

It's curious what the psyche settles on when what was once deemed real is no more: the smell of the air, the feel of the earth, and the glimmer of sunlight playing off her hair. But that too—all of it—was a different kind of real. Here the air smelled of roses, the earth felt timelessly mysterious, and her shimmering white hair crowned her like an angel's nimbus. My perception of this world would never again return to what it once was—like dying but without the loss. I was unspeakably grateful. That was the heart of it, an indescribable gratitude for the brilliance of her unconditional grace.

"Siddhiprasada!" I affirmed. "The blessed grace of a true Devata.*" She nodded in acknowledgment.

A full minute passed in silence before I asked, "That experience—the one when I was that boy watching you and Master Rambala—the entire experience seemed . . ." I searched for the right words. "It was more than a memory. I was as real as this, here and now. I remember things now, things I hadn't thought of before, things I couldn't otherwise have known. I'm grateful for what was going on there between you and Master Rambala. But there are now other feelings. When I was watching you, I sensed an uncomfortable combination of disenchantment, grief, and even some resistance. Please tell me what you know. I believe those feelings had to do with my mother passing away in that life. That's one of the reasons you wanted me to see that, isn't it? That experience you gave me had something to do with my mother dying." Finally, I added, "I sensed that you weren't the only one watching me. I felt her spirit there, my mother from that time. I can still feel her, even now."

*Deity

"Young master, I didn't choose that time, you did!" She continued, "In the akash, all past impressions are indelibly kept. The akash rests between the streams of manifest change and where time is whole, absolute. The past, the present, and what might yet be are there. Everything is, whether realized or latent, whether it is attained wisdom or wisdom's promise; it's there. Some of those impressions are attractive. In that life, you failed to embrace the greater truth of your mother's existence. That was impressed in the akash as incomplete knowledge. That's what drew you to it, for you to liberate it. What remains unfinished in time wakes again and again, troubling the spirit from life to life, obscuring many related perceptions, the way dust obscures the passage of light. Inevitably a time comes when these incompletions must be attended. It was this unrealized karma that inspired those feelings. The time had come!"

"Can you tell me how she died?"

"Your mother fell to the bite of a mountain adder. Her passing was a difficult ordeal for both Master Rambala and you. Rambalaji struggled ceaselessly, grieving for months on end. He asked me to help him overcome it, but it was only when his heart could no longer endure that I decided to intervene. Had I not done so, *pramoksa* would have been delayed."

"Pramoksa?"

"Liberation!"

"You mean enlightenment?"

"Yes—samyaksambodhi! Over time, grief left unrequited turns to illness. But first it gathers into a concentration of mental pressures, a *ciri grantha* that forms in the back of the mind. What you glimpsed in that ceremony was its dissolution in Rambalaji—the removal of his final limiting attachment."

"I sensed that. It's why I straightaway felt so grateful."

"Your mother's time here on earth was complete; she had more to do elsewhere. Once the ciri blanketing his reason was no more, he found her again. He witnessed her standing in her true nature—a vision adorned with the light of immortality."

She leaned forward to peer more closely into my eyes. "The *amaraprakash*, the shine of eternal life . . . in its light, grief is instantly transformed to gratitude. Every being must one day come to that!" Her voice took on a new and more powerful quality as she said, "Look before you now: the dawn has come. You are standing at its door!"

Looking her in the eyes just then, I forgot myself altogether. Their pull was too compelling, too gripping to resist. I was literally engulfed in her depth. The world came to a stop, my thoughts all vanished. The silence was nearly complete. Only a vague sense of something mysterious remained, a hint of a call that rose like a wave and then crashed into a feathery roar like that of a thousand whispers, more ancient than anything I had ever sensed. Clearly she was that dawn!

Like the gentle breeze that suddenly rose to brush over our skin, her voice came forward in a honeyed sweetness, "In his Oneness, Master Rambala came to realize that she is and will always be with him. He unveiled her there in the eternal heart. There is but one true heart. She who was once his wife and your mother has long since entered the song of her waking bliss. Now he is always in her embrace. In the divine turning, when the illusion was no more, all that remained was her *amrita*, the blessed light of the one Goddess."

"I see that now. But then no matter how much I knew and had been blessed with, I just didn't want to let her go. Maybe it was because she was such a perfect incarnation of love. It seemed so incongruous to be here in this valley and to lose her like that. She was so very pure and deep, like fresh snow on an ancient mountain. And yet the great masters living here let her pass. I feel differently now. But back then I secretly held that as somehow unjust."

"That shadow trailed you through three lives," she said. "Now it is done!"

"It is!" I said. "Like Master Rambala, I can see her too. She's there in your eyes, in the amaraprakash—in the immortal light. But not just there. I can feel her in my heart, in that space that opens when I surrender to her. I knew it back then, but I resisted. Her incarnation was only a mask, a momentary gift meant to entice my heart into her lila. She's eternal; she always was. That realization, which rose between that past life and now, that's what you wanted for me. To see that. Thank you!"

A soft scent of roses started to fill the air. "A gift from her," she said.

She continued, "In life, or when facing *mrityu*—death—the desire to possess another can easily blind the mind to the true nature of a soul. The law of karma is clear: 'To the degree that one possesses another, one is possessed.' The essential purpose in being in this physical life is not to use it to hold on to what we are given but to delight in the love it invokes, and to delight in all that life brings or takes. When an earthly love falls from our sight, our love remains, so we might transform it into something higher."

I said, "I can see how that affected me as a recurring theme. The difficulty in holding on and the pain of letting go—a truth half hidden or a falsehood half seen. Holding on to satisfy a lack in the end only affirms that lack. To see someone as an object of possession, or equally to be possessed by someone, or anything—those are real dangers."

She said, "To covet is a plight all beings endure for a time. Its sacrifice is a vital part of the waking. Until the want of the mind is extinguished, everlasting life cannot be attained. And so it is with a genuine delight; it is only realized when personal desires are selflessly relinquished. Some come to realize this, but this release cannot be puritanical nor can it be a rejection of the sensual life! Those are the mistaken paths of the misinformed. Truth can only be won when the sacrifice becomes a complete and unpretentious deliverance from the hunger to possess."

"Until now, I hadn't heard it said so perfectly."

She answered, "Unity is the everlasting rule of time. Change and diversity are merely its game. The Self is beyond any one incarnation; it is neither a verity of a becoming nor can it die. It is a circumstance of an eternal life. Of all that we might value, the highest must be Oneness, not the many faces in it. A true life constitutes and upholds diversity; diversity does not uphold the Oneness."

"Brilliant, that's exactly it!" I said. "I'm not that boy, this body, or even this mind, but the One who reveals these potentials so that the One can live in this life!"

"Yes! Until the high Self is realized as one's only true reference, the mind continues to bind its service to a reference forged from the body, the mind, or remembered past events. Until then we are burdened, just as you were compelled to share in the insufferable trappings of the world for three lifetimes."

I said, "And then there's that step in which to sacrifice the false for the real, which poses a less obvious challenge. Realizing our true reference is not the same as claiming it."

She answered, "The last danger is in desiring to possess the high Self. A conclusion is drawn and a claim is set, a conclusion destined to fail. Time, like a fire, cannot be held too long. Self-realization cannot be limited to a mere broadening of ideals. In the passage from darkness to illumination, the invitation to possess the high Self is the final test!"

"You called it an invitation . . ."

"Young master, there is intelligence in darkness, cloaked in temptation. In accepting or in denying its offer, liberation is either found or lost."

"Temptation is the final test," I repeated. "Like a rose, pick or attempt to possess this Self and we instantly feel the stab of its thorn warning us. I suppose we could say that the same is true of love. If we make it an object of our desire and try to claim it, we soon lose it. But if we set it free, let it fly, it returns to us to show us its higher form. But in this world the desire to possess is, all the same, so predominant."

A fire seemed to fill her eyes. She declared, "This is what the children of this world must come to learn: The truth of existence cannot be quelled by the mere glitter of illusion. When illusion has run its course, it is truth that lives on. Nor can an unenlightened mind still the redemptive nature of the heart. When blinded in desire, it is not emotions but the pure call of the heart that must be heeded. Only in true surrender to unconditioned love will the inner eye be freed. It is faith that must illumine it. Its glory can then stream down to fill the heart's chalice. But faith is not easily won. It wakes only when the hunger is foregone. It can then rise through the silence to sound the eternal way and wake the flame of a greater Power, and so light the beacon that guides the Will of the One. This is how faith enters life."

She paused briefly and then continued, "Begin now. Acceptance is the first turn of the key. Accept what is and whatever comes as part of the great calling. But do not covet what has come or will yet come. Accept the guiding hand; let live the Supreme Will. And let it destroy the heart of human desire so the true heart can live. Worship love above all else! Devoted solely to love, Self-realization is assured. Love is the seer's first and final grasp of truth. It is through the union of these two, faith and love, that the hand of fear is burned to cinder. Too much fear rules this world; too few find their way back to love. It is for this reason we of this tradition are here and why we adorn the emerging teacher with our favors: to illumine the way."

She asked, "Is it wise for the children of an omnipresent parent to splash about, serving the meaningless pursuits of a misguided belief? Isn't it much wiser to use the time they have been given to discover the everlasting treasures waiting in the Lotus Land of Divine Being? The Mother does not direct her children to their wanton pursuits. She offers them a world of true treasures. How much grander is the wish of Divine Mother. Success for all rests in a mere turn of devotion, for devotion is the first door to truth.

"Many lifetimes have passed since I vanquished the ruse of death. Today I am the oldest woman on this earth. People are often overcome with awe when I reveal to them my true age. I was already quite old when I became Rambalaji's teacher. It is believed that you are fortunate if you live one hundred years. What is one hundred years? A mere splash in the greater truth of existence. Many generations have come and gone. I have watched as multitudes have fallen asleep in this wintered age. But one day all must return to this sacred path to the sun. I know them all. I know their hearts and minds and all their relationships. Young master, hundreds of years ago I held the one you now call your beloved in these arms, whispering the lure of wisdom into her ear. And so too I have inspired guidance in the heart of the one she now calls her mother. Many teachers today will try to say life is merely a dream, that it is nothing more than an illusion. But what is a far greater illusion is death."

I added, "Breaking free of the cycle of rebirth to reclaim eternal life isn't so easily accomplished."

Nil'Amma Tara replied, "Ending the deception of death is only feasible if the grip that is strangling the heart is released. This begins in sacrificing all trivial pursuits and attending to the higher purpose.

Quell the bidding of the ever-thirsty ego. The way is found in receiving the Will of Supreme Self as the only true motivation. Many will say, 'Come eat this or do this practice if you wish to live a long and happy life.' And these things may lengthen a life, extending it a few more moments, but death will still come. Love is the only way to conquer it! If life is the voice of love, death cannot take it away. Uncover this mystery; remove the shadows that bind in life. Remove what possesses, cast aside the need to possess, and then the task is nearly done. Then become what this world is praying for. The Mother will stand by you and she will say, *Now you are ready, enter my heart, drink of eternal life—no more splashing about.*"

"Nil'Amma Tara," I asked, "why do you stay if you have already conquered all that life has to offer? You are awake to eternal life. Why don't you simply let go of your body and fly to the upper worlds?"

"Ages ago, when still quite young, I was blessed to have an *amara stri'guru* as my guardian. Having attained *amritavapu*, the eternal form, she lived far beyond what was believed possible even among the great Amarta ancestry. On the fourteenth year after my birth, I asked her that exact question. I will now tell you what she told me: 'It is illusion that must take flight, not the Self! The one Self is everywhere.' My dear, if I am everywhere, what need is there to fly to another world?"

"Many have called me Ambadevi, mistakenly setting me apart from them. And yet it is I who ignites the purifying flame in every mother, father, and child, for I am the sun of love that nourishes this world. Amma Tara sees through the eyes of all creatures. This body does not bind me. If I keep it, if I dissolve it, whatever is my whim, it will be so! This body you see before you is only a glimmer in my eye. It is *amritaka*, the nectar of the eternal that flows through these limbs. If I believed I was merely this image, I would surely die here and now. Immortal life is my lila, my delight; all doors are mine to open. To truly know me is to find the one home. There are many rooms in this temple. I am forever free."

17

MASTER PHOW TSENG THAK

His long, silver-ashen hair and thin, wispy white beard
reminded me of the midafternoon mists that would gather
around the surrounding peaks.
The pupils of his eyes were dark, penetrating, and clear.
The upturned age lines encircling his eyes
created a bright, joyful look—nature's record
of having lived a good life.

In Amarpura, in the lives of the Amartya masters, the signs of aging seem to be altogether missing. Rather than showing the common indications of old age, the masters are vital, disease free, and—as with Nil'Amma Tara and Master Amir—exhibit an extraordinary physical beauty. The Amartya concept of immortality is exclusive to these masters.

In our world's long history, extended life has occasionally come about naturally. Examples include Jeanne Louise Calment, a French woman who lived to be 122 years old; Shirali Muslimov, an Azerbaijani mountain man who lived to be 168; or Javier Pereira, a Columbian Indian native who lived to be 169. Others have lived unusually long lives through medicinal supplementation or through Taoist long-life practices. Such people include Li Ching Yuen, a Chinese herbalist and martial arts master who was reputed to have lived 256 years.

Immortality has been the ultimate object of human desire for millennia. Huang Di, the Yellow Emperor, was China's first prominent authority to bring credibility to the concept of immortality. During China's legendary golden age, not only did Huang Di give his people agriculture, teach them how to heat and cook with fire, and harvest silk from the silkworm, he also allegedly developed a secret elixir of immortality. Legend states that after he alchemically transformed himself he vanished from the world, taking with him his entire entourage of attendants to the world of the immortals. Knowledge of Huang Di's success eventually spread around the world, inspiring a kind of alchemical renaissance that was practiced secretly for hundreds of years in both Europe and the East.

Throughout recorded history, successful life extension—whether the product of good fortune, the results of medicine, advanced Taoist practices, or the secret Rasa Siddha practices in India (wherein special herbs, metals, and charms were formulated to alchemically extend life)—has always been accompanied with the common ravages of old age. People that live beyond the normal range of old age nearly always look equal to their years or, at the very least, *old*.

I woke before daybreak to find a quiet setting in which to reflect on the numerous changes I'd already undergone since my arrival. I found my spot in an alpine wildflower meadow. I sat back against the trunk of a solitary old-growth tree, a perfect place in which to gaze up at the sun's first rays as they fanned out in reds and gold behind the eastern peaks. I was thinking of my first meeting with Nil'Amma Tara in the forest when just then I spotted her meandering down through the wildflowers in my direction. In the morning light, wearing a flowing ivory wrap, she was the vision of an angel. She appeared so deeply contemplative I wondered if she'd even notice me sitting there. Just as she was about to pass, she stopped to look at me with eyes that seemed to be elsewhere, possibly weighing out something meaningful or distant.

I reflexively broke the silence by stating the obvious. "Such a lovely morning."

She acknowledged my greeting. "It's a lovely reminder that our real beauty always rests in our purest expression."

"I think that's what makes this morning seem soothing," I added.

She answered, "Discovering the beauty in love is the secret desire behind all desires. In Sundari's presence, nothing—not you or I—can exist divided. The beauty calls us in and fulfills us only when the heart opens to its purpose. If we find there the splendor of our Oneness, then through that one Self she shines her expression into form."

The morning sun spread across the meadow to ignite the green leaves above me with an orangey glow. I closed my eyes for only an instant to drink in the warmth as it touched my face for the first time. When I opened them again, Nil'Amma Tara was already far away, with only the scent of roses left behind.

Master Amir had left the valley for a few days to attend to a matter beyond its borders. Master Janjuran's whereabouts were presently a mystery. But Master Rambala had been especially available, making sure all my needs were met. He took particular pleasure in reacquainting me with a variety of natural sights and walking trails. After returning from our first extended walk, I asked him if I would in any way interfere with their standing of reclusive anonymity if I used their names in my writings. He explained that the masters had already discussed the possibility. They had all agreed that I should be the first for hundreds of years to speak or write about Amarpura openly.

"But," he continued, "one condition must be kept."

"Amarpura's whereabouts must not be revealed to anyone!" I guessed.

"This valley is an unspoiled realm, shielded to preserve its rare virtues," he replied. "It has been of great advantage to us that none can find it unless we wish it."

I asked if anonymity was the primary reason for the sthagmudra.

"There are many reasons," he said. "We don't require recognition or renown for our works. The search for fame or glory is the pursuit of fools. Our influence is most always received unseen, made all the more powerful through our anonymity. Whether we are acknowledged or not, our work is felt around the world. We walk among the people of this world listening, inspiring, and altering the essence of their misconceptions, but rarely do they know. It is not necessary for a devotee who seeks the knowledge to come here. It's only when the knowledge is introduced to the world by a teacher that recognition becomes necessary."

I said, "On the other hand, I found my direct connection to this tradition deeply influential and inspiring."

He answered, "Yes, tradition must be honored. A devotional connection to the masters of this tradition is highly auspicious. But it is not necessary to limit that devotion to the physical form."

"I completely understand what you're saying," I said. "It is easy to feel in the purity of one's own heart the light of that Self, which is so gloriously expressed through the life of the masters living here. I can also see how a kind of projected separation can come about when the physical form creates the illusion of another. And yet I was so grateful to finally be in your company."

Master Rambala laughed musically. "Yes," he said, "to see the teacher is a pure joy for the sincere. And when the time is right, we do appear, but not always in the common form. Each being requires requital in his or her own way."

"I've often felt the presence of the masters in my personal life. I suppose that's because I've never really doubted."

He said, "Faith is the most powerful connection to the teacher. Without it, little is gained."

"Even in my distant part of the world I consistently felt your influence."

"Because you trusted the Knower! When skepticism rules the mind we are rendered invisible to the seeker. So too when skepticism rules, the seeker cannot receive the gifts of the teacher. In faith we can be known! *Abhishradadhati, aham asmi*—believe in stillness—*I Am*. This fundamental understanding is the basis for coming to know us, the path to our door. The Knower who moves the master is also the One who graces the devotee."

"You said there are many reasons for the sthagmudra, the protective seal that guards this valley."

"Many indeed! But it is the ambitious search for power that most often poisons a well. Time and experience have provided an irrefutable testimony. Traditions and religions have come and gone, but the Amartya Parampara has endured. Why do you suppose that is, young master?"

"Because in many of those traditions the sacred was left open to reinterpretation, often in the hands of the ambitious!"

He said, "Some would argue that in making Amarpura visible to the world harm could be prevented. These are not the contentions of those who have experience with these matters. They are the inexpedient assertions of the uninformed. Amarpura would surely suffer the pains of exploitation. The Divine does not take up residence where truth and falsehood, light and darkness, or greed and generosity are allowed to dwell as brethren. In the house consecrated for the Divine, truth alone can dwell."

He asked me to envision what those who are obsessed with attaining power and eternal youth would do if they believed they had found the means to attain these things for themselves.

He said, "Many know this tradition is not a myth. Only a few generations back a number of the Himalayan tribes still sang their songs of us. But much is different now. Presently the pursuit of fortune rules over reason. The human heart has not yet claimed victory over the lower pursuits of the mind. For more than a thousand years, an affluent secret society has searched for Amarpura."

"But why?"

"They search for power. These are not the rightful bearers of power or knowledge. They are driven largely by their desire to acquire the coveted *lapis philosophorum*. These beings have long pursued this ill-founded ambition, driven by lust and mistaken perceptions. Our conditions of anonymity have kept them at bay."

"Lapis philosophorum—the philosophers stone?"

"They are not alone in their search. Others have hoped to find here the waters of life, believing our ability to overcome the dominion of death is merely an alchemical achievement."

I said, "Isn't it alchemical when life extension pertains to some kind of physical transformation? Certainly there's a physical change, a turn in the biological progressions that would otherwise cause bodily degeneration?"

"There is!" he said. "An alchemical transformation is definitely involved, but it is not for the reasons these societies believe. Whether spiritual or material, the attainment of immortality is foremost a verity of the high Self and not the result of manipulating atoms or sipping the waters from a fabled life-regenerating fountain."

I said, "I can understand why people might believe that. Particularly when it comes to the fountain of youth. Our world's history is full of accounts where it was pursued. And here in the East there are also those scriptures that pertain to drinking soma, the sacred nectar of the gods. And, of course, there are stories of amritaka, the nectar of immortality. Those could easily be related to the waters of life. Particularly amritaka."

He said, "Amritaka is the true fountain of youth! But it is not a gift of the earth or matter; it is the blood of the Divine. It flows only from above and only when the corridor that links the one Self to physical form is rightly purified."

I interjected, "So they continue to search for this place because they're just not able to understand."

"Aaravindha, they refuse to understand; they are far too consumed with their lust for power. They have no real interest in the purification or the greater knowledge. They seek only to affirm the beliefs that suit their ambitions."

Since arriving in the valley I had often speculated on why, in this region of the Himalayas, the Amartyas have chosen Sanskrit as their primary language. When I asked Master Rambala, he told me they use Sanskrit because of its accuracy and subtle potencies.

He said, "No other language can so perfectly explain the deeper spiritual meanings involved in the great knowledge."

He told me that in most of the stories once told in this region the Amarta were referred to as Xain. He said the word *Amarta* is in principle the same as Amartya, Amara, and amrita, all of which relate to a state of everlasting life. *Amarta* simply means immortal, while *Amartya* means divinely immortal. *Amara* delineates the immortal condition as permanent, indicating a final and lasting state. *Amrita* differs only in that it refers to an immortality derived through the sacrifice of the lower life tendencies, in order to infuse the mortal form with amritaka. Amritaka is secreted like a celestial hormone at the peak of the central meridian in the crown of the head.

He said the name Xain originated in the Chinese Tang dynasty. It initially related to the Ba'xain, the legendary Eight Immortals. He said the Ba'xain myths were created around the lives of eight masters who once gathered on the island of Penglai Xiantao, which had long ago vanished into the Bohai Sea off the northeastern coast of China. I told him that while I had heard of the Eight Immortals, I had believed they were just a metaphor designed to represent the Eight Pieces of Brocade, a Neijia internal long-life practice that involves eight chi-developing movements used in the practice of Baduanjin qigong.

A wide grin spread across his face. "Many today believe that we too, the Amartya Parampara, are a myth. And, of course, being a myth does have its advantages."

I said, "But maybe my writings will change that." I added, "I don't believe knowledge of this tradition will strike any two people the same way. I believe people will only believe or recognize what they want to or are ready to."

He reached over to absorb my hands in his. "It is a part of your calling, my dear. You are fortunate that you can feel your dharma so vividly. To pass forward the knowledge of our tradition—you have long had my blessings."

I asked him about the man I saw with the children on my first morning.

He exclaimed, "Ah, Master Phow Tseng Thak! He has been anticipating your visit. If you go now, you will find him seated in meditation near where you last saw him."

It was a short walk following the streamside trail to find Master Phow. He was resting in peaceful meditation near where I'd last seen him, exactly as Rambalaji had said. He was seated on a small wooden bench that stood on a thick green felt blanket in the shade of a large tulsi bush. Beside him a small, blackened ceramic bowl was smoldering with the scent of sandalwood. Up close he looked much smaller than I remembered. Careful not to disturb him, I sat down soundlessly on a nearby patch of sandy earth to wait. I was about to close my eyes and join him in meditation when he partially popped open his left eye. The quiet in his face immediately shifted into a welcoming smile.

The sight of him surrounded by the green forest conjured up a sense of being in a fairytale. His skin was leathery and cracked, his hands boney and thin, and his posture appeared slightly bent like that of an old sage in his late seventies. He wore a thin, purple wrap over his narrow shoulders. His loose, ankle-buttoned, mossy-green pants resembled the kind of garb I had seen the men wearing in the village where Amir and I had stopped on my way here. A bright, multicolored cloth belt was wrapped twice around his rounded belly, its end tied neatly into a tasseled knot at his side. His long, silver-ashen hair and thin, wispy white beard reminded me of the midafternoon mists that would gather around the surrounding peaks. The pupils of his eyes were dark, penetrating, and clear. The upturned age lines encircling his eyes created a bright, joyful look—nature's record of having lived a good life.

It was quite an effort to adjust my hearing to his eccentric use of English. Though I soon learned that he spoke French, German, Tibetan, Mandarin, Awadhi, Thai, Sindhi, and Arabic, but—oddly—very little English. All the same, after a few minutes of humoring me with his mixed English, I was able to glean most of what I needed to understand him.

Master Phow immediately told me that I was fortunate to have found the valley so easily. He seemed to want to impress on me that it was rare for anyone new to be allowed to come to this valley. He had a gentle and humble manner, loving and grandfatherly.

I asked him if he would share a little about his life. He seemed almost apologetic when he said his life hadn't been an extraordinary one. He said when he was just a boy his parents convinced a revered Taoist teacher named Phong' Lei Kham to take him in. Phong' Lei was an accomplished master of the Xainzi, belonging to the Jade Flute tradition. Under Phong' Lei's tutelage, Master Phow studied a variety of advanced internal and external martial arts and gradually mastered a number of Taoist longevity disciplines. He said he had devoted the greater part of his life to following those practices. Phong' Lei had on occasion spoken about the Valley of Immortals, telling his students that the highest spiritual knowledge could only be learned there. At other times his old teacher would go into phases of misgiving when he would openly express that the valley could never truly be found or possibly didn't even exist.

He added, "Regardless of what Phong' Lei believed, I never failed to believe that it existed."

Master Phow said that at that time his name was Phuenzi. Master Phow had a number of devout students who came from far away to study with him. Phong' Lei passed into death at the age of 116 when Master Phow was already quite old—ninety-two. Master Phow said that he had gone as far as he wanted with the Taoist systems but was not yet convinced that he had achieved what he had been destined to learn.

He then made up his mind. He said goodbye to his followers, gave away all his possessions, and set off in search of the fabled land of the immortals. For the next ten years he wandered through the Himalayan mountains, but with little success. Only on a few occasions did he come across a hopeful story or a small lead that would inspire him on. At the age of 102, Master Phow had become too weak to continue.

He told me that, unbeknownst to him, he had come within two days walking distance of the valley. He settled into a tranquil place in the forest to surrender his body back to the earth, knowing that he would surely die there. And though he was alone, Master Phow said it seemed fitting to die free from the grief of others. He said he was at peace; he believed he had lived a good and true life. He had never intentionally hurt another soul, lived as a vegetarian, and believed steadfastly in a higher guidance. Though his breath was shallow and his limbs were barely able to move, he performed one final ceremony of gratitude to the Jade Emperor, and then laid his body down to let it drift toward death. But then the miraculous happened.

To the best of my understanding, and considering his poor command of English, here is my translation of his story: Looking off into the distance as if to remember, he recalled, "I was curled up on the forest floor for two days. The five life elements had withdrawn from my body. At first I was afraid. The cold and dryness had come; my life was in death's grip. I had fallen into the unknowable darkness. I could no longer hear; I could no longer see. There was nothing left to hold on to and I could only fall further into the emptiness. Nothing existed beyond the hollow blackness. There were no sounds, no feelings, and no sensations. I cannot say how long I was lost there. I had no thoughts. But then, all at once, I was surrounded in *dakar lampa*, a brilliant whiteness. I knew then that it was over. I had died. I did not think it; I knew it! There was no pain, no fear. But there was something there, brighter even than the light. That was when I saw him for the first time. The brilliance was almost too great to bear. I could not hide; there was only my essence, no form or place to go. A blue light came to me through his eyes. And then it was clear to me what he wanted. He wanted me to remember my life. Immediately I felt my body; a feeling of warmth filled it. I heard a wonderful sound. Someone was chanting. With each word a new wave of blissful blue light passed through my blood, my bones, and the muscles of my body."

He continued, "My only thought was, how can this be? I am alive again! My lungs gasped in a breath, drawing in the sweetness of life. Before opening my eyes I was greatly blessed—I saw myself as I truly am. I am not the one who had died in that broken old body. I am the One! The blessed ones had come to carry this Self beyond the reach of death. I was free! My karma was forgiven. What can touch this Self, I thought. It is eternally pure. It cannot grow decrepit or old. I saw my old body behind me and my new body healed. I had only love for it, only love. There was no more pain in my old bones. I was new. Opening my eyes, I saw my beloved companions for the first time. The beautiful Mother, Nil'Amma Tara, held this old head in her arms like a baby. And Rambalaji's hands rested on my chest, warming my heart."

He paused momentarily to wipe a small tear from the corner of his eye and then said, "Master Amir—it was he who had whispered the sacred chant of life into my ears. Master Amir is incomparable. He is Vag'Isvara, the lord of the secret language. I grew stronger and stronger as he sweetened my ears with his breath."

He said, "Young master, one can only awaken from death this way once in eternity. My search is now complete. *aham kratajata, aham sadananad, aham preman*—I am gratefulness, I am everlasting bliss, and I am love.

I asked him when this occurred. Master Phow said it was in the autumn of 1949. I added those fifty-seven years to his age, 102. He would turn 159 this year.

I asked, "Was that the moment you realized the Amartya lineage as your own?"

He told me he had found this tradition late in life. It didn't truly begin until he was awakened from his belief in death, which was due entirely to the compassionate grace of the masters.

Master Phow continued, "This is why I have lived so long. They made it possible." And then in a gently humble voice he added, "I have not yet washed away all of the impurities that cover the clear light. There is still more for me to realize. The masters have given me the time I need."

He told me that early in his life he followed the teachings of Master Phong' Lei, hoping to gain mastery of the vital life currents in order to conquer the aging process but added, "There are limits to that path. Controlling the mechanisms that sustain physical life is not enough. It's also necessary to completely awaken from the dream. This is all a great dream! You and I only appear different because these bodies are living in the mind of God. As long as there is fear we are not fully awakened. I have realized much, but there is still a subtle stain on me. It is very thin, very thin indeed, but there is still a small fear that death will come again."

Master Rambalaji had told him that it would only be a few more years before his mastery would be complete. Master Phow added, "He has seen ahead to my moment. Young master, for that I am infinitely grateful."

"Why do you and the others call me young master?"

"Because you are very young! And you know the high knowledge. Before you arrived I was the young master. Now it is you!"

He chuckled. "I am three times older than you, but I am still quite young compared to the others."

18

MASTER RAMBALA

He gently engulfed Ravisu's little arm with his large hands.
Surprisingly Ravisu didn't murmur a single word.
After a moment of silence, Rambala closed his eyes
and sang a soft and lovely chant.
Within seconds, little Ravisu closed his eyes too
*   and joined in*
with a voice that sounded nothing short of angelic.

The scent of moist earth and moss saturated the air as I wandered up a soft, rain-soaked trail to an old temple ruin made all but invisible beneath a tangle of twisting vines and brushwood. A broad-armed grove of maples guarded it from the sky and wind. If it hadn't been for a narrow path that pointed to its worn, brown wooden doors, I could easily have missed it. A snarl of black, snakelike roots conveniently pushed up through the dark earth to replace the otherwise fragmented stone steps.

I had found it yesterday evening searching for a sunset outlook, deciding the instant I opened its doors to make it my new place to write, remember, and meditate. I learned that the ruins were nearly five thousand years old, originally built to honor a Tibetan belief in the Supreme Mother, Qomolangma, a goddess commonly associated with Mount Everest. Although the outer walls were weather-beaten and thoroughly camouflaged with lichen and stone-splitting vines, the temple's inner structure was surprisingly well preserved. The cobble floors were swept and most all cobwebs kept at bay. Presumably someone had taken it upon him- or herself to care for it. Earlier I had come across a sagely old woman lost in song, meandering along through the forest while sweeping its grounds. The people living in this valley tended as much for their natural surroundings as they did their homes.

The temple interior smelled musty, like damp earth spiced with a hint of burnt incense. Two Buddha-like faces, streaked black with smoke stains, were embossed in a thick rock wall in the first of two rooms. A large, stone altar stood between the heads on round, hardwood posts. A coat of red and white candle wax filled in the small depressions on its pitted surface, endowing it with a subtle translucence. On the opposite side from the temple's entry, a small square doorway opened into a brighter sunlit room, possibly once used as a vestibule, which opened to a lushly greened courtyard. What had in another time been a domed ceiling was now open sky. A short row of windows was set at a thirty-degree angle into what was left of the southwest-facing wall, most likely positioned that way to let in the warming midday sun. In the misty afterglow of vaporizing rain, the rays coming in through the fragmented dome and windows produced a soft sacrosanct sense of holiness, transforming specks of airborne dust into flickering bits of gold. On the room's farthest end, a large crumbling archway framed a far-reaching panoramic view of the southeast stretch of the valley. Regardless of the number of people living here, so little could actually be seen of their homes. What impact there was looked fairly well blended into the natural fauna and trees—a model for environmental awareness. Edging the view stood a large poinsettia tree in full bloom, boasting an abundance of bonnet-sized pink blossoms. Inside the archway a worn stone bench had been aptly placed to offer any fortunate onlooker a perfect place to take in the view—an ideal setting for my late-morning meditation.

I had been transcendent for a long half hour before I sensed someone's eyes watching me. A quick look around and I found Master Rambala sitting in the shadow of a large niche just a few steps away. Somehow he'd managed to come in without making a sound. Like a child caught in the midst of a lark, he threw me a playfully prankish smile.

"So how did you do that without me knowing?" I asked.

Master Rambala said nothing. He simply smiled, a soft twinkle lighting up his eyes. Then he told me he had deliberately stayed silent in order to better witness the pranic currents as they orbited and pierced my twelve life centers, which he referred to as the *dvadazinchakras*. Master Rambala said he saw that I'd mastered my meditation practice. I responded by telling him it was still a source of pleasure for me, a personal indulgence like diving into a restorative balm of silence.

I said, "There's no time I'm more at peace then when I'm in that luminous silence. When everything falls away, there's just the One. There's an indescribable charm there, a blissful presence beyond description."

"Indeed," he said. "When one's awareness absconds the confines of the thinking mind, *maheshwari* confers a luminous grace."

He had purposely used the term *maheshwari* to affirm his meaning. In relation to one's divinity, *mahesh* means "great," and *ishwari* means "personal."

"I can feel that ordering grace flowing through me, but I can't define that presence it comes from," I said. "It just is!"

He offered, "Who can say what that is? How does one define a timeless supremacy dreaming a ceaseless play in an infinite realm of possibility?"

"I'm glad you've come," I said. "I so adore being around you and listening to you." I paused and then said, "Rambalaji, if you'll indulge me, I have a few things I had hoped to talk over with you that just happen to be about the meditation practices I'm doing—the *pavanas*. I'm sure you're aware that I've been teaching these forms."

"We are aware of it. With exception to the few times you were unnecessarily concerned about having been too quick in passing those practices on to rushed or ambitious students, you've done very well."

"So you know what I want to talk about?"

"You've been uncertain!" he said. "Set your heart at rest; there's little need for concern. Planting a seed a bit too soon happens more frequently than not, even among the finest teachers. A pure heart often acts impulsively on the compulsion to relieve suffering. There is no wrong in that. While the right timing is ideal, consolation for offering it a bit too soon comes in knowing that a seed will only sprout when the ground is fertile. An apple turns red only when the sun has given it enough light. A bird can only fly when its feathers are matured. And high spiritual knowledge can only be understood when the initiate learns to hear purely. This is called *satya sravanam*. If the *cetas*—the thinking mind—is tarnished with *asmita ragas*—ego desires—the initiate's time has not yet come. For the mind to be nourished by the seed of truth, the path of hearing must be rooted in humility; it must be receptive and pure."

He added, "I understand what else concerns you. It is true that you are introducing methods of practice that have been previously considered too advanced for the common devotee. So your teaching methods will be unique, particularly in these present times when people believe everything can be had in an instant."

I said, "I'm aware that these techniques have long been kept as pure temple knowledge and were only taught to the most advanced initiates, and probably under the strictest guidance. Until now, I haven't been able to fully intuit if teaching these techniques more openly has gone well with our tradition. Previously I taught a number of the world's most advanced meditation practices: mindfulness, mantra, *kriya*, and so on. And I've watched people progress with these techniques according to their abilities. But—"

"But you realized that these techniques were not always enough, that they were largely intended for the common householder, for those who had sought advancements within easily manageable margins. Few live long enough to gain their full benefit. This disparity caused you to remember that there are more advanced methods that can bring results more quickly."

"Exactly! I knew that I'd have to find the core knowledge, the most essential forms, which brought me to the pavanas. I discovered the techniques through my saumedhika drishti seeing and formed the appropriate systems. I didn't ask the masters of this tradition for their permission."

"Young master, take solace in knowing that you've managed this all accurately. You have distilled these methods very well. They are exact in every detail. You withdrew these methods from the one great vault of knowledge, the *nabho gyana akasha*. The knowledge is there for anyone who knows its secrets. But finding this knowledge is only a beginning; it requires a pure hand to fully grasp it. If you have been given its keys and you have grasped the mysteries it holds, the secrets of the nabho gyana akasha are thereby in your care. You must then use that knowledge as you deem fit."

I continued undecidedly. "When I look back over the span of my life, and now over my former lives, I can't help but wonder if I've made too many mistakes. You said only a pure hand can grasp this knowledge. Is there anything *truly* pure in life?"

"It is not for anyone to say. What may to some seem wrong is to others right. What matters is the truth—what the Supreme Self knows!"

"Until now," I said, "I had to make these decisions without our tradition recognizably standing beside me. Please don't misunderstand me. I felt your presence my entire life, but not once have I felt any of the Amartya masters tell me what I must do, other than to come here. To an extent that's created a kind of uncertainty. Obviously there's responsibility that comes with offering techniques this potent, techniques that can have a profound influence on the practitioner. I struggled a long time with who should or shouldn't be initiated. On the one hand, I believe deeply that everyone has a right to all knowledge. On the other hand, I intuitively know some knowledge can't be given to just anyone. Finding the demarcation between these two has been my conundrum. I've accepted the task and I have done what I thought was right, but there's always that gray area. I mean, I can draw knowledge or most any technique from the nabho gyana akasha, but it always comes down to a human moment—a decision made in thought—that determines how that knowledge should be used."

"Indeed, those are valid concerns," Master Rambala replied. "On the one hand, there is knowledge that can be taught and understood by most anyone. Clearly you understand this. On the other hand, there is an exceptional high knowledge—knowledge this world inherited from the stars, *nakshatravidya*. This level of knowledge must be sheltered from those who are not ready—protected to ensure its survival—in order to uphold the traditional and future passage from teacher to student."

"Which entails an ongoing guardianship, doesn't it?"

"Yes! Long ago, at the beginning of this age when widespread greed and ambition came to overrule reason and moral character, the great masters collectively chose to withdraw the most valued and advanced knowledge. They did this to protect it from the heedless abuses of the unaware. This decision was difficult even among the elders. However, this knowledge must in time find its way to the ready initiate. The 'gray' is that no absolute rule can measure when a student is ready to receive it. Every student is unique. The concept of eligibility is always inimitable. Knowledge is easily communicated, but not wisdom. Among the Amartya masters, one tenet has long been used to weigh the suitability of an initiate: satya sravanam, the ability to hear humbly, which is the best sign that wisdom is dawning. Sravanam is the ability to hear beyond the asmita, the ego's ignoble desires. When sravanam dawns, wisdom takes hold!"

"So, respectively, advanced knowledge can't be taught indiscriminately to the masses or to the uninitiated. It requires more care," I responded.

"You have the keys to the vault in your hands," he added. "The charge and responsibility for carrying on this knowledge is now yours. In the near future it will also be in the hands of those who have learned this knowledge from you, and so on. That is parampara; that is tradition!"

Master Rambala asked if I would join him for a stroll through a part of the valley where most of the fruits were grown, adding that he wished to show me something related to sravanam.

After wandering down a long set of stairs chiseled into a sheer vertical cliff, we passed through a series of tall larch and pine trees. The canopy eventually opened into an area where a variety of rock-lined water culverts were cut level with the forest floor. Each culvert distributed a stream of clear spring water to where a copious variety of fruit trees stood. The site was agriculturally idyllic with plenty of sunshine and rich, absorbent soil. A number of earthen berms ascended in tiers across the upper hillsides to protect the groves from erosion. A handful of locals were up on ladders picking fruit into wooden buckets. A few children sat happily along the trailside eating their fill. Master Rambala picked and then offered me a deep yellow fruit he called *lakuchi*, which looked like a blend of tomato and pear. Mixed into the grove were a variety of other fruits—apples, yellow pears, and cherries. The dominant smell in the air was that of yellow plums, which were scattered about in plenty, baking brown in the midmorning sun.

The teeming sound of whistling beetles and the hum of honey-bees and birdsong combined to produce a natural operatic harmonic beneath the bustle of pickers. But there was something else, something less concordant blended in—the sound of a child sobbing. Tracking its source, I soon spotted a young mother sitting on a low branch of a large tree. She had an unpretentious and lovely face. Dressed in a simple white-and-blue-striped cotton wrap, she cradled a young boy in her arms with his head resting against her shoulder. His petite frame fit seamlessly into her reassuring embrace.

There was clearly something wrong. Even at that distance I could see the little boy's face was flushed and teary. A white gauze bandage engulfed his left arm. A lissome young man immediately rushed over to greet us. While gathering his long hair to tie it back from his face, he said something in an obviously frenetic manner. After a moment of listening, Master Rambala turned to explain that the man's little boy had accidently pulled a large teakettle of boiling water down from their stovetop and severely scorched his arm.

Rambala gestured for the mother to bring the boy over. It was only when she came close that the little boy first noticed what was happening. The moment his eyes caught sight of Master Rambala they widened to reveal his awe. He started to squirm in his mother's arms, forcing her to let him walk to Rambalaji on his own. He was a lovely, pure-featured child perhaps six years old, maybe younger. He looked very much like a folklore fairy—small, shirtless, narrow-shouldered, and finely featured. There was pain in his teary eyes. But more than pain or any other effort in his face, there was an overt expression of admiration. His mother knelt to brush his tears back with her thumbs, but he took no notice. Wholly absorbed in a look of wonder and surprise, he didn't once take his soundless stare off Master Rambala.

Master Rambala dropped to one knee and compassionately spread his arms. He said, "Ravisu, *kairan kusu debho yimbai?*" I assumed this meant something like, "Ravisu, how are you feeling?"

Ravisu stepped forward and without a word gave Rambala his arm. He understood what Rambala wanted. After carefully examining the bandage, Master Rambala slowly untied its bindings and pulled back the surrounding cloth to uncover a second wrap made of medicinal leaves. I could see by the boy's expression that he was trying his best to fight back the pain, particularly as Rambala cautiously unrolled each leaf from around his little hand and forearm. The condition of the burn was instantly obvious. On parts of the forearm and hand the skin had peeled away, leaving raw strips of red-blistered flesh. It looked as if he would be scarred for life. I stepped forward to settle down beside Rambala. He offered me a benevolent smile.

He gently engulfed Ravisu's little arm with his large hands. Surprisingly Ravisu didn't murmur a single word. After a moment of silence, Rambala closed his eyes and sang a soft and lovely chant. Within seconds, little Ravisu closed his eyes too and joined in with a voice that sounded nothing short of angelic. As they sang together, Ravisu's expressions gradually transitioned from fighting back pain to sporadic moments of smiling. I looked around to see that the locals, who moments before had been picking fruit, were now standing on the ground with their eyes closed. Their hands were all in prayer mudra. Within a few seconds, one after another joined in to sing along, creating an unbelievably beautiful chorus of harmonic rhythms. I marveled at how Rambala's manner stayed so sweetly unchanged as he sang. A short while later both he and the boy's voices faded to silence. Ravisu, looking up at a gentle angle with eyes closed, appeared astonishingly serene, like that of a sleeping cherub.

The people all stopped singing as well. The wind blew softly, the birds sang melodically, and the leaves went on whispering their forest secrets. When Rambala finally removed his hands, the skin on Ravisu's arm and hand showed absolutely no signs of having been burned. All that remained was a hint of redness and a radiant glow shining through the face of the child. The father, who had fallen to his knees beside us, immediately began thanking Rambala over and over.

Turning his attention to the father, Rambala stood and pulled the father up with him. He paused to look him directly in the eyes and stroke his thanking face with the back of his palm the way a loving parent might. When the father again tried to thank him, Rambala gestured for him to let it be. He then nudged my arm and we quietly walked on.

After we left the grove behind, I said, "It was such a beautiful thing to watch you heal the child like that."

"Was it I who healed his arm, my dear? I merely showed the boy his way."

Master Rambala pointed to a bench resting beneath a pair of large, broadleaf trees. It was deep green and quietly tranquil there, with barely a breeze brushing over us. The bench was carved from a red cyprus wood covered with a soft blanket of moss.

I said, "So please tell me why you wanted me to see that."

He answered, "I knew someone once, quite a long time ago—a child not much older than Ravisu. One morning I found him sitting up there in that old temple."

"The one we just came from?"

"Yes! He was sitting exactly where you were sitting this morning. When I found him there he told me, with a sad look on his face, that he would wake every morning and realize that he had been with an angel. I asked him why that made him sad. He said, 'When I open my eyes and see the world around me, the angel is gone.' I asked him if he could tell me something about the angel. He answered, 'I only know I was with an angel, but I can't remember anything about him.' I asked him what he would like to do about it. After thinking about it for a long time, he answered, 'I will sit here on this spot and meditate until the angel returns.' And I said, 'Very good,' and then left the child to himself. I returned the next morning to find the boy still sitting there—he'd meditated the whole night. He was so engrossed in his meditation he didn't even hear me arrive. So I shook his little arm to get his attention. Once he opened his eyes, I asked him to tell me about his experience. He said, 'When I stopped listening to the world I could again hear the angel.' I asked him how that felt. He said, 'I don't know, I couldn't feel him.' I asked the boy what he would like to do about it. He exclaimed, 'I will sit here on this spot and continue to meditate!' I returned the next morning to find the boy still sitting there. Again he didn't hear me coming. But this time he was so deep in his meditation that even when I shook his arm he didn't feel it. So I stretched open his small eyes. Once he realized I was there I asked him about his experience. He told me, 'When I stopped listening to and feeling the world around me, I could hear and feel the angel.' So I asked the boy what the angel looked like. He said, 'I don't know.' I asked him what he would like to do. He replied, 'I will sit here on this spot and meditate!' I came back the next morning with some water and food to find the boy still sitting there. But now he was no longer meditating. His eyes were open and his look of sadness was gone. He had a soft, blissful smile on his face. I asked him if he could now see his angel. He said, 'When I completely stopped listening to and feeling the world around me, and let go of seeing it too, I could finally see the angel.' So I asked him, 'What did you learn?' He said, 'When the world is gone and there is only silence, there is only one Being. I learned that I am that angel.' And I said, 'Very good!'"

"That's why you wanted me to see this!"

"My dear, I shared this story with you to remind you, rather than tell you, what sravanam is. This is how Ravisu's healing occurred. These people living here have a strong faith that God participates in everything that occurs in their lives. From the time of his birth Ravisu was enfolded in the truth of our existence. The outer world has not tainted his vision nor stolen away his trust that the Divine exists in all things. His parents had told him that a man of God would come to heal his arm, that he had nothing to fear, and that the pain was merely a message that he should make himself ready. Ravisu had no doubts; his faith was strong. When he saw me coming he did not see the man; he saw only the presence of God coming to help him. When he surrendered his arm to me he consequently surrendered himself to the healing light of the One. When he closed his eyes it was the sign that he had let go of the world to let himself be transformed. When he heard the voice of God singing a song of the beloved—of devotion and surrender to the perfection—he innocently joined in, and in turn opened his little heart to the grace of God. From pain to bliss, from darkness to light, from ignorance to truth—that is the healing! In this outer world there is only imperfection, but in the One there is only perfection. In his surrender he realized that Oneness, the perfection. Then his healing was certain."

I said, "So what was true for Kubitha's mother was also true for Ravisu. His faith healed him."

19

DEVA'BHAG

Peering down over the cliff's edge, a warm updraft blew
over my skin.
The atmaka, the rainbow essence, seemed to have
grown brighter
while we were talking.

Our human love for beauty is that indescribable madness that the soul rouses to realign our psyche to its rightful path. True beauty is far more than the obvious superficial kind of beauty; it is our love shining through our feelings, truth shining through our thoughts, and joy shining through our works. When we abandon ourselves to the allure of that kind of beauty we innately slip into a current of bliss, an inwardly calling ananda. When trying to write about Master Amir's beauty, I kept revisiting the idea of breadcrumbs left behind on the path by Hänsel and Gretel to mark the way home.

On first sight, it's always Master Amir's physical beauty that catches one's attention, but as one draws closer it quickly becomes obvious that his beauty is simply too esoteric to limit with a physical description. It might be better to point to the haunting magnetism that draws one into the endless depths in his amethyst-blue eyes. Or maybe it has more to do with the broad, synchronic way he moves, always in perfect concord with nature's surrounding elements, like a soft wind barely felt but somehow effortlessly able to move an entire forest. Whatever way it manifests, his beauty is foremost a deeply spiritual thing, something that always moves from within. It might initially come across as physically exquisite, but inevitably his beauty always seems to invoke some deeper sense.

I had been laboring my way uphill for over an hour, tracking the path Master Amir had previously asked me to follow in order to join up with him that afternoon. I hadn't yet explored this direction and appreciated the idea of another adventure. He said the trail would lead to his choice view of the valley.

I found Amir indulging a pleasure along the path's grassy edge, sitting cross-legged in the shade of a broad overhanging tree. The air was filled with birdsong. A small flock of mountain finches took turns landing on his outstretched arm. When he glanced in my direction the delight in his face was palpable, bridging that otherwise elusive narrow between playful innocence and being a man of extraordinary mastery. He brought one of the less colorful female finches in close to his face, carefully stroked the feathers on her head, and then lifted her back to flight.

Standing up, he smiled. "It's a bit farther up. The walk will be steep but well worth the climb."

And it was steep, and narrow, and treacherous; in places the drop-off side of the trail plummeted hundreds of meters to the forest below. The air was sweeter and cooler this high up. The last stretch of the path transformed into a narrow ledge handily etched into the sheer cliff wall through the natural erosion of wind and water. It wasn't long before our ascent leveled off onto a rolling alpine meadow. The view was even more dramatic here than Master Amir had promised. Impressive vertical, mica-flecked, dragon-tail rock formations stretched from the meadow all the way up into the barren peaks where blue-gray mists curled like giant breakers over the upper altitudes. Below, the visible parts of the valley twisted and turned through ravines to form smaller enclaves and aquatic basins. A few towering waterfalls fell from above, some misted white while others formed soft double rainbows in the bright sunlight. We sat in the sun looking out amid the moist, fragrant grasses with our backs pressed to a cluster of granite boulders.

Within a few minutes a newborn fawn wandered out from within a small group of wind-shaped pines and for a little while gazed with curiosity in our direction. It then sauntered over to Amir and nestled down at his feet. Farther back under the trees its mother continued grazing without the slightest concern. I remarked that the deer seemed to be uncharacteristically fearless, even tame.

He said, "Unless we intentionally create one, the creatures of this world have little cause to fear us. Animals approach when they sense we've laid aside that tenacious human need to rule and when they recognize in us a spirit that cherishes life."

I said, "And perhaps all creatures are drawn to an awakened heart."

He added, "All creatures find comfort at the feet of the Master—that is true. But one need not be a master to gain an animal's trust. There is little so enchanting to a wildling as the sincere virtues of acceptance and recognition. Having no intention to do harm is the highest of our attractive virtues. Ahimsa, harmlessness, is a goodness anyone can strive for. Too few in this world understand that mastering the art of ahimsa coincides directly with self-mastery. In the not-so-distant future there will come a time when harmlessness will once again be revered; then even the hungry tiger won't cause one harm."

"Perhaps that's because animals still intuit that people are destined to be the world's stewards."

"A fact too many have forgotten!" Amir replied. "In the oldest of the Amartya shastras it states: 'The Supreme gave breath to man and woman so they might tend this earthly garden and keep watch over all its creatures. Most fortunate are they who work to comfort and relieve the suffering, for it is only they who will find, through their acts, liberation from the suffering they may have caused. A path of darkness awaits those who live for themselves alone, but the caretakers of life's garden will, through their virtues, be lifted into heaven's grace.'"

"I'd like to read those shastras."

He said, "You have read them—long ago! The process of reincarnation fades memory, but what was of core value to you was nonetheless assimilated. There is no need for you to read them again. You've realized the ways of ahimsa, thus the way of nonharming is easy.

Harmlessness, truthfulness, and compassion—ahimsa, *satya*, and *karunya*; these are the three noble virtues."

I asked, "Would you indulge me a bit? I would love it if you would share with me a little about your life."

"What would you like to know?" he replied.

"Everything! When did you come here, where did you come from, and what brought you here?"

For a while Master Amir looked reflectively off into the distance. "A considerable amount of time has passed!"

"How long would you say that is?"

"I have lived in these mountains through three of your lifetimes. Aaravindha, I am a very old man."

Suddenly it struck me. I realized I had unwittingly let an adaptive, pragmatic part of my mind shove off the fact that I was sitting with a master who's actually hundreds of years old. I said, "It's hard to keep up with how old you might actually be. My instincts tenaciously run back and forth to reorganize my perceptions in their effort to match you up to the familiar circumstances that I'm accustomed to. Before long I find myself relating to you as if you're as young as you look. Interesting—to know something and yet still have the psyche work automatously in the background to reestablish the familiar. I suppose a more focused mindfulness and humility are the only way through that."

He replied, "The rational mind may be a loyal servant, but in its dedication to the familiar it often mends the wrong fences. Perceptions are as mutable as water, but it commonly takes some time to annul the auto-mechanized responses that are inherent to our mental constructs."

Master Amir continued, "Our surroundings often play a vital part in sustaining or shifting our views. When humanity comes to believe something, it predictably demands that it must be real. Then even the aware are bound to contend with the results of those demands. This regulating effect is referred to as *prajjavritti*. Life and death coexist in this world; that is natural law. But regardless, just as there is a higher rational mind and a higher Self, so too there exists a higher life beyond the reach of birth and decay."

I replied, "Those influences are strong. To break free of their bias and our dependency on the familiar, it seems that some kind of absence is required—a mind-purifying retreat from the outer world. Is that what you experienced when you came here?"

"Most definitely! The collective prajjavritti has no authority here. When sharing in the world's dream, the dreamer is highly susceptible to the dominant influences. Withdrawal and humility are the grounds for the shift in perception, but not a humility that makes one insignificant or unworthy. It must be a humility that allows for all possibilities. A master once said that 'the meek shall inherit the earth.' But that word *meek* is a dialectal misinterpretation. It is the humble who shall inherit the earth, for only in humility can a person hear the truth, bend to change, and mature. Defensiveness, aggression, and violence are the vices of the fearful and arrogant. Some say humility is an emotion, nothing more than a product of the mind, but that would be grossly unjust. It is arrogance that is a product of mind; humility affects its release. Others will say humility is defenselessness, a kind of vulnerability, and they would be right. But in the end, it is just that sort of vulnerability that transforms an ignorant man into a sage."

He paused. "When I first came here, I had completed the fifteenth year of my birth."

"You were young. Master Rambala told me that when you were born thousands of doves gathered to greet your arrival, filling all the trees around your home in a broad circle—a phenomenon never before seen."

"Then you already know a little about my life!"

"A little. Rambala said it was a proof of divine will." I added, "He also told me your mother died shortly after your birth."

"Not after; she died during my birth. Some call it a tragedy, but those are the opinions of the naive. It was *svarudha*; she ascended on a wave of bliss to the *aditya loka*, the solar world. There was no pain in her dying, only *parasantosh*, divine contentment, and *shraddha*, faith, were there. She had fulfilled what she was born to accomplish."

He told me that his mother was born Aramean; she lived in the same ancestry as the master she followed throughout the length of her life: Yehoshua, son of Mariam.

"So she was a Christian," I said.

He answered, "No. She was Master Yehoshua's disciple. There is a clear distinction. Arameans who followed the line of Yehoshua Meshikha trusted they were the master's disciples. This lineage of Arameans believed in their master's words: 'Those of you who believe in the works that I do, you will do also; and many will do greater works than these.' They called themselves Talmidah, not Christians. Arameans were the first to accept Christianity as a religion, but the greatest number of Talmidah, many of whom lived in Turkey and Persia, chose not to accept the proselytization of their beliefs. They served their faith as free Gnostics."

As an Aramaic woman, his mother was controversially outspoken. She chose to live in Turkey because at that time it was more liberal toward women than many of the more patriarchal regions. When his mother was still very young, during times of prayer she would experience vivid visions of Master Yehoshua and Mother Mariam. In one of those visits, Master Yehoshua told her that she would one day meet an Egyptian *athravan*, a Zoroastrian priest whom she would marry. The idea of marrying rested uneasy in her heart because she had already promised her life to her purpose, which she believed was to bring reprieve to the poor, sick, and suffering. Nonetheless, she fell in love and the marriage came true. Shortly thereafter Mother Mariam appeared to her again, informing her that her time on earth was nearly complete. Mariam told her there was one important deed left for her to fulfill. A year later she became pregnant. A few days before Master Amir's birth, Nil'Amma Tara appeared to her.

In her last vision, Nil'Amma Tara showed her the body of a newborn male. She told her that she wouldn't otherwise have seen him. And there was no need to be concerned for his well-being, as she herself would take him into her care at the age of fifteen. Nil'Amma Tara told her he was Maryah of Eloha, an avatar whom she would watch over until he was fully grown.

Amir's father was born in a region referred to as Faiyum. He moved to the Nile Delta near Heliopolis and then traveled on to Cairo. In the earlier part of his life he lived in Alexandria where he studied

Mazdaism and was nobly ordained as an athravan, the highest station a priest of that faith could attain. However, because of his universal spiritual insights, he was later recognized more aptly as a nonsectarian seer and mystic, a reputation that didn't affect his Zoroastrian followers but grew to trouble many of the more conservative members of the surrounding Muslim communities. A small group of radical clerics soon perceived him as highly threatening and a blasphemer.

Amir's father often refused to remain content within the suppressive values of the dominant religions, occasionally rebuffing the strict controls of a few influential clerics. As a result, Amir was just thirteen years of age when his father was murdered in his sleep by the followers of that group. The cleric who had sent the executioners had taken offense when his father publically accused him of being too puritanical and despotic in his rule.

Orphaned, Amir left Egypt immediately thereafter. Wherever he went, people would greet him with kindness, often feeding and housing him before he ventured on. At fourteen, he left civilization behind and wandered into the Himalayan mountains. After a year of searching, he came across Nil'Amma Tara meditating in the forest.

At eighteen, Amir had already mastered the Eightfold Heart-lotus siddhi, the *Ashtamanimat Hridyamboja* siddhi that transforms the human heart into a perfected medium for divine will. He advanced so masterfully in his esoteric abilities under Nil'Amma Tara's guidance that Grandfather Pitamah eventually gave Master Amir the revered and authoritative title, *mahashaya'atarkyasahasranatha*—the master of the thousand impenetrable powers. By the time he was thirty-three he attained *Amara'samyaksambodhi*, the highest of the three levels of spiritual enlightenment.

I asked Amir how he felt about the men who had murdered his father.

He said, "When I came under her guidance, the first truth Nil'Amma Tara blessed me with was carried in these words: 'Worship love not with a selfish want or with a half-guarded heart but with your whole being. More virtuous even than the search for enlightenment is a sincere sacrifice to love all that would be said in judgment or bitterness, or might be done in spite or anger. Love is the one virtue required of us all. No greater truth can be bestowed. Without love, life and meaning would cease, for love bears within it the very reason for existence.'"

I said, "And equal to one's love, one forgives."

Master Amir's gaze shifted toward the valley below and he asked, "Aaravindha, do you remember the morning you departed from your home to begin this journey here?"

"To what are you referring?" I asked.

"That morning, when you looked out over the sea before leaving your home, what did you see?"

After a moment of searching my memory I told him that I remembered seeing a rainbow over the water. I thought it unusual as it wasn't a typically arched rainbow, but a bright pillar of rainbow light—like a sundog but lower in the sky, hovering just above the water. It was particularly odd as there wasn't any mist over the ocean that morning; the air was crystal clear.

He said, "It was a blessing bestowed by the masters for your journey. It was a *saunimitta*, what you might call a good omen."

While we talked I watched a slow and soft veil of clouds start to form around a few of the distant peaks. He said the people in these mountains refer to the resulting misty glow as lotus light.

"Like your name, Aaravindha—Lotus Light," he said.

Amir's attention returned to something below in the valley. He asked me to look toward an area that he called Deva'bhag. The term *Deva'bhag* can be translated as "Garden of Spirits." In the purplish-blue backdrop of a part of the valley's steep walls, a fractured white line stood out brightly, a line created by a narrow cascading waterfall. Small pools formed at the base of each fall, forming ghostly vapors that transmuted the afternoon sunlight into small rainbows. He then pointed a bit farther into the valley's green undergrowth, a few hundred feet from the falls.

He said, "Do you see that—a *surahdhanus*—another sort of rainbow pillar? There, along the lower part of the stream."

I answered. "I see it. It's not arched; it's like the one I saw over the water. It's brighter than the others—the spectrum in the darker shadow is more vivid."

And then I realized what I had said, something that didn't make sense. In the darker shadow there wasn't any sunlight; a tall, craggy peak blocked out the sun. And neither were there any nearby waterfalls. The stream was running slow and flat there.

"There's no sun there!" I exclaimed, barely believing my eyes. "How's that possible?"

"It's not a common rainbow," he said.

"Then what is it?"

"It isn't!" he laughed.

"It isn't? What does that mean?"

"If something isn't there, then it isn't."

"Then it's a mirage, some kind of illusion?" I puzzled.

"No, he's not a mirage, nor is he an illusion."

I looked questioningly at Amir. "Did you say he? Is that pillar of light caused by a person?"

"Yes, but not in the traditional sense."

"Not in the traditional sense? I'm at a loss. Then is it a visible aura, a man's aura?"

"It's not his aura; it is his *praatmaka*, his essential light."

I squinted my eyes to better focus and asked, "Like a Dzogchen rainbow body, a *'ja'lus*?"

"Yes, somewhat like that. The rainbow *atmaka* you see below is the result of a *siddhivrddha*, a highly advanced discipline that involves the deliberate withdrawal of the five life-materializing elements that constitute the aggregate human form. This siddhivrddha drew the elemental aspects of his human body back into its pristine, nonmaterial essence."

"That's fascinating! Who is he?"

"He isn't!"

"Okay, then who was he?"

"A few *gurujans*, elders who live in our surrounding regions, have erroneously come to believe this is what you thought it was, a 'ja'lus. They believe this is the 'ja'lus of Master Tshering Moba Mingma. Master Tshering was a shamanic mystic of the Sher'wa people. Those who have seen it had long ago cultivated the myth that it must be him.

But only a few have actually seen him. This is a rare sight, appearing here in the Deva'bhag just two or three times a year."

"The Sher'wa—are they the Sherpa who migrated from Tibet to Nepal?"

"Yes, they roamed south from the Tibetan region of Kham; many settled in Nepal. Master Tshering came here in search of this valley over a thousand years ago, during the reign of Padma Gyalpo."

"Padmasambhava?"

"Yes, Padma Gyalpo was Padmasambhava's original incarnation. Master Tshering spread a form of esoteric Buddhism into many of the nearby regions. In his old age he felt the strong urge to find this valley. His sudden withdrawal from the world and his followers created a mystery that started the stories that he secretly retreated from the world to transform his body into a 'ja'lus."

He added, "This is not Master Tshering, although he lived here as a devoted disciple of Grandfather Pitamah. He dedicated the last of his life to our lineage. As a result, he lived through two centennials before leaving his body behind in his spiritual ascent. What you see below—this atmaka—is another more reclusive and less known mystic who had, over his persistent practice of radical disciplines, attained an advanced level of skill. Only a few still know his actual name. It was Master Khandro Tseh Whang. He was a highly intelligent *bodhana* guru who had familiarity with this valley hundreds of years before Master Tshering came here. Master Khandro was an indirect disciple of Mahasiddha Kukuraja, a forefather of Garab Dorje. Garab Dorje was a central predecessor of the Dzogchen teachings. At the age of eighty-six, Master Garab Dorje withdrew the five elemental emanations to create a 'ja'lus, ascending from this world into the heavens."

I asked, "You said this rainbow body is somewhat like a Dzogchen 'ja'lus but not the same."

"What is similar is that through his disciplines Master Khandro, like Garab Dorje, developed mastery over the five primal emanations. He too withdrew the five primal layers of his physical body, but only until his individuated self-light, his *atmaprakash*, was all that remained. What you see down there in the shadows is his resulting realization."

"And the difference is?"

He answered, "Master Khandro followed the teachings of anatman, the belief that anything that is perceivable through the five senses is not valid, and that only the unbound and unchanging is real. Anatman is not a belief in a void but in an unlimited and indefinable self—a manner of no self. Followers of the anatman dogmata believe liberation is attained only when all aspects of form, even consciousness itself, is transcended and existence is brought to its final absolute state. Anything that is transitory by nature is not considered real. Master Khandro disciplined himself to attain that state of final liberation, which he believed was the complete release from all causal forms."

I said, "This sounds very much like the concept of laya yoga, the yoga of dissolution in which one's consciousness is withdrawn from all outer emanations and expressions to bring the observer to rest in an absolute state."

Master Amir answered, "It is a concept that is still followed by spiritual devotees around the world, particularly in the East. But it is rarely understood. To misunderstand this conviction can have dire consequences."

I said, "And that's now what was once Master Khandro—the end result of his efforts."

Master Amir answered, "His knowledge wasn't complete in its wisdom. Master Garab Dorje carried the anatman knowledge and its associated Tantra disciplines to the next level. He developed the means to attain sambhogakaya—an ananda kaya. The invitation you received to come here during your retreat—the master who appeared to you—that emanation was an example of sambhogakaya."

"You also called it an ananda kaya—a bliss body?"

"Yes! Sambhogakaya is a bliss body; it's an unbound, subtle body that can exist in a variety of alternate worlds, or in some cases it can also manifest when needed as a light body in this earthly realm."

"The 'ja'lus—is that what I saw around Nil'Amma Tara when I saw her levitating in the forest grove?"

"You saw something similar. It was the praatmaka of her *bhradamara* kaya."

"I don't recognize that term."

He answered, "It is the essential immortal body, the amaraprakash, the immortal light of the unlimited body of Mahat."

I said, "I've always understood Mahat to be the bride of Purusha, the first nature of the one Divine Person."

"Yes. A few of the Amartya ancestors have referred to Mahat as the Great Mother's body because She is the Mother of *prakrithi*, the sole manifesting nature that bears in Her womb the potential expression for all possible forms. She births all. All beings drink from Her well, making real the expression of infinite probability. There is but one bhradamara kaya."

"So that would be the same as the *devatapratima*, the prototypal image of God/Goddess, the immortal high Self."

He answered, "Often advanced siddhis—siddhivrddhas—are accompanied in their manifestations by a display of rainbow light."

"Is that because advanced siddhis, particularly those that require one to shift the natural laws surrounding their physical expression, implement those methods through the akashic field?"

"Very good, Aaravindha. Indeed, you are remembering. When a siddhi is expressed through the etheric field, the four descending and manifesting elements—air, fire, water, and earth—are restructured in their most primal levels of expression. This can cause a resulting phenomenon of rainbow light to appear. This phenomenon rests on the akashic field but can also be seen in the material realm. You saw it arising through Nil'Amma Tara's crown. It is called the *surahkirita*."

I said, "A nimbus of rainbow light—a celestial crown."

He continued, "There are three rivers of consciousness that feed, sustain, and dissolve the human form."

"Rivers? Streams of consciousness?"

"We call them *nadi*. These nadi originate in the all-comprehensive realm of pure awareness beyond the reach of the thinking mind. They initiate in the bhradamara kaya. They constitute the three cyclic spokes in the wheel of time: conception, conservation, and termination."

I stood up to stretch and take a better look at the rainbow body below. Peering down over the cliff's edge, a warm updraft blew over my skin. The atmaka, the rainbow essence, seemed to have grown brighter while we were talking.

I turned my head and said over my shoulder, "This is spiritual physics; you're talking about the core quantum realm of consciousness, that place where Oneness edges the diverse forming of life."

He nodded. "This knowledge is elementary to the Amartya tradition and central to the actualization of eternal life. The Amartya masters apply aspects of this knowledge correspondingly, but it isn't limited to the founding disciplines in Dzogchen, and it is even more dissimilar to the path Master Khandro chose."

I said, "So there are a number of possible ways to use this light-body knowledge.

"There may be many ways, but there is only one method to ascend beyond all aspects of limitation, including the limitation of no self."

"The idea of no self is limited, isn't it? I've always believed that."

"Oh, yes. The Amartya Parampara bears the oldest and purest record of this knowledge. The methods discovered by the early Dzogchen were long before already resting in the archives of our Amartya tradition. This knowledge was brought to this world in the hands of the foremost *Nakshatra* masters. Mahasiddha Kukuraja managed to cognize a part of the knowledge—due to our surreptitious contribution. Garab Dorje then carried that knowledge on through his realization."

"Nakshatra masters?"

"The star-born, the Eka'Amarta!"

"Star-born?" I repeated, half hidden in my breath.

"Aaravindha, human life did not begin here. You have always known this."

"I believe I have! But this is so very lovely to hear you talk about it. I feel that I've known about the Nakshatra my entire life. I've had numerous internal glimpses of them, but for the most part the broader body of knowledge involving them has been hiding just out of reach beyond my memory. I can feel it there sometimes, sleeping in the innermost heart of my mind—in the stillness—waiting for me."

A loving look of approval spread across Amir's face, like that of a close and supportive friend. He said, "The three nadi are *devanada*, *patinada*, and *mokshanada*, which respectively inspire, sustain, and liberate life."

"Are these nada-rivers associated with the three primary *randri*, the uppermost meridians in the crown of the head?"

"Yes. These rivers not only create the foundation for mind, but they also they maintain one's essential experience of reality. In other words, they bind one to the cyclic stream of time and all that the probability within change can express or take."

"Our secret umbilical cord to the great Mahat-Mother."

Master Amir's face lit up with a blissful smile. He said, "Master Khandro chose to direct his disciplines toward the attainment and mastery of the mokshanada alone."

"In other words," I said, "he focused on just the one river rather than the three. He set his aim purely on the task of dissolution or liberation."

"Exactly. But to understand his choice of direction it's also necessary to comprehend the enduring belief that brought him to it. Master Khandro was faithful to the one-sided concept that all aspects of manifest form are an illusion and are, as a whole or independently, a cause for suffering. He believed that only the realm of absolute timelessness—unbound consciousness without form or experience—is real. And that all else is nothing more than a mere glimpse of the greater truth."

"I see the problem!" I said. "If he believed that any part of creation is an illusion, then he didn't completely comprehend that the two—life and its source—are fundamentally one. He didn't fully understand that the absolute state of consciousness is never separate from its parts. I've always seen this idea as similar to the idea that the wave is not as real as the ocean, when in fact the ocean is the wave. It's a mental thing and shouldn't be designated as statistical. Regardless of whether life is transitory, life is still the nature of the one timeless Self, and the Self's will revealed through change."

Master Amir laughed appreciatively. "That understanding is the fundamental difference between those seeking everlasting life and those who merely seek to escape samsara—what they believe is the cause of suffering."

He added, "Through his disciplined practices, Master Khandro established nirvana or, more appropriately, a state of sustained *nirodhyama samadhi*. Nirodhyama is—"

I interjected, "The stilling of all mental obscurities, thoughts, tendencies, habits, and cultured perceptions—and essentially all *vritti*—through a process of transcendental release."

He tilted his head slightly and continued, "When he established his samadhi, he realized *rtamprajja*, which gave him direct intuitive cognition of the five essential emanations. Thus he was able to sequentially retract each of the five emanations. In nirodhyama, he withdrew the forces sustaining earth, water, fire, air, and finally moved to withdraw ether—*akasha*—into mokshanada, the river of dissolution."

"You said the three rivers inspire, sustain, and liberate life. So it seems that in order to attain his 'ja'lus, his consciousness must have stayed at rest in nirodhyama samadhi the whole time, during which time his individuated state of being touched the source of life. He had to sustain that state of rest so that the inspiring and sustaining nadi would be completely curtailed or stilled, while also holding a pure intention to liberate the five emanations solely in the mokshanada. That's quite a disciplined feat—to carry through with the withdrawal of all five elements. And yet while this seems so very extraordinary, in my heart it also seems somehow tragic. I don't see in that effort or accomplishment a complete realization of our truth of existence."

Master Amir said, "In his attainment of 'ja'lus, he came to rest upon the surface of *nirodyapralaya*. What can be said of nirody-apralaya is very little, as it borders the indefinable absolute realm of unspoken possibility. It represents a near but not complete absorption into the great primordial enormity. An initial splendor in the intimate approach and recognition of the true nature of the Self arises from that vastness. But in its end, the bliss is suspended there. This is because awareness requires the force of the inspiration nada, the patinada, to yet be available. But he had curtailed this force. Nirodyapralaya, the complete stilling of consciousness, is similar to *rtambharat prajja*, the truth-expanse wisdom that exists between absolute consciousness and the causal impulses that form life. But it's not the same; it lacks the essential impulse of life."

Astounded, I said, "I've never heard of anything like this before. You said Dzogchen had taken the state Master Khandro created to a higher level in creating a bliss body, so that they could escape this world's samsara limitations but could also continue to exist. But Master Khandro didn't create anything. He merely withdrew all there was, and that would mean he is neither here nor there. Like you said, he isn't. Then what did he accomplish?"

"Nothing at all, my dear! We cannot accomplish what has always been, nor can we attain what already is. In his act of dissolution, has he accomplished what he was created for? Is he any more sacred as a result? Is he any freer than before? Is the Self satisfied now? Will the eternal act of creation finally come to rest?"

"What will become of him?" I asked.

"When the time is right, we will awaken him, return him to the current of life. A divine wind brings him here. Soon the dawn will rise. At that time we will set him free to realize the true jewel—everlasting life. The final transformation, the awakening, occurs in the delight of the One for the game, not in the pursuit of an end. That is the secret to living this divine life."

20

MASTER JANJURAN GUNA'SAMPAD RASHANTHI

The moment I began turning its pages
I knew I had found what I had been searching for
since first setting foot in this world.
I had never before witnessed the lost secrets
of our human origins
so perfectly revealed.

Miracles are seldom a contradiction to natural law; miracles are almost always explainable events that only appear remarkable when they're placed within the world's mainstream frames of what is or isn't real. We too often forget that our ideas of what can or cannot happen are constantly changing. One day much of what humanity has believed to be incredulous will become commonplace. Bearing in mind that our human consciousness is rooted in a quantum field of infinite possibility, it stands to reason that the only real difference between life's everyday happenings and those rare and unbelievable wonders is in the way we elect to see.

In the Amarpura valley, events that would undoubtedly be considered impossible in the outer world are everyday occurrences. It took me the first few weeks of being there before I fully adapted to the difference. In our world's run-of-the-mill collective mind, it's easy to stay asleep and to live our lives half-lit under an overriding custom of limitations, most of which are based on facts and restrictions that are handily drawn from the pragmatic notion of *if you see it, it's real; if you don't see it, it's not*. But then seeing doesn't always equate to believing. For most, if a phenomenon doesn't fit into their familiar range of understanding, it must be impossible and therefore an illusion, or it has come about through some grander influence beyond our human reach, that is, a miracle. To the hard-headed realist, miracles are seen as either shams or delegated solely to sleight-of-hand magicians and tricksters. And though people are typically aware that the acts are tricks, they nonetheless flock to such performances, perhaps secretly hoping that some aspect of the magic might be true. Could it be that most people harbor a secret belief that anything might be possible and in some way yearn to find that freedom? And, if so, isn't it also possible that this yearning might actually be based on a glimmer of truth?

After arriving in the valley, I actively sought out the company of the masters in a typically social manner. But I soon found that they were all predictably unpredictable and were rarely in one place for any length of time. In order to keep up, I opted to find a more effective method for meeting with them. Rather than searching them out, I discovered that when I closed my eyes and allowed myself to transcendentally feel for the most predominant attraction in the moment, and then let it become the object of my focus, I had much better results. Once I sensed who it was I should visit, I simply let my desire settle effortlessly on that silent field of inner presence as an open offer. Each time, the master who had been the object of my focus would soon thereafter come to visit.

With exception of Grandfather Pitamah, who continued to be an incomprehensible and unrivaled enigma, Master Janjuran proved to be the most elusive of the masters. Occasionally I'd spot him wandering through the forest, most often at a distance. Whenever I would walk over to speak with him, he'd offer me a sly smile and fleetingly vanish into thin air behind some tree, rock, or bush. Rather than taking it personally, and after assessing his clever smile, I quickly realized that there had to be some sort of game afoot. I decided to put my mind to the task of figuring it out.

Both Nil'Amma Tara and Master Rambala had said that Master Janjuran and I shared a common talent: our saumedhika drishti skills. My intuition told me that the game he'd started had to do with that affinity. Consequently I made him the first of the masters on whom to try out my new *silent offer theory*. I inwardly focused my intentions to visit him without making the slightest effort. As predicted, after just five minutes of doing so, his face appeared in my inner sight. Along with it I right away sensed he wanted me to come visit him at the cliffside structure where I'd first met him. I was sure now: this subtle way of connecting was a part of his game. Thus I began my new method, which I continued to use successfully for the remainder of my stay.

Meandering down from the temple ruins to the cliff involved a pleasant experience of taking an unavoidable shower in warm dewdrops. Before dawn, a gentle summer rain had drenched the forest, leaving the earth muddy and the branches hanging low and heavy. Here and there, curled fingerlike ferns and rounded black stones pressed their shimmering faces up through the evaporating mist. The sun breaking through the trees and the combination of misty scenes generated a feeling that I was walking through a glistening, fog-layered dream.

Entering the cliffside courtyard, my clothes were soaked through, so much so that I could literally squeeze the water out with my hands. Heading toward the main entrance, I stopped to investigate the underside of the vines draping down the wall. Parts of the reliefs were missing or broken away while others seemed fairly intact.

I was unexpectedly halted by a faint and perplexing hum. Listening for its origin, I soon discovered that steady streams of nearly inaudible whispers—subtle ghostly chants—were coming through the cracks in the stone. When I pressed my ear to the cool blue-gray rock my touch instantly caused the chants to fall silent. When I pulled away and for a few seconds remained perfectly still, the sounds slowly returned. I tried the same technique of touching and releasing a few more times. Each time the sound would stop and return again a few seconds later. Something deific or fairylike was definitely alive in these stones. A few days ago, when I had asked Master Rambala about the subtle harmonics I felt active here in the valley, he remarked that it was to some extent due to the *yaksha*, benevolent nature spirits. I wondered now if these sounds were a sign of their presence. The only other sound was an occasional billow of air passing in and out through the main entrance.

Puddles of warm rainwater had spread across the courtyard slate, providing me a convenient means to wash the mud from my bare feet before stepping through the entry. Once inside, a narrow foyer opened into a large, inner chamber possibly twenty meters deep. On the entry-wall side, slightly above eye level, a row of ten narrow glass windows let in a soft blur of light, just enough to give the room a subtle but evocative glow. Inside the entrance, two round, white stone pillars stretched up to the unevenly chiseled ceiling. On the other end of the room, two more pillars stood on either side of a polished granite stairway that led to a small landing. The landing divided into opposite directions, which led to two separate arched wooden doors. The room was Spartan-like, with no décor or furniture other than a few benches pressed against the entry wall. The only sign of life was a flock of small rock doves—a few paced nervously back and forth along a high narrow shelf. The bounce of their melodic coo and the echoing sound of water dripping farther back in the room gave the space a solid, hollow feel.

With Master Janjuran nowhere to be seen, I decided to wait on the bench nearest the entry. I closed my eyes and soon found myself questioning if I'd received his message correctly. The same mysterious sound of whispering chants I'd heard coming through the outer walls started to haunt the reverberant ambiance. The more I listened, the more it sounded like a fluttering breeze filled with manifold layers of breathy mantras. In a little while I was completely rapt in the sound, following it further and further into a spacious depth that seemed to transcend the room altogether. Then, in a jolt to my senses, the burdensome echo of a heavy door creaking open shattered the peace. My eyes darted to the sound.

At the top of the stairs, a taller than average man was beaming a Cheshire-Cat smile: it was Master Janjuran. He looked somewhat different than when I'd first met him. Maybe it was just the angle of perspective and low light, but his long hair and beard seemed longer, falling farther down over his narrow shoulders. The faint touch of blondish-red in his hair was also more pronounced, dominating the white and gray. The distinct cheekbones in his long, thin face were also less noticeable—more padded—giving him a younger and more graceful handsomeness. But that mythic Baltic look, which previously reminded me of the Latvian Vanemuine sea wizard, was all the same still there. A silky, thin red robe with long, wide sleeves draped down in soft, velvety layers over his narrow frame. His deep purple, loose-legged pants showed an even darker purple waterline around their cuffs. He must have already been in the forest.

There was a spry and joyful revel in his stride as he walked down the stairs to greet me, though his words were nonetheless lax and soft. "Please forgive me," he said, "for being late. The morning air is refreshing—full of prana. Lovely morning for a walk. Shall we?"

The instant Master Janjuran's welcoming hands touched mine, the potency of his inner sight became apparent. A flashed vision lit up my thoughts. I saw him and me sitting in a small gazebo-like structure surrounded by a grove of black-limbed maples. A pair of woven bamboo chairs and a wicker table stood at its center, bearing a basket of fruit. Unquestionably, the vision coming out of the blue like that indicated that he must have purposely communicated it.

He confirmed that theory when he said, "A few of the children have set a table for us a short distance from here in a sunny forest meadow. We should go now. I would very much like to share one of life's lovely treasures on the way."

Rather than follow a traveled path, Master Janjuran led me through the wet underbrush, seeming to take special delight in the water splashing down over us. A few hundred meters into the forest, he came to a sudden stop and raised his open hand in the air, which I assumed was his signal not to say anything. He turned his head slightly as if listening for something. I quietly joined in. Nearly lost between the hundreds of delicate forest sounds, I heard the rebounding echo of a captivatingly beautiful birdcall. After a brief silence we walked on. Barely two minutes passed when he stopped again; he repeated his previous signal for silence. His raised hand slowly shifted from a halting gesture into a kind of divining tool. Slowly turning his hand, he pointed in the direction from where the birdcall had previously come. His searching expression shifted into a radiant smile and his gaze narrowed toward the shady blue-green mists that were still veiling the more distant trees. Working to see what he was looking at, I soon spotted the faintly blurred shape of a bird flying toward us out of the mists. Navigating the umbrellalike underside of the woven branches, it quickly closed the gap between us, slackened its flight, fanned open its wings, and then executed a perfect swoop, landing on a bent maple branch above our heads.

It wasn't so much the bird itself but the sweet glimmer of delight in Master Janjuran's upturned face that most held my interest. His eyes were nearly aglow with a tangible sense of joy. For that brief moment I saw in this highly advanced master what I had now seen a few times before in the faces of the others: not the stoic indifference the world often associates with a master but the heartfelt sensitivity of a young child.

The bird was about the size of a common crow, but there wasn't anything common about its thick, downy-white underside and its stunning, dark-black wing feathers that shimmered streaks of Persian blue when it darted its head from side to side. Its tiny, jet-black eyes studied us fastidiously as if we were as fascinating to it as it was to us. Master Janjuran responded by closing his eyes and touching his two forefingers to his lips and then affectionately blowing the bird a kiss. The bird puffed out the tiny white feathers on his pear-shaped chest and began bobbing up and down. Master Janjuran let loose a soft laugh and then gestured the bird off with an upward wave of his hand. The bird took that as its cue and flew back into the misty forest from where it had come.

Pointing toward the bird's retreat, he said, "You see, Aaravindha, as I promised—one of life's lovely treasures. He comes here every year for a few weeks to search for his companion."

"So that call we heard earlier—it was for her, his mate," I said.

"Yes, but he won't find her here," he answered. "She left this world nearly six years ago. But this little fellow's heart is quite large. And one day he will find her, likely not as a bird.

I said, "Love is that tie that connects us all."

He added, "Regardless of what new face or form we might dawn."

"You said he searches for her unsuccessfully year after year. That seems a little blue."

"No!" he insisted. "Sadness is a personified interpretation. This little one's heart is full with love. You see, it's not in the object of love but in its realization that we find fulfillment. When the heart is open, what use have we for sadness?"

I flashed back to the few times I had lost a family member or a friend to death, and then remembered just how old these masters must be. All of them have seen their family and companions slip away in death.

I said, "Blessed by the realization and recognition of love in our hearts, it would be a lovely thing to have those who have lost a friend or family member remember that."

"And to sing their love out joyously," he said in a hearty voice, "like this small bird, to openly declare it. That would be a glorious world indeed."

A short while later we entered a small garden courtyard, the exact place I had envisioned earlier. The floor of the gazebo had been freshly swept clear of leaves and the bamboo chairs were fittingly dressed with small, red silk pillows. A porcelain platter with two small, white cups and a simple silver pitcher smelling of floral herbal tea was waiting for us.

"This will be a good place for us to remember," he said. "Friendships are not made; they are remembered!"

After a leisurely conversation he turned to me the way someone might if they were about to say something important. "As you know, this talent you and I have is a bit unusual. Even between your use of it and mine, it has its differences."

I said, "Your use of it must be unique unto itself—you're an Amartya rishi. As far as most of our outer world is concerned, your life shouldn't even be possible. And I've used my saumedhika drishti up close, mostly one-on-one with people; you've used it at incredible distances. Undoubtedly you've mastered it fully. And there's also the time element. You masters all call me young master, and that must be the first real difference: I'm young, at least compared to you and the others. If anything, I've learned that this talent gets better and more profound with time. Given how old you are in comparison, I must appear like a child."

"Not at all!" he exclaimed. "You may be quite young in your body, but we would be mistaken to measure your talents by your age. You believe I have mastered my skill fully, but in truth it's not possible to realize it in its entirety. There's no limit or end to its reach, although it took me many years to develop it to where it is now: 122 years, to be precise."

"One hundred twenty-two! That fact alone humbles me."

"In my case, the time was necessary," he replied.

A moment of stillness followed as I watched his face become more thoughtful. He said, "You know already that too many believe that what the master has attained is impossible for them to attain. No doubt you have seen this trait in some of your initiates. Too often there is the mistaken belief in separation. Too long has the dark lie been perpetuated through the doctrines of a few misleading religions, their dogma proclaiming that there is but one child of God born solely of a divine origin, while the common person is born of a mortal origin. Thus mere people are limited to serve a lesser truth. No truly illumined master has ever claimed that. Nor has any true master ever asserted that their attainment is above or beyond the reach of those who will follow. All beings are children of a divine origin. To say anything different only prolongs the greatest lie ever told."

"That's a robust statement."

Master Janjuran answered, "What greater darkness can be set upon one's heart than to sever it from the truth of one's existence?"

"Actually, I appreciate you saying that. I've often felt I might have been a bit too fiery in believing just that."

"Then together we will change this lie," he said teasingly.

"Could you say more on the differences you mentioned between your use of saumedhika drishti and mine?"

He answered, "Though it is now mine to do with as I see fit, it was originally a skill I had to attain or, more correctly, to remember, as saumedhika drishti is inherently a part of every being. But unlike you, I wasn't born with it; and a learned skill is different than a congenital talent."

"I'd like to hear more about that," I said. "I've searched for a way to teach others this skill but haven't yet found the right techniques. It seems to involve at least five siddhis. How did you learn it?"

"I initially discovered the means when I was still very young—a young master!" he joked. "I was invited to a remote *ambara 'mandira*, a sun temple built into a mountain not far from here. A *Sramana* born of a noble house had long ago chosen to spend a summer season there. By right of birth he had authority over the scriptures amassed in its archives. He knew me well; I had spent a part of my childhood with him. During that time, he came to appreciate my burning desire to awaken my spiritual way. He granted me a very rare privilege: I was given access to the mandira's most secret scriptures. In my search through the archives I uncovered a thick, ancient book sealed in a gold-clad cover, authored thousands of years ago by a highly accomplished Amartya master. His name at that time was Mahattara Amamriprabhu, although he has had many other names. I am sure you have already speculated about him." He pointed to the mountain that Master Amir had said was Pitamah's home.

"Grandfather Pitamah wrote the book? If he wrote it thousands of years ago, just how old is he?"

"Old beyond description. His exact days are unknown. He doesn't allow anyone to know his true age or his birth origin. But Ambadevi—Nil'Amma Tara—may know. She knows a great many things."

He continued, "The moment I began turning its pages I knew I had found what I had been searching for since first setting foot in this world. I had never before witnessed the lost secrets of our human origins so perfectly revealed. I spent days reading it, completely unable to eat or sleep. All I could do was study page after page. My dear, I discovered in those endless texts the most ancient spiritual practices known to our tradition."

He adjusted his chair and leaned slightly forward. "I will now tell you a little secret, one I have never spoken of. This book did not contain an ordinary writing. There was *aidha* in the words."

"Aidha?"

"Aidha is very rare! It is a lustrous power embedded in the letters, established there to initiate a realization of the knowledge they express. Directly!"

I said, "I'm not sure I understand. Are you saying the words were luminous and that the words themselves had a power?"

"I am saying more than that. The words emitted a knowledge-endowing light as they were read. Aidha bears a *bhavana bashkaravac*, a transmitting light that directly bestows the essence of the written word. Aidha is meant to reach through the reader's surface intellect and call up from the source of their being an intended realization, invoking a pure and direct experience of the knowledge."

"Grandfather Pitamah wrote that?"

"Yes, the aidha was embedded there through the power of his illumined will. This sacred scripture revealed the living truth-light. It not only revealed to me the most sacred and protected knowledge of our tradition, but it also provided me with its direct experience. The *shakti-prajja* blazing through those words destroyed all obscuring shadows in my mind, until my last belief in what I had previously held in limitation was overcome. Thereafter my outward reliance on seeing and hearing changed. With my mind clear, I heard the waking roar of the combined *Ek'Akshara* just as the ancient master Sramana rishis once had. I knew then that any knowledge could be found; it is all contained within the causal structure of that lion's roar."

"The Ek'Akshara . . . do you mean the original Sanskrit letters?"

"Oh, Aaravindha, it was far grander than just the combination of those letters! It was the pure sound of our origin, the thunderous command of the Supreme One, the cradle-sound in which Sanskriti is merely a shadow language. I was so overtaken by that experience that I immediately and willingly surrendered my entirety into the hands of Pitamah, the great master. Burning within those ancient parchments I found my true path, which also led me here to his feet. You see, young master, by the grace of Mahattara Amamriprabhu I was able to gain what I was previously told was impossible."

While he was speaking I saw in Master Janjuran something I hadn't noticed until now, something resplendent but still indefinable forming in the air around us: a faint quivering distortion of light, like a mirage.

He asked, "Do you understand the true meaning of *darshan*?"

"I believe it's the revealing of the presence of the Supreme One through a providential moment, effectively for the initiation of another. That's to say, it refers to an illuminating moment brought on through a heightened revealing of one's divineness."

"Exactly! Do you also know the meaning of *drishti*, its authentic meaning?"

"I believe it might have several meanings in different Eastern traditions, but from what I have heard Master Amir say about it, in the Amartya tradition it refers to a power of insight that reveals pure knowledge. More exactly, it's a focused ability to transcendentally draw into one's awareness an experience of truth-knowledge from a time, an event, a person, or a possible experience."

I sensed his unwavering gaze deepen and intensify. He then unexpectedly tapped the top of my head with his forefinger. At that exact moment a jolt of light shot through my entire body. My thoughts momentarily went into a spin. While I tried to regain my focus I heard him say, "Saumedhika drishti is the means to realize darshan of the highest order."

His unexpected touch had started something that seemed to be accelerating on its own, regardless of my attempt to refocus into the moment. It was having an anomalous effect on my perceptions, which caused me to feel suddenly thrust outside of my normal intellectual boundaries. My linear sense of time had begun to break into incremental fragments, triggering me to echo back and forth between my thoughts and an unlimited sense of expanse. A strongly increasing sense of being pulled free from my physical body was quickly overcoming any sense of wanting to hold on. Why this was happening was beyond me. My initial thought was that Master Janjuran had restarted the game he had played with me earlier but on a much deeper level. A knowing smile had claimed his face. He quickly pressed his hands together and then opened them again, turning his palms in my direction. At that moment it seemed as if the space around and between us was splintering into mirrorlike particles.

He whispered, "Remember, Aaravindha, She gave you this atisiddhi so that you could find Her."

Whatever Master Janjuran had just initiated, it was intensifying too quickly for my thinking mind to follow. I heard him say, "Let go—remember!" I slipped into an effortless abandon; my breath began streaming out of my body, emptying all sense of physical limitation. My body soon lost its solidity and then became completely motionless. I had passed beyond its reach. And yet my awareness felt more free and alive than ever. Who I had been a moment before seemed distant and small.

I have experienced some of my most precious and profound meditations when I have perceptually let go of my surroundings and found myself transcendentally enveloped in a pristine silence; this was most often followed by intermittent surges of streaming bliss light. But this experience was quite different. My awareness was free-floating somewhere deeper inside—not in my limited self but in a realm where my seeing, feeling, and hearing were completely free of their confining limits, opening my awareness into virtually every direction at once. Whether my eyes were open or closed no longer mattered. The only remaining objects of my awareness were Master Janjuran and a complete availability of my open-ended awareness.

A subtle, blue-white light similar to the blue I'd witnessed around Nil'Amma Tara started to shimmer over the surface of his face and hands. A soft upsurge of rainbow light lit up the space above his head. In seconds, the light seemed to weave us together and sweep us into an ascending whirlpool of intensity. My sense of being in a moving spiral invoked a feeling of being pulled deeper and deeper into an inner vastness, which seemed to border on the infinite. From somewhere far off I experienced my mind reaching out for me. A moment later, which could just as well have been an eternity, everything faded into an absolute silence. I was the silence—without shape, thought, or definition. All that remained of me was a subtle inkling of desire. But this desire wasn't a mere human desire; it soon grew into a grand ubiquitous desire, one greater than any I could have imagined—a desire more ancient than time itself. It was a pure, untainted desire to be and, at the same time, to know. Like a great storm forming, it soon expanded to fill and consume the silence that I was, and then it burst into a free roar, which felt like a thousand ocean waves crashing all at once. My whole being was suddenly engulfed in the all-consuming thunder. I watched the way silence watches, as the thunder articulated into thousands of undulating rays of bliss-filled light all passing through and from me, spreading out into every direction.

I felt like laughing, yet my experience was just too expanded. But then somewhere in the distance I heard my body laugh. The roar started to subside and I found myself standing in a rain of light, each drop seeming to sing out a pure tone, separate and yet in harmony with all the other tones. I was more the space that held it all rather than a perceiver in it. Soon even the space that was watching was aglow. Remembering the world, I immediately saw all beings in me and all minds in mine. Simultaneously I saw myself as a baby, a child, an adult, and an old man. I saw my friends, my family, and an endless stretch of former lives. And then I heard Master Janjuran's previous words echo through me, "Remember, Aaravindha, She gave you this atisiddhi so that you could find Her."

That brief moment of reflection gave me a sense of location, a place I was watching from that in turn allowed me to focus on something that was forming in my awareness. I saw the hands of Grandfather Pitamah writing the aidha words of light that Master Janjuran had found in the sun temple. What Master Janjuran had seen in those words I now saw, and what he had learned I also knew. He and I were one and the same, a single ray of golden light resting beneath a thousand-flamed lotus that grew brighter and brighter. Again I heard Master Janjuran's voice, "Remember . . ."

Then, all at once, everything was gone—only perfect silence remained. So perfect that all I had left was a simple and pure awareness of being, not the kind of silence one might imagine as soundlessness. This was perfect and whole silence. My bliss was complete in this place, but it couldn't be described as a place—it was a consummate presence. Time was irrelevant now, but then in a moment of self-recognition I felt it all begin to stir, as if the immeasurable was coming to life. There was a ripple in the immovable. I felt a soft and divine breath embracing me.

The most wondrous moment of my life had arrived. I was blessed to view Her astounding glory. I was graced to see the ineffable. I felt my body in a now tiny world, somewhere far off, weeping with joy. In this sublime embrace, my soul was lit up as bright as a sun. The ripple in the silence had come to carry me through it to a sacred shore. I now saw before me Her blue lotus world. I cannot endeavor to describe the depth of luminous brilliance and sublime love that was unveiled in her presence.

Looking back at that moment, I might only attempt to tell you of Her love, Her resplendence, and Her beauty. But in truth I am left without a voice that can truly describe Her. I simply cannot find the words. We can only know Her if we are willing to sacrifice ourselves fully into Her love.

I can't say for sure how long I was there. But eventually I rediscovered my mind waiting for me. But I had flown the course of Her river and I could not return to what once was. I looked across at Master Janjuran, smiling. His game was now complete.

21

A STARLIT PAST

I could hardly believe my eyes.
I was looking directly through the space where his hands
  had been,
down to the sand and pebbles below.

I n hope of becoming more acquainted with the previous succession of Amartya masters, I asked Master Rambala if he would offer me some insight into the legendary history of the Amartya Parampara. In our past conversations I had come to recognize that there were certain themes that Master Rambala was particularly fond of. Noticing a raised eyebrow and a new twinkle in his eyes, I could see that this subject might be one of his favorites.

He said, "Aspects of the parampara's most distant history remain unclear even to us. Only Grandfather Pitamah still holds knowledge of the most distant reaches of our tradition. The Amartya Parampara is greater than a thousand scholarly voices can convey or that can be assimilated through a hundred dutiful lifetimes. Our forebears have passed it from teacher to student through an endless line that predates all known time frames. It exalts the ultimate truth of our existence. For those who have been blessed with the means to hear, it bequeaths an unending and incomparable wisdom, offering a glory unmatched in this world or in any above. The parampara has been referred to by our Amartya ancestors as the *ashirya hemasutraka*, the invincible succession that links the *acarya* of our tradition to the difficult-to-understand *Nakshatra Amaragana*, the original architects of this world."

I said, "This is the second time that you've mentioned the Nakshatra—the star-born—but this time you referred to them differently. I don't believe you're talking about the same star beings that some Mayan elders have claimed are their star ancestors, are you? Or the Sirius star connection that the North African Dogon tribe speaks of?"

He said, "No, I am not speaking of those claims." He put his hand on my shoulder and continued, "However, I will say that the *tanusmrti*, our biological memory, which could also be called our genetic code, is in all humans an extraterrestrial and terrestrial mixture. We have known this for thousands of years. However, this extraterrestrial influence arrived later, long after the arrival of the Nakshatra."

"So does that mean that humans today are all descendants of the Nakshatra?"

He said, "No, my dear, that's not quite it. Not all who inhabit physical bodies are from the Nakshatra Amaragana succession; many here are *Bhaumya*, earthborn. The Bhaumya have developed along with this earth's forming." He shifted his gaze to the sky and said, "There are, of course, others, those who have migrated here from former worlds. Some of those worlds still exist and some do not."

"Those who migrated here," I asked, "did they originally come here as physical or nonphysical entities—in human form or as astral bodies?"

Furrowing his brow, he answered, "Astral bodies? The correct term would be *khasharirin deha*. *Astral body* is a theosophical term. *Astral* can be related to the term *ethereal*, but *ethereal* is more correctly related to *akasha*. Khasharirin deha is the akashic form. In other words, when alluding to the ethereal foundation of the human body the proper term would be *khasharirin deha*."

He then added, "A few who came here did so in physical bodies that would be referred to as *bhautika deha*. Long ago, some of those who had come here in a similar human form as these bodies we now inhabit had mixed their tanusmrti—their extraterrestrial genetic information—with the tanusmrti of the Nakshatra descendants who were already here."

"The Bhaumya inherited the genetic information of those who came here from other worlds. I've always believed that."

"Indeed, all who live here on this earth have!" He added, "Prior to that mixing, the Bhaumya spirits evolved through a succession of ascending animalistic inhabitations, what we would call the *Brahanta-Bhaumyaviyakta* ascent, which in the end led the Bhaumya to their superior human incarnations. The Bhaumya in particular are more inclined than any other inhabitants who have come here to this world to feel a spiritual alliance to the earth as their Mother. This is due to their hereditary earthborn tanusmrti, which drives their survival concerns more than any rational form of logic. For those who have ascended through the Bhaumya line, their kinship to this earth is strongly interreliant."

What he said about the Bhaumya and their kinship to the earth ignited an entirely new line of questions, particularly as I reflected on the many native cultures around the world that interact with animal spirits and seem to prefer the natural ways of the earth to many of the world's alternate celestial theories.

He continued, "However, an unalloyed Bhaumya birth is no longer possible—the extraterrestrial tanusmrti was, over time, integrated into humanity worldwide."

I asked, "So the original ascent of their souls or spirits moved from animals to apes, and then to prehistoric man, and then rose in scale to become contemporary human?"

"Yes, but only in part! Another distinction must be made. This human body in its fundamental state didn't evolve from the ape or prehistoric man. Animals, monkeys, apes, and prehistoric bodies were what they were, and are still what they were. This human body is much older in design; it is an *anunirdesha*, an ageless exemplar. It existed similarly in multiple worlds before this one was even a cluster of elemental stardust. Prehistoric people have long been extinct—a trial of genetic manipulation that did not survive the test of time. The final phase of the Brahanta-Bhaumyaviyakta ascent—the migration of the Bhaumya through their animalistic forms—wasn't complete until they progressed into the human form as it is today."

I followed, "Now that's a controversial concept for anthropologists! It seems that the modern world is adamantly divided between evolution-oriented scientists and biblical, man-created-by-God theologians."

He continued, "Everything and every being has a divine origin. But that fact should not negate our sciences. You see, my dear, this human body doesn't evolve; it adapts, just as the earth or our environment adapts to shifting seasons or earth changes. It acclimatizes to changes in environmental circumstances, and from generation to generation amends itself to the earth's natural regulating conditions. This issue has plagued those narrow-minded Darwinists and biophysicists endlessly. It is really very simple. The evolution of the soul-self and the process of physical acclimatization are not the same! It is the self-aware consciousness that inhabits this material and follows the evolutionary path. The human body is merely an adaptive vessel—a somatic gateway for consciousness. It is solely a convenience that provides a localizing point of reference. The indefinable Self that inhabits this form is effectively always free and can exist in and beyond its limits simultaneously. It's this freedom that allows it to evolve toward a greater consciousness in whatever vessel it finds itself. What evolves is the soul's ascent from limitation to freedom, from obscurity to clarity. A music lover may say, "Oh my, your violin has evolved greatly; it plays much better than before." In truth, it is the musician, not the violin, who has evolved."

"I deeply appreciate what you're saying. You're affirming so many of my beliefs."

He answered, "My dear, I suspect you initially hoped to ask if this body is a creation of a higher extraterrestrial intelligence or if it is a divine manifestation."

"Yes! Thank you. That's it exactly."

He continued. "Initially it was a divine manifestation, later it was influenced by extraterrestrial tanusmrti. I can say more on that later. First let me complete my answer of your earlier request. The Mayan were not Nakshatra descendants; they were a pure example of the Bhaumya, the earthborn. Over five thousand years ago, and again three thousand years ago, they were briefly ruled by an extraterrestrial race known as the Kabuvil. These were otherworld visitors whom the

Mayan people both respected and feared. The Kabuvil were of two minds: sympathetic and kind, or exceedingly cruel."

"And the Dogon?"

"The people of the Niger River cliffs?" he asked.

"I believe so," I answered. "I don't really know very much about the Niger River or any surrounding cliffs. I've not been there before. I've only learned that the African Dogon people lived in either Niger or Mali and are somehow connected to the Sirius constellation through their ancestral beliefs."

He replied, "The Dogon natives were once blessed by benevolent visitors known as the *Nommo Pashei*. These were aquatic masters from the silver-water planet in the Lubdhaka cluster: the Sirius constellation. They rarely left the water, communicating with the Dogon tribe elders from the banks of a Niger lake. Their soft, blue-gray skin, similar to the ocean's aquatic mammals, was ill-suited to the dry air of that region. Compared to the Dogon natives, the Nommo Pashei were quite small. Like that of an eight-year-old child, they measured just over a meter in length."

"This is too fascinating." I replied. "But when you referred to the Nakshatra Amaragana, you weren't talking about a class of beings, an extraterrestrial race like the Kabuvil or Nommo Pashei."

Master Rambala burst out in laughter. "No, no, my dear, those are the extraterrestrials—two sorts of the space people that our conventional world is so obsessively intrigued with. The extraterrestrial influence arrived later, long after the Nakshatra arrival."

"I have to admit the extraterrestrial influence is intriguing to me as well. And considering the constant flurry of UFO sightings, it seems we're still being visited."

"Visits are ongoing and frequent here!" he said. "Yet humanity should be more cautious in these matters. Many that visit here are not doing so with noble intentions. There are those who have chosen not to interfere with humanity's progressions, but there are also those who are notoriously deceitful and dangerous to humans, and quite desirous of claiming dominion over this world. We have long been aware of these immoral beings."

"And the—"

"Yes, the Nakshatra!" he interjected. "The human form is a physical expression of divine principles inherited by this earth. It is the corporeal expression of the Divine in humankind, a marginalized replica of the greater primary structure of supreme creative intelligence."

"So, in principle, this body is the divine image, the devatapratima, the prototypal image that is a fractal representation of our greater Self?"

"Yes, though it is always somewhat altered by its inhabitant and the adaptive conditions of its material surroundings," he concluded.

I stood up to move and stretch my body. We had been sitting together since dawn on the banks of a shallow stream. This place was quickly becoming my favorite spot to visit. It didn't have the extraordinary view of distant waterfalls that Master Amir had shown me when I witnessed the rainbow phenomenon; very little I have witnessed in life could compete with the beauty there. But I had come to associate this streamside with a number of previous conversations between Master Rambala and me over the last few weeks.

The water coursed by dreamily, creating a soft rhythmic flutter between the thin, grassy reeds growing in its midst. The tiny stalks piercing up through the water's surface created silky ripples, which crossed over each other downstream to create a sparkling array of imaginary, sunlit diamonds. I stretched my arms to the sky, took a slow deep breath of the fresh morning air, and then bent down to sort out a few flat stones. I skipped one low and fast across the water's languid surface.

"Five jumps!" I exclaimed, turning back to face Master Rambala.

He gazed at me with an amiable smile. In that warm moment, it came across like a loving gift more from a dear friend than a watchful master.

I said, "I'm not yet completely clear on this. If the human body wasn't brought here through an extraterrestrial contact, how exactly is it that it came to our world?"

He pressed his palms together and touched his lips contemplatively with the tips of his fingers, waited a long thirty seconds and then said, "I suspect you know the answer, Aaravindha, but I will nonetheless indulge you. This body is a dream; a superlative Will holds the forces of this dream in place. We can examine it with our senses and say, *No, no, this is no dream; I can feel it, see it, and smell it.* But our senses are equally a part of the dream, thus they stand in agreement with the great Dreamer's Will, which makes this seemingly physical experience appear very real. But truly what you see before you is not what it seems to be."

He waved me back from the stream's bank and asked me to sit down directly in front of him. Once I was seated, he said, "My dear, let me show you."

He held out both of his hands, resting them in the air with his palms facing up. He said, "Now I want you to look carefully at my hands. Be still and do not blink your eyes or shift your gaze!"

I agreed. "I'll do my best."

A few seconds passed as I wondered what it was he wanted me to see. I relaxed my eyes and felt no strain. But when the seconds became minutes, I started to ask what it was I should be looking for. Before I could say a word, he stopped me with a quick "Ssshh!"

Immediately, the color of his hands shifted to a faint, sky-blue hue and then they instantly disappeared. I could hardly believe my eyes. I was looking directly through the space where his hands had been, down to the sand and pebbles below. Even his wrists were all but invisible, having become so indistinct that I could no longer make them out. I looked up to see Master Rambala smiling blissfully, his eyes closed. The instant I looked back to his hands they were no longer transparent.

While searching for a plausible explanation for what I'd just witnessed, he said, "You see, my dear, this body really isn't what it seems."

I was about to say that I'd never seen anything like that, but then I flashed back to my original vision of the master appearing in my tent when I received the invitation to come here. And then I remembered Master Amir's appearance in my bedroom as a child. Those events could very well have been similar in context to what Master Rambala had just done.

He interrupted my sudden rush of thoughts, saying, "Our perception of material form—in this case, your and my perception of my hands—is perpetually upheld through an existing covenant between your and my mental arrangements, and the sole Will that initiates, sustains, and dissolves the five streams of our sensory awareness."

He lifted a finger to touch me on the forehead and then said, "There is an eye above the eye of the mind; all sentient beings partake in the perceptions that arise through it. In this *devadipa caksu*, this eye, the streams gather to initiate our mutual sensory experience."

I asked, "Is that in the Sadayatana chakra, above the Ajna chakra—the true third eye?"

"That's correct," he said. "This eye rests upon a sleeping bed of *shakyata*."

I cut in, "Shakyata?"

He replied, "Shakyata is pure potential. It is roused into expression only by the high Self's undying desire to be. But this is not a human desire, my dear. It is a *daivika kama*."

"A divine desire?"

He agreed and added, "One that is shared fractionally within the inmost seat of consciousness in all creatures. It is the divine-will-to-be that acts as the pivotal force that draws into expression this latent potential, which becomes our perceptions of life. But in truth these perceptions are only potential. Shakyata appears real only when it is assimilated into *prajjabodha*." He added, "When it is touched by our pure awareness."

I said, "So prajjabodha, pure awareness, is our primary manifest-ing power. And that level of pure or unbound awareness lives above our individuated consciousness. So it isn't limited to one person; it's fundamentally shared by all beings simultaneously."

"Yes," he said, "and therein rests the answer to your question. A mate-rial object is not merely a static entity. It is upheld through a dynamic stream of shared perceptual evolutions that cycle through pure aware-ness within an unlimited field of shakyata potential. What is made possible through prajjabodha enters expression and then returns to its source. These cycles give the thinking mind its sensory experience of time—of movement—driving forward the experience of life. In prin-ciple, each cycle is another moment unfolding. Which to the mind appears as a surging stream of continuance and change."

I said, "And thus we experience the process of life—we see, hear, feel and so on. I believe I can see where you're headed with this."

Master Rambala tilted his head slightly and waited.

I offered, "All material perceptions in their embryonic causal states are governed by the one underlying Will. That high Will is life's binding force that initiates, sustains, and calls back to itself everything that is put into manifest expression. When our awareness is at rest transcendentally in the devadipa caksu—in the eye above the mind that interfaces shakyata to our unfolding life perceptions—it's actually possible to suspend the three phases of evolution, the cycles that carry our life experiences. Through your example of showing me the invisibility of your hands and from what you've said, you demonstrated that it's entirely possible to alter our mutual experience of reality, even redirect our experience of time through suspending a part or all of a cycle."

I paused to probe his sparkling eyes and asked, "That's what you just did, isn't it? Just now when your hands vanished, you held back or intercepted a perceptual cycle!"

He smiled approvingly. "You see, my dear, consciousness is like a river that springs into form in the sea and must repeatedly return to its essence in the sea. It is this way so that life can continue. Every perception that passes through the mind is bound to this rule."

I looked to the ground, pausing to sort out the right words. I said, "Doing that with your hands really brought this all home. Not theoretically, but concretely."

He nodded.

I continued, "If it's possible to curtail the evolutions of perception, then it's also possible to alter our physical experience of reality. Not just in withholding the cycles or interfering with them but also in manifesting alternate or new perceptions! What I am getting at is that it's possible to introduce a new intention into the five streams, which would result in a perception that wasn't there before. This would mean that the human body itself could be dreamed into this reality. The only real difference in this happening all the time in our lives—or through the hands of a master, no pun intended—is in the varying levels of awareness. The difference is in whether a perception is direct or reflective. I understand now what you meant by the Nakshatra Amaragana being divine architects."

"You see," he continued, "the answer to your question is far more interesting than what any extraterrestrials coming to this world might invoke in our imagination."

"To say the least," I interjected.

He added, "The long and slow journey of the Bhaumya changed significantly when the Mother Taras descended from the upper worlds to give birth to the first human beings. A great leap in consciousness occurred."

My ears were suddenly on fire. "The Mother Taras?" I asked. "I don't think you're referring to the twenty-one Buddhist Taras, or the bodhisattva Tara manifestations, are you?"

He answered, "The Matra'Taras are similar in some ways, yes. But the Buddhist Taras you mentioned are not the Dvadashamatarka Taras I am now referring to. The Buddhist Taras—the metaphoric *Vajrayana* and *Tantric Taras*—have provided a prodigious blessing to their devoted monks and nuns. They have provided good ideals for many acarya to realize their inner and outer virtues. In particular, the virtue of *maitri*, which includes the qualities of compassion, friendliness, and kindness."

"Dvadashamatarka?" I asked.

"The Twelve Birth Taras," he answered. "Dvadashamatarka is translated as the "Twelve Holy Mothers." Every year, shortly after the summer solstice, a group of twelve illumined women assemble in a sacred *mataragrha*; it is the original place of the first births. The temple has long been protected in an undisclosed location, not far from here in these mountains. Each luminaress upholds a seat that homages one of the original Matra'Taras. This tribute takes place every year as it has for too many millennia to count. Nil'Amma Tara, our beloved Mahamatra, holds the most exalted seat; she is the blessed Maugdha, the living grace of Adilokajanani, the first Mother. From a time long before my birth she has carried this seat. This ceremonial day of *Tara Purnamasa* takes place on the first full moon after the summer solstice."

My mind was suddenly reeling with exotic images inside imagined, elaborate settings. I asked, "Rambalaji, you said this temple exists near here in the mountains?"

"Yes, my dear, it stands in secret, inside the fold of a snow-covered peak that is only accessible for a short while every summer. It rests upon a powerful *devasthan*."

"An earth power point?"

"One of the most powerful; it stands as a bond between the heavens and earth. Before this present human race arose, this great temple was created. It cannot be found or seen by the impure of heart. It is quite near this valley, very high up in those distant mountains." He lifted two fingers to point low beneath the morning sun.

"Before this human race? That must be quite a story to tell. Is it possible for me to travel there to visit it?"

"No, no, my dear. It is forbidden for any man to ever set foot in the Matrachakra. Only women of great purity are able to enter it. At its heart rests a great birthing hollow—the *svarsvayoni* chamber. Not a place for a man."

I said, "Too bad. I would have loved to have seen it."

He chuckled, "Perhaps, if you incarnate again as a woman."

I asked, "If people hadn't yet arrived, then who built the temple? I assume from what you said that the Matra'Taras came here to plant the seed of humankind. But then who prepared the way?"

He answered, "A very astute question, Aaravindha. The *Shubhrasura*, the White Spirits, built the temple. These were beings of extraordinary intelligence and moral depth—true hierophants of wisdom."

I asked, "Are they the legendary tall people?

"The tall people?" he asked.

"Yes, the Sau'Re, our world's prior race."

"Prior to this past twenty-four-thousand-year epoch, Sau'Re was one name that the White Spirits were known by. The White Spirits were our solar forebears, the disciple votaries of the Nakshatra Amaragana. Indian Vedic legend alludes to them as the *Aditya*. Prior to the Veda, their feminine counterparts were venerated as the protectors of the *pratibhakirana*, the divinatory ray. These feminine counterparts of the Shubhrasura were known as the *Saurama*, who became this earth's first *shalisau* and *stririshis*."

"I know what a stririshi is—a female seer. But I don't know the word *shalisau*."

He explained, "A very ancient name for the watchers, the once unequalled caretakers of life. These Saurama shalisau, through their flawless wisdom and heightened insights, were they who summoned the Dvadashamatarka, the Birth Taras, to this world. Above all else, they worshipped the Blue Taramati, the first Mother Tara of the great Sun."

I confessed, "Talking about this knowledge with you, I feel as if a world of ancient memories are streaming into me. So much of what you're telling me has been pressing its way into my mind in pieces for as long as I can remember. This is kindling a new appreciation for everything I have learned so far. I cannot tell you how grateful my heart is right now."

He smiled in acknowledgment. "A great deal of our ancient history has been lost to this world."

I said, "Considering that Sanskrit was only created a few thousand years BC, I can't help wondering what the original names were for these ancient beings."

"That's true," he said. "There was an unparalleled language, a Daivika language, spoken then; you could say it was angelic. It was withdrawn from the world approximately twelve thousand years ago. Its alphabet is much larger than any other ancient or modern language. It contains a scale of 144 ascending phonemes, which held in them the secrets that were drawn directly from the actualizing sounds of creation."

I said, "Like the phoneme-*bijas* in mantra lore."

Master Rambala's face dawned a new smile. "Yes, very much like that."

I asked, "Then is it true that we have those ascending phonemes encoded into our human structure?"

He said, "There are 144,000 pranic movements in the human body. Each one thousand movements has a governing value that is represented by a single phonetic. These 144 movements have an alpha-numeric value that can be divided into twelve subsystems of tonal knowledge, each of which can serve as a possible key in creating the divine-to-material manifestations. Sanskrit is a mere shadow of this much superior language."

"I can see why it was withdrawn into secret," I said.

He added, "A vast and authoritative science is embedded in this language. Long ago it was debated and decided that it was too sacred to carelessly divulge to the uninitiated. The withdrawal of this kind of science from common view is not an unusual practice. That is why so many archives of knowledge are hidden in secret hermitages around the world. This science can bestow a great power to those who are able to master it. We live in a divided world. It is a knowledge that is sought not only by those who work for the betterment of humankind. Now it is spoken only in the Amartya temples. Only a select few still know it."

"Do you know it or use it?"

"We do know this language. It is the central and also most revered language of the Amartya tradition. But to know it, one need not speak it."

I said, "I assumed that much. It seems to me that it isn't solely a reflective or audible language."

"That's correct."

"I believe I've often heard it," I said. "Not with my ears but in a more direct cognition, primarily during my deeper meditation practices. I've been able to associate it with intermittent surges of bliss, which has given me an appreciation for its aliveness."

"Yes, through drishti," he said, "Saumedhika drishti!"

"Rambalaji, there's something else I hoped to talk to you about. On occasion I feel as if other Amartya masters are living here in the valley. I can't entirely place why I sense that. I know they're not actually here. But I am aware that there have been a number of other masters living here in the past. At times I sense that their presence isn't altogether gone. I can feel them even now, in particular when we talked about the past. What I'm sensing is more than a mere impression, isn't it?"

He answered, "The footsteps of every master who has lived here is lastingly emblazoned upon the earth. When we speak of the parampara, the never-ending tradition, it is meant to imply that the force of every previous master who carried the flame of knowledge in this lineage is still available to the *Amara'acarya* or any future master."

"And that's what I've been feeling."

He added, "There was a time when sixteen *Amara Devata* were living here. Over the last few hundred years, all but those who are

213

presently here have set their earthly forms to rest in the ancestral interment caves. To this day their bodies rest there in silent serenity, unblemished by the decay of time. Each body rests in the manner in which it was left behind, alongside the few Sau'Re bodies that were abandoned there many thousands of years ago."

"Their bodies are still there—intact—resting alongside the corpses of the ancient Sau'Re? That's astonishing. Here in the valley? I actually had no idea that these caves existed."

"No, my dear, not here. At quite a distance from this valley."

"But in the Himalayas?"

"Yes. As you know from your travels, the Himalayas are quite vast. A good many secrets are buried in those mountains."

I said, "What fascinates me most is that you said they're not affected by decay. Considering that the Sau'Re are not even from this era, they must be tens of thousands of years old."

He said, "Bodily decay is the common way for most all creatures after death. Outside of the Amartya mastery, beings in this realm of existence are bound to live within the turning transitions of the *Triguna.*"

"The Triguna—sattva, rajas, and tamas."

He added, "Those few masters who have vanquished the shadow of death, when they choose to set their bodies down, rajas, the fire that drives life, is allayed. When rajas ceases to hold sway, then so too the decay of tamas is negated. Then only the sustaining quality, sattva, remains. A body sustained in the light of sattva remains pure, free from the defilements of aging or decay. You see, my dear, whatsoever the perceiver in the body comes to accept as the rule of existence is also what the human body comes to resemble."

I asked, "So is the lack of decay in the bodies resting in the interment caves similar to the Christian definition of incorruptibility, which the Catholic Church assigns to saints whose bodies don't break down after death? Like those of Teresa of Ávila, Padre Pio, and Clare of Assisi, and, of course, like Paramahansa Yogananda, whose body showed no signs of decay for the first twenty days after his death?"

Master Rambala said, "That sort of incorruptibility is also witnessed in Goa, in the body of Francis Xavier. Many unknown graves around the world hold bodies that can fit into that definition. However, although the decay is lessened in some of these bodies, they all do show variable amounts of decomposition. Those bodies resting in the interment caves do not!"

After my time with Master Janjuran, in which I had ventured with him into our exploration of saumedhika drishti, my awareness of virtually everything became more sensitized. I now constantly sensed small shifts in the air around me, felt people thinking about me, even sensed when a bird or small animal was watching me from a hidden place in the trees or brush. But more than anything else, I could feel when one or more of the masters living here wished to talk with me. I now sensed just that. I pushed myself up to my feet to take a look around and right away saw that I had been correct. Master Amir was walking in our direction from upstream, wading barefoot in the water on the opposite shore. His sandals dangled in his left hand. He offered me a hailing smile.

I wondered if I would ever get acclimated to the sudden rush of energy that flowed through my veins in those moments when I would first see him. I can only compare it to a feeling that might come up if I saw a great angel descending through the clouds. There was so much power—Shakti—in his aura; it seemed to affect everything around him.

After offering us his greeting, he waded the stream and sat down beside Master Rambala. He shared a few words with him in Sanskrit, too fast for me to translate or keep up with. All I could glean from what he said was that it had to do with Grandfather Pitamah, some kind of ceremony, and me. In sync, they both stopped talking and looked over at me. For the moment I was taken a bit aback, uncertain about what they were going to say.

"What?" I felt a tad awkward.

Master Amir gestured with a nod for Master Rambala to tell me.

He said, "You probably already know that we have been in contact with Grandfather Pitamah in regard to granting you a visit. He extended his invitation to you today."

"That's incredible!" I said. "I had little hope of seeing him, considering what I've heard about his reclusive nature."

Master Amir added, "This invitation, it's quite rare. Grandfather hasn't accepted any visitor other than the Amartya masters living here in this valley for a very long time."

I felt my heart start to race but tried my best not to show it. I was sure my face was a bit flushed. No doubt I looked as surprised as I felt.

Amir continued, "Young master, there will be an *upayana*, an initiation, that is required to prepare you for your visit."

"An initiation, like a *dikshana*, a transmitted blessing?" I asked.

He said, "It's a bit more than that. In receiving you, Grandfather is also offering you his ongoing blessings. If this calls you, we will proceed with the initiation."

"You already know my answer," I said.

He laughed, "I do, but this manner of approaching you is tradition."

For the next hour, the three of us talked together about what would be involved in the initiation process, though parts of it were kept purposely vague.

The two days of waiting passed more quickly than expected. The hour was near. The sound of a conch resounded somewhere far off in the distant hills to announce the coming nightfall. It rang out every evening around this time, but for some reason this time it seemed especially reminiscent of another life. Its wail was followed by a ritual evening prayer, which echoed a hauntingly supernatural intonation as ageless as this valley it now possessed. The moon, ready to claim the sky, glowed coral pink, nested low in the hazy horizon like a fairytale egg between two equally pink, snow-capped peaks.

While I was out, a long, white kurta and a matching pair of narrow-legged pants, folded skillfully over an improvised bamboo hanger, had been left for me beside my sleeping cot. A warm, sweet-scented breeze wafted through the forest, promising a balmy evening ahead and no doubt another brilliant firefly performance. The warmest nights seemed to bring them out in large numbers. My hair was still moist from bathing in my favorite waterfall. I finished my shave, using up my last bit of shave cream, and carefully wiped away all remaining traces. I tossed my razor in the washbasin, pulled my new shirt down over my head and shoulders, traded my khaki shorts for the pants, put on my only pair of sandals, and leaned back against the thatched wall behind my cot.

Feelings of nostalgia and gratitude were vying for prominence in my heart. I saw myself standing at the edge of my life, witnessing a kind of imaginary line that I was about to cross—a line I had secretly sought for what seemed an eternity. I gazed introspectively into a small, wooden hand mirror, reflecting on what the experience of being ceremonially initiated at the hands of these great masters might be like. I was sure that I wouldn't see the world through the same eyes after this night was over. Everything was about to change, irrevocably.

My musings were cut short by the sound of feet crunching down the path. I jumped up to greet them before they made it to my door. Just as Master Rambala had foretold, two *hotre*—Kuru priests—were on their way to escort me to the place of my initiation. He had referred to them as *Devarha-hotre*, which I assumed meant they belonged to a high spiritual order. Both men were similar in stature, average in height, and handsomely slender—most likely in their midthirties. And both had short black beards, long tied-back braids, dark Asian-brown eyes, and clear tawny-brown skin. So too they were identically dressed—ceremonially—in long, silvery-gray, near floor-length robes with V-shaped purple collars.

They must be brothers, I thought as I watched them draw closer. They certainly looked the part. I pressed my hands together, bent slightly forward, and stepped ahead to greet them with a universal namaste-style salutation.

Master Amir had said he requested their attendance to participate and to learn the ceremony—a ceremony that hadn't been performed for hundreds of years. He had told me they were a part of the last descendants of a secluded clan that broke off from the Vedic Kuru tribes approximately three thousand years ago. Rather than joining the larger tribe that settled in Uttar Pradesh, this clan migrated north into the Himalayan mountains, over time becoming as reclusive and mysterious as the interior mountain winds.

We walked in silence under moonlight for close to an hour. On occasion, one or both of the men would gesture for us to turn onto a new path, but they continued to say nothing. Following a notably less traveled trail, we soon passed out of the main valley through a narrow crevasse that headed directly to a massive solid stone hillside. We trekked up the hillside to a meadow basin that rested in the moon's shadow at the base of a sheer rock mountain. Somewhere up on that mountain a special devasthan—a sacred power point—linked the earth to the heavens above. Amir had said that there were only a handful of earth points this powerful in our world, and each has long been kept hidden from the uninitiated.

We crossed the meadow in a matter of minutes and then hiked up the base of the mountain using a steep, storied switchback cut into the stone. Our trail leveled off outside the entrance of a dilapidated, cliff-dwelling ruin. The ruin was comprised of a half dozen fragmented buildings cut directly from the sheer cliff walls. The forward-most buildings were mostly collapsed, leaving exposed a number of inner chambers filled with heaps of fallen rubble and the tangible hauntings of a long-forgotten people. Once we'd passed through the ruins, we followed a narrow passage to a mammoth, overhanging ledge; a low-ceiling cavern passed beneath it. On its far side we stepped into a round room encircled with walls made of large, chiseled bricks. The walls stretched up like a deep well toward the open sky.

I was glad that the Kuru brothers didn't speak English, though it may have been that they were merely instructed not to talk to me. I wanted the time to reflect and feel into the rising sense of what might be waiting ahead.

Slipping into a small, round access hole just big enough for one person to pass through at a time, we entered the main body of the mountain. The space quickly widened into a tunnel. We descended a steep stairway that narrowed again to an uncomfortable width, barely broad enough for us to walk in a single line. Careful not to fall, I felt my way along through the dark for about fifty meters, at which point we were able to follow a gradually increasing glow coming from somewhere farther ahead.

Our walk here seemed somewhat archetypically metaphoric of life's journey: Ascending a steep rise, the passage became more and more internal, becoming a path of one. And then at the deepest and most unknowable point of the path, it turned up toward the allure of a distant light.

The glow turned out to be a candle-lit stretch of the tunnel. The air felt significantly cooler and smelled as old as time. Charcoal-black drawings of interacting hawks, deer, tigers, and people were spread along the walls, though most were faded to near obscurity.

We pushed open a final wooden doorway. The stone threshold, thick timber doorframe, and massive wood doors were elaborately carved with ancient hieroglyphic symbols. Stepping over the threshold, we entered a large amber-lit hall at least twenty meters across. The walls were outwardly ballooning and stood nearly two stories high. Their unusual concave shape amplified back to us our every sound. Above, the walls straightened into a sheer, vertical rise that stretched to the stars, reminding me of a smaller version of the Cave of the Swallows in Mexico.

A dozen or so thick, white candles were uniformly spaced all around, set back into small, roughed-out niches. The floor was blanketed end-to-end with white sand, bits of it sparkling gold under the soft candlelight. On the opposite end of the room, partially shrouded in blue shadows, Masters Amir, Rambala, Janjuran, and Nil'Amma Tara were already waiting, each sitting silent and cross-legged on separate flat boulders.

The thick, wooden doors closing behind me created a loud echoing clang as the rusty metal latch fell into place. The Kuru brothers split off like practiced guardian sentinels, taking up their positions with their backs to the wall on either side of the entry. The room fell silent. Except for the sound of my breathing and an occasional crackle of a candle, nothing stirred.

And then I noticed it—a subtle upward pull—like a wind, but not a wind. It started in my legs and soon spread up through my whole body, and then passed through the crown of my head, leaving behind a sensation as if I might literally lift off the ground. After a brief instant of dizziness I let myself relax into the feeling, which transformed it into a delicate sense of weightlessness.

This was one of the only times in my life that I felt this vulnerable. But at the same time, the vulnerability felt like a great relief. Master Rambala had not said much about the actual procedure, focusing primarily on it being performed at the request of Grandfather Pitamah, and that it was necessary for me to receive it before visiting him.

After Master Amir had left us that day at the streamside, Master Rambala had said, "This will be a highly auspicious initiation."

He did explain that it was an *Amarta savitra'upayana*, an initiation to act as an aligning bond to Grandfather's ongoing *radhas*—blessings—and that it would bond me more intimately to the older Amartya masters, thus giving me greater access to the blessings of the entire lineage. He also told me some of it might be uncomfortable, as it would change me both energetically and physically.

I joked, saying, "Psychic surgery." It unsettled me a bit that he didn't laugh.

He added, "Even for someone well acquainted with the mind-purifying surges of liberated Shakti, it is difficult to bear the intensity of Grandfather Pitamah's proximity. Even a momentary glance coming through his gaze is highly life-changing."

He told me that the outpouring of *vibhuta*, the power through Grandfather's aura, is so forceful that this preparation was deemed necessary to open the last of my untapped *caksu nadi*, the inner-eye meridians.

When he told me these things, rather than feeling concerned or worried I was instantly drawn, even excited, at the prospect of going through the process. But now that the time had arrived I felt uneasy. Not so much in a frightful way, but with a growing sense that I was facing into new territory.

Master Rambala had said this would change me, in a tone that seemed to say it would be more than I could understand until it was over. He pointed out that a few meridians that are not known to other traditions would be activated and brought to their full potential under their guidance. He added that to attempt opening these particular meridians by myself would be too daring, as it posed a number of dangers. The process would increase the flow of *shaktidadatyam*, which he said had to do with sensitizing the will of the mind to divine will.

After sharing the saumedhika drishti experience with Master Janjuran, I had come to believe my inner-eye meridians were already cleared. I no longer felt any of my previous binding limits. So I had no real sense of where this new step might take me.

I asked Rambala if Grandfather Pitamah would also be there for the initiation. He said, "He will be, but you won't be able to see him in person until later. After the initiation, when you are able to sleep again, you'll be given directions to his home. Your ability to sleep will be an adequate sign that the procedure's integration period has settled. During the interim, you will feel particularly sensitized in your perceptions. It is very likely that you will feel a brighter and more attractive light calling you, so much so that you may very well lose all interest in being in this world. It may be that you will be called to leave this world for the higher worlds. But that will pass."

He went on to tell me that I wouldn't desire any food, water, or sleep during that time, as I would be sustained through a lingering connection to the *nisprana amritham*. When I asked what nisprana amritham is, he explained that in order to sustain our lives we depend upon an external life force, an environmental prana. We take it in through food, water, air, and so on. This is the dominant life-supporting force that all living beings rely on. But there is also an internal fountain of life force that can sustain life indefinitely. It is the founding source from which all life originates.

Standing silently deep inside the middle of this massive rock mountain, the mysterious ceremony was about to begin. The first sound that rose through the hush was Master Rambala's soft footsteps in the sand. He stopped in front of a centrally placed round, flat-topped sitting stone and then silently gestured for me to come forward. I walked halfway around the seat and dropped down to a cross-legged sitting position. The brother priests came forward carrying a pair of triple-tiered oil lamps similar to the arati lamps I had seen used by the Brahmins in Varanasi on the banks of the Ganges. They carefully placed the lamps on either side of Master Rambala, on two stone pedestals rooted in the sand. Nil'Amma Tara came forward to stand directly behind me. Next, Masters Janjuran and Amir came to stand on either side of me.

A long minute hung silent in the air. The masters closed their eyes; I closed mine, as well, and let myself slip as intimately as possible into the center of the moment.

22

THE WAY TO PITAMAH'S MOUNTAIN

I wasn't aware of the protocol—
should I knock or just open the door and walk in?
Then the words "Come in" sounded in my mind
as clear and distinct as if they'd been spoken.

I woke to find myself suddenly alone. I looked up at the stars; my head was resting on a small, pebble-filled pillow. I was lying on a cool, stone slab between two thick, wool-quilted blankets. For a brief instant I wondered how I had come to be here, and then I remembered that during the end of the initiation I had entered such an expanded state of blissful awareness that I had lost all reference to time or place.

The moon was long gone and judging by the twilight in the horizon, dawn was less than an hour away. Across a deep ravine, possibly seven hundred or more meters as the crow flies, a small campfire flickered brightly against a dark mountainside. Though it was quite far off, the fire was bright enough to suggest the standing forms of two people. *Possibly the Kuru brothers,* I thought.

I was somewhere above the valley. The air was cooler and thinner; my surroundings were barren. The only notable shapes were the few boulders spread out arbitrarily on the stony earth around me. Although the light was still predawn and dim, I could make out where my initiation had taken place far below. Farther off, in the more distant horizon, I recognized the dark indigo silhouette of the mountains that surrounded the valley. I had no memory of having climbed up here. It made no sense. But at present I didn't really care. Under the open sky I was satisfyingly at peace.

During the initiation I had somehow been transported into a golden bliss so intense that I had lost all body consciousness. I became so expanded in my awareness that it escapes every manner of description. When the bliss waves finally calmed into stillness, my first sensory experience was my eyes opening to the glittering stars above. I have no idea how long the initiation may have taken; hours must have passed, although it felt in some inexplicable way more like lifetimes. The process had been much more penetrating than I had expected, and at times even painful. At times the pressure became so penetratingly intense that I thought my skull would effectively split apart or explode. But each time the bliss waves would return to flood over my awareness, filling me with a shimmering balm of white light, which was bright beyond anything I had previously imagined possible, like that of a thousand burning white suns. Master Rambala had told me that the details of the procedure should never be revealed casually to anyone. Accordingly, I carry its intimacies as a closely guarded secret.

Like a slow tide, the morning twilight washed across the heavens to claim the nocturnal sky. I soon realized I was on a high mountain ledge that jutted out horizontally from a sheer cliff wall. The ledge dropped down a near fifty meters to a more gradually descending hillside below, where a trail led from a small clearing off into a field of boulders as big as houses. Behind me, attached to the cliff with rusty, metal fasteners and aged rope, a weathered wooden ladder rose another ten meters to a second ledge that fronted a small, cave-like depression.

With my first physical effort, my body felt almost too heavy to move. It felt gross and burdensome like a lead statue, compared to my much-preferred weightless state of expanded awareness. All the same, I made the effort. I folded my quilt over my shoulder, tucked my pillow under my arm, and scaled the ladder.

Beside the cave's entrance I found a cloth satchel filled with cinnamon rice balls and an assortment of fruit. Next to the satchel stood a small tin filled with sweet milk covered with a thin layer of ghee, and a corked water gourd stood nearby. For the time being, neither the food nor water held any appeal. The idea of eating or drinking seemed oppressive and crude.

For the moment I wanted only one thing: to close my eyes and return to the freer and more expanded states within. A smooth sitting stone had been positioned in the rear of the cave. I folded my quilt to act as a cushion, placed my pillow underneath it for more comfort, and settled in. The cave was just shallow enough that my view was still open to the valley below and deep enough so the hot sun crossing the sky wouldn't touch my body. A feathery, white mist had moved in to blanket the valley, creating a feel of being suspended in a separate world above the clouds.

I was alone, but I didn't feel alone. An undeniable impression had been left behind by the Amartya masters who had—at some previous time and for reasons of their own—sat in this exact spot. When I shut my eyes, my awareness instantly expanded so hugely that it seemed the world as a whole was nothing more than a tiny blue jewel floating in my inner currents of boundless bliss.

Again and again I lost body awareness, at times disappearing altogether in the bright white waves. And each time I inexorably found myself back in my body, discomforted with having to contend with the weightiness of being once again so physical. Whenever I opened my eyes the world had changed a bit more. It seemed more and more thin, and then all at once it shattered into fragmented luminous particles. When I let my sight relax into the view, the particles would at times part, letting me slip between them to touch something else, something higher.

It was in those moments that I encountered one of my life's greatest challenges. In that less defined space, I heard a beckoning call so powerful it rendered me entirely defenseless. Not a fear-causing call—it was blissfully ecstatic. Nor was it verbal, though it did seem hauntingly musical, as if at times I was inside a great hall of celestial echoes. Each time I let go to it, a deeper and stronger upward pull would arise, recurrently causing my spine to arch and quiver and flashes of lightning to burst through my inner sight. The challenge first appeared as a strong feeling, one that caused me to be less and less willing to stay in my body. I knew I had been brought here to acclimate. Master Rambala had told me I would need a few days to integrate back into a more stable state of awareness. But I wanted only to go further, to fly deeper, to drown in the ocean of sweet bliss.

For the next three days I didn't sleep, eat, or drink. I faced persistently into the unsullied puissance, which streamed into me like a golden rain falling from above. And then the final contest arrived, bearing the intense, rapturous feelings of a long yearned-for homecoming. I knew then that I had passed through the gates of the upper worlds, the world of the ascended immortals. I had found my true solar home. I had but one desire left: to let my body go.

But then something held me back. The moment I felt it, the yearning started to subside. In its place a sudden rush of love broke open a previously unknown chamber in my heart. I heard myself say, *I Am! I am all that I have ever sought.* But this realization wasn't merely a thought, an idea, or a hope—it was real. Then for a brief moment I saw Grandfather's face, his eyes radiant with love. I heard him answer my words, *"This love is the home of all hearts."*

Simultaneously, I heard the unspoken, yearning whispers in the hearts of all my friends, my students, people I hadn't yet met, people I might never meet. And then I felt all around me an embracing support of the Amartya masters, past and present. A new depth of peace flooded over me. Slowly my body lost its gross feel, the world outside lost its weightiness, and my earthly senses came back. On that third night in the cave, I sipped some water from the gourd and let my body fall asleep.

When the sun rose in the morning sky, I knew even before I had opened my eyes that Master Amir was standing in front of the cave entrance. He was beaming that now familiar smile that I had so come to love.

I had fallen asleep sitting up in my meditation. Stretching out my legs was a bit slow and difficult at first, but with a little effort I was soon standing. After Amir's warm embrace, we climbed down the ladder to where I had first awakened three nights ago. A thick rope ladder with hardwood rungs was draped over the stone slab. We carried the heavy mass of rope and wood to the drop-off, tied its ends to two rusty, steel pegs that were lodged in the stone, and let it unravel bit by bit until it reached the floor below. I looked over at Master Amir with one question in my mind: How did you and that ladder get up here?

He laughed robustly and then I laughed as well. It was lovely to be in his company, and there was no need for him to answer.

The sun blinked in and out between the broad, overhanging trees as I scaled steadily higher in elevation. Grandfather Pitamah's mountain home had appeared much closer than it did now in walking there. I had loosely estimated that it would only take me an hour to get there, but it was now well into the second. I didn't really mind the extra time; it gave me more room to reflect on what I might actually say or ask when I arrived. When I first came to the valley, I had tried to learn all I could about him. Each of the masters had shared something unique and awe-inspiring, but to my consternation I also learned that he rarely accepted visitors. No one from outside the Amarpura valley had been invited to see him for generations. My optimism for visiting this enigmatic being had grown thin. I had nearly given up. But now I was on my way.

The upayana initiation had been the only requirement, which I readily accepted. Four days later I still found myself shying away from food or water, and whenever I closed my eyes my whole body continued to experience intermittent surges of bliss. And while Masters Rambala and Amir both seemed confident that my acclimation was going well, at times I still found myself perplexed and occasionally halted in my tracks by the unexpected shifts in my normal way of seeing. I occasionally experienced a transparency of material objects and periodic gaps in time. Now and then the environment would become prodigiously clear, even microscopic, and other times distant.

My trek started out fairly easy; the first trails were all effortlessly navigable. But once I left the central valley behind it became far more demanding. Trails were fewer and often faded into brush. I relied mostly on the soaring peak of Grandfather's mountain as my guiding point of reference. Passing through an extensive stretch of brambles and hardened undergrowth proved to be more than laborious. It also presented a slim degree of uncertainty as to what might be resting out of sight beneath the foliage. On one occasion, I startled a green snake warming itself in the sun on a shoulder-high branch. Had it not hissed as I came close, I could easily have collided with it head-on. Another time I had to rush hurriedly to get out from under a broad cluster of large spiders, a type that drop from their branches when disturbed. My biggest surprise came when I nearly tripped over a large, sleeping boar, which fortunately ran off snorting and squealing in fear rather than turning on me in anger.

Relief finally came when I found a shallow stream to follow. From there I passed through a growth of sappy pines, which filled the air with a fragrant aroma of warm pitch. I came upon a large, mazelike field of elephant-sized boulders so thick in number that it was virtually impossible to see more than twenty meters ahead. I followed a narrow trail that snaked into a small meadow basin. The earth was moister there due to the cooling shadow of a large, sun-blocking crag and a small spring that gurgled up at its center. On the far side of the meadow the trail ascended toward a final grove of trees. In the hills above it, a distant segment of the trail climbed through a series of steep switchbacks toward a V-shaped recess pressed up high between the two nearest abutting mountains. I knew it had to be the place where I'd find Grandfather waiting.

Master Rambala had told me that once I arrived in this part of the valley, an *apsarapala* would temporarily delay me. He said I would need to have her permission to go any farther. What he said took me by surprise. It didn't seem so odd that I might need permission or that someone might be guarding the entrance to Grandfather's domain. What surprised me is that in Hindu and Buddhist folklore, an *apsara* is a mythic female like the celestial damsels in European legends who are often referred to as water or sky nymphs. In the East and West, they're most often depicted as temptresses—extraordinarily beautiful and bearing supernatural abilities.

When I jestingly asked Master Rambala if he was referring to a mythic apsara, he looked at me obliquely. "Myths are fables," he asserted.

"No one living here on this earth can qualify as mythic; if she was a mere fable she wouldn't be real. She is an *amarastri samrakshin*, a female guardian devoted solely to serving the will of Pitamah."

More earnestly, I asked, "So she has the means to deny me if she so chooses?"

"Yes. She may not appear how you might imagine a guardian. But she is nonetheless a formidable samrakshin. If she believed you were unworthy, she would not let you pass. The world assumes that power involves brute strength. She doesn't require physical strength to prevent entry; she would employ other methods."

"Other methods?"

"She would distract you," he answered, "beguile your senses. Few in this world have the power to resist an amarastri's charms."

I looked at him in wonder.

He said, "Don't concern yourself, young master. You were invited. Maintain the purity of your intent. There's no more required."

A short distance into the trees, I came to a circular clearing that held a small cabin in its center. A pair of grazing miniature goats raised their heads above the daisy-speckled, knee-high grasses and then frolicked toward me, bleating like a duo of excited children. The cabin was built like an Eastern fairytale *matha* made entirely of stacked stones and hand-split beams. Half of it was built on land, the other half on stone pillars that stood in a crystal-clear lily pad pond. A narrow, wood-plank dock hugged the waterside of the cabin. A flat floating bridge connected the dock to a small, grass-covered island in the center of the pond. On the center of the bridge a stunningly beautiful young woman was sitting with one foot in the water. Seemingly unperturbed by my arrival, she waved me over with a relaxed gesture of her hand. When I came near she motioned for me to sit down beside her. Up close, she looked even more striking. She was scantily dressed in a simple white wrap. Her long, shiny black hair was loosely braided over one shoulder. Her skin was copper-bronzed and flawless, and her eyes shone like dark, perfectly shaped jewels.

I was about to present myself when she lifted a hand to cover my lips. Her soft fingers smelled slightly of jasmine and the fertile scent of forest.

She smiled with a hint of coyness and turned her head lightly side to side. I stayed silent. She pulled closer a small, wooden bucket, loosened a ladle that was fastened to its side, and scooped out some water for me to sip. The water tasted floral, instantly inspiring a fond memory of a honeysuckle bush that grew alongside my home as a child.

I started to thank her, but again she stopped me by swiftly lifting a finger to her lips. A bewitching twinkle gleamed in her eyes, which had a hauntingly mesmeric feel and caused me to intuitively look away. When I glanced over again, she gazed at me with the innocent smile of a child. After a long silent pause, during which time she seemed to be scanning me for something, she offered me her hand and led me to the end of the dock on the far side of her home. She lifted my hand with hers to point to a steep trail that ascended up the mountain. I looked over once more to see if she wished to say something. She only nodded.

It wasn't until I was well out of her sight that I realized just how oddly entrancing those few moments had been, as if I had just passed through a beautiful dream, and I wondered if it had even been real.

For the next half hour, the ascent became increasingly steeper, testing every muscle in my legs. The surroundings gradually morphed from a green lushness into a barren array of high alpine foliage. Then, around a final bend, a stone block wall nearly twice my height came into view. A large, timber-frame gate was braced open with angled wooden blocks to allow entry. I scaled a set of worn stone stairs that passed up through the gateway and led to a terraced courtyard, which I then realized was equal in height to the walls I'd just come through. The view behind me was enormous, stretching all the way across the valley and beyond. At the far end of the courtyard two massive boulders projected up through the earth, creating a formidable barrier to the next level up. Between them stood another open double doorway, which offered the only way higher. I followed it up a long, curved stairway beneath an overhang of weather-cracked vines that were, all the same, blooming bright red against the midday sky. The stairs ended on a landing at the temple's main entrance. Beside the doorway stood a large, iron temple bell with some sort of inscription that I couldn't identify. The temple's forward wall was built entirely of massive old-growth timbers. A heavy, intricately carved roofline slumped and extended in a slow curve beyond the walls.

I wasn't aware of the protocol—should I knock or just open the door and walk in? Then the words *"Come in"* sounded in my mind as clear and distinct as if they'd been spoken. I pushed open the thick, wooden doors and stepped into an entry foyer. Another set of closed doors was waiting. The smell of amber resin and sandalwood was profuse. I set aside my daypack, took off my shoes, and then paused to calm my pulse and steady my focus.

Since I had left the cabin below, I had felt a growing sense of stillness in the air. Every step had felt increasingly more hallowed. But here at Grandfather Pitamah's door, the feel of sacredness nearly took my breath away. There wasn't anything particularly noticeable that made it seem so holy—no sacred art on the walls, statues, altars, or anything visual. The feeling was purely a feeling, but, all the same, it was quite a profound feeling. I pushed open the second set of red, paint-blistered doors, ducked below a low threshold, and stepped into a large, high-vaulted room.

23

PITAMAH

He drew in a breath and let it out slowly.
"Ghatayate mrityu—I have put death to death.
It is of no value to one who has secured the eternal."

Seated in the middle of the room was the soft silhouette of a man. Daylight spilled in from above and behind him through a pair of rippled glass windows. The gentle light set his long, thinning white hair aglow and brightened an already perceptible bluish-white aura that outlined the contour of his body.

He sat with his eyes closed and his face angled slightly up, so still it caused him to appear as if he was frozen in time. Church bell-sized, ornate metal bowls packed with ash-covered sand and thick incense cones burned on both sides of the entry, filling the room with a thin layer of smoke that hung low and motionless in the air. True to his name, his serene and silent face appeared genuinely grandfatherly. His eyes were crowned with bushy white brows and an equally thick, white beard rolled down in a silky wave to his chest. He was wearing a light, sand-colored vest over an ivory-white shirt, which looked like it had been fashioned in another era. A downy, ivory blanket with delicate gold embroidery was draped over his legs. A simple wooden table rested by his side; on it stood a golden chalice next to a florally carved and polished bone-white cane. A stunning palm-sized opal served as the cane's capstone.

I was weighing whether I should just sit on the wooden bench that was waiting a short distance in front of him when I heard, *"Ciramitra,** come closer."

*My beloved; one who is dear to my heart

I hesitated briefly. Were my senses still adjusting? He hadn't moved his lips, or for that matter a single muscle. He was sitting as still and tranquil as a statue. *No,* I thought, *I definitely heard him.* He had sent the message clairvoyantly; there simply was no other explanation. I sat down on the bench, pulled up my ankles, and crossed my legs. As soon as I was settled, a peculiar sensation spread over and through me, like a flood of warm sunlight that penetrated to the heart of every cell in my body. The small hairs on my arms and neck stood on end—there was some kind of charge in the air.

Looking at Pitamah sitting there unmoving and silent, I wondered what it might be like to be so old. The masters had said it was this man they now called Grandfather who first came to this valley so very long ago to establish Amarpura.

He lowered his head to face me but continued to keep his eyes closed. In a gentle and slightly cracked voice, he said, "*Sahapathin.** It is true; I am very old."

He drew in a breath and let it out slowly. "*Ghatayate mrityu*—I have put death to death. It is of no value to one who has secured the eternal."

I said, "Thank you. Thank you for allowing me to come here. I know it's rare for someone to be given this opportunity."

He tilted his head vaguely. "And why would anyone choose to visit an old man like me, and so far away in these mountains?"

I answered, "I don't know all my reasons. I followed a feeling, a strong feeling. I just know I needed to see you."

He said, "You could easily see me without coming here. If you look closely, you could find me in the eyes of any living creature. And if you could not find me there, then look to the wind, the waters, and into the earth. *Meh priyatma,*** merely summon my name and I am there." He smiled subtly, "But now that you see this old man, you do *not* truly see me."

I said, "Grandfather, I came to see you in your true state, not as an old man but as you truly are."

"Ah yes, as I truly am," he whispered.

*Fellow traveler

**The delight or pleasure of my spirit

I said, "I believe that if I could really see you, I would see more of myself through you. And I could put an age of searching for you to rest. But now that I am here, I realize that I haven't wanted to visit you *just* for myself, but for all those I love and will still come to love."

"A virtuous quest," he answered. "To ask sincerely for oneself is indeed wise, but to ask for the benefit of others is both wise and noble. Sahapathin, I may yet show you what you seek, but to truly receive you must first surrender yourself and become nothing."

I answered, "I don't desire to be someone. I abandoned that search long ago. I don't see a value in pursuing a mirage."

Another hint of a smile spread between his dimpled cheeks. "Meh priyatma, in humility one finds the door to knowledge; in sincerity one breaks free from the forces that bind. You have done well to tell me what I wished to hear."

A moment of deep silence passed between us. He said, "I accept your request. Now look to me and behold me as I am!"

He opened his eyes unhurriedly. A soft twinkle flickered briefly in the dark center of his irises. And then there was something else, something I hadn't expected. Barely visible strands of light diffused out from the corners of his eyes, similar to the way light strands might form around a shiny object when one's eyes are blurred wet.

The instant his eyes locked onto mine, a surge of incredibly intense white light struck me so profoundly it nearly knocked me back off the bench. Startled, my hands instinctively flew to the sides of the bench to steady myself. I felt my heart start to pound and blood surge through my veins. And then an almost unbearably loud rumble crashed like a huge ocean wave through my head. It felt as if the air had been sucked out of my lungs. I struggled to focus, but it was of no use; the intense whiteness had temporarily blinded me to everything but the white.

Within a matter of seconds, a whirling wind-like sensation flooded through my body, bringing with it a torrent of gathering sounds: echoing celestial bells, layers of shimmering chimes, and then a chorus of low chants followed by thousands of whispers of people praying. Just as I thought the sounds might be too much to bear, they stopped and the whiteness faded, leaving in its wake a gentle sense of extraordinary lightness. But I could no longer feel my body or any real sense of where I was. I was somehow free-floating in a deep cobalt-blue firmament filled with shimmering stars. It was as if I had been thrust somewhere out into the universe. And then I saw his face appear, faintly at first, and then like a ghost rising into form through the blue. In the bottomless pools of his steady gaze I saw my reflection, and then I saw in his eyes my eyes. And in these eyes I perceived an endless cascade of faces, and then people of all sorts: fetuses of the unborn, newborns, children playing, and then men and women laughing and weeping.

I heard Grandfather say, "Priyatma, look now behind you." I felt a sudden sensation of turning and I instantly saw before me a dark and ominous sky. Beneath it was a gray and gloomy landscape. As the scene came more into focus, I saw that it was filled with millions of lifeless corpses, mountains of bodies that stretched off into the most distant views. Then he said, "Ciramitra, you will not find me there. Now look to your heart."

I did as he asked and let myself feel undefended to receive what might be there. At first came a tremendous surge of unbearable pain. Next I felt the world as a whole, as if it was there in my heart, along with the endless lamentations of all those who are suffering: the sick, the dying, the poor, and the suppressed. The more I saw there, the more the pain increased. Soon only one thing was left standing as more intense than the pain: my desire to reach out and offer some kind of relief.

"Meh priyatma, now come to me," he said.

In an instant, another world seemed to open up before me. I saw a great hall so large it was like a world unto itself. In it were thousands, possibly tens of thousands of meditating monks; they sat side by side, and all were swaying in slow, synchronized spirals. How it happened I cannot say, but it somehow felt incredibly real. I suddenly found myself sitting among them. Looking around me, I realized I was surrounded by hundreds of the previous Amartya masters, many I then remembered and many I didn't. The stream of images then came so quickly that I started to lose all sense of reference.

I closed my eyes and recalled what Grandfather had said: "I may yet show you what you seek, but to truly receive, you must first surrender yourself and become nothing."

Disconnected from any real or tangible body awareness, I abandoned myself entirely into a deepening sense of gratitude and reverence. Before long I was fully immersed in the still presence of a pure and unconditional love. Slowly his face appeared again, radiant with an indescribable tenderness, and then his face became my face, and then I could no longer differentiate a difference. I had entered a Oneness so sublime it was inexpressible by any use of words.

A long time surely passed unmeasured while it seemed the universe was breathing through me. Gradually I started to feel my body again, and then began to smell the aroma of incense. At first the space around me appeared hazed over and blurry, but in a little while my eyes cleared and I could see him again—the old man—conveying the same grandfatherly kindness and compassion that I'd perceived in his face when I had first arrived.

I couldn't immediately ground myself enough to feel if I was actually localized again, nor did I really try. My body felt amorphous and my thoughts were few and weightless. My perceptions were spread out in virtually every direction. It was an exquisite feeling; I would have willingly stayed this way for a long time. I realized now why the masters had me go through the initiation. I had had no idea how truly intense and profound it would be in his company.

He said in his gentle tone, "Meh priyatma, acquiesce your awareness with mine and we shall enter the heart of our parampara as One."

It's not possible to adequately convey in written words the true content of what he showed me then, as it wasn't received in the intellect's predictably linear manner of listening. At best I might say that his intentions became my cognitions, and those cognitions metamorphosed into visions. Many of my previous realizations, new marvels, and a number of unrequited questions that had been half-buried for too long to remember were satisfied. I realized again that to find God is the same as finding one's true Self. To realize the sublime and wake into the pure lands waiting for us in our spiritual heart, we must before all else truthfully yearn, even mourn, for our lost and forgotten divinity. Only in that surrendered receptivity can we call back to us what we've lost. We are all the heirs of a powerful, manifesting dynamism that allows us to dream our lives toward either the promise of a greater light or a lesser darkness. And because we have free will, we can also easily fritter away our given time in the pursuit of things that will, in the end, always fail to bring us any lasting fulfillment.

We can comply with the demands and doctrines of our societies by running away from the challenge they present and by passively hiding in a world of insignificance, or else by actively seeking out our roles, fortunes, fame, or glory. Or, conversely, we can become nothing, give up the labor to be someone that we believe we must be. We can willingly transform our never-ending desires for the glitter of transient things and in its stead learn to listen the way a pure moment listens for the next. We can return to our natural, inborn humility and open ourselves to the most ancient of all reasons—to wake up from the dream of shadows.

The first step toward a true enlightenment is, before all else, to be still. But as it so often is, the path of silence may be too obvious for the thinking mind because the human intellect is nearly always committed to the driving pursuit of desire. To the ego-ridden mind, stillness represents boredom. But to the illumined, stillness is the open door to the possible and the true source of everything.

I know now that I will forever have Pitamah looking through my eyes, and just as he had said, I know I will find him peering back at me through the eyes of others. Sitting across from Grandfather, our forms and our separateness had become completely irrelevant. I knew him to be the One teacher—the living light in all our hearts. The more I relinquished, the more I was given. Soon we were soaring like a sole swan through the clear skies that live between the upper worlds.

Pointing to the heavens, Master Amir had once said, "To fly free like the swan, one must first learn to be as silent as the space between the stars." Now in this freer world above the mind, I had discovered how the masters can come and go between endless other worlds.

As I took in all I could bear, Grandfather said, "This grand reach of seemingly endless realms is only one of an infinite number of possibilities."

In his mysterious manner of communicating beyond any use of words, he conveyed to me that at the summit of our ascending existence lives the Great Blue Realm, the *maha loka*. The maha loka is the true origin of all downward-cascading *lokas*, or realms. Directly below that rests the golden *sarvaga loka*, and below it exists the seven worlds of Mahat—the *Vyarthi*. I remember even as a child dreaming of a great blue world above ours. Now, together with Grandfather, I was able to see it in its astounding beauty—not an earthly beauty, but a spiritual beauty, a *saundari*—a beauty that belongs to the soul alone.

He conveyed that at the apex of consciousness, the maha loka is home to the first Mother, Anma. The seat of Anma is the blue jewel of the eternal sky, the *Nil'Ambaramani*, the source of all order that makes possible the linear expression of the akasha and the many universes it holds. This blue jewel is the one spiritual sun and the great primordial womb from whence all possibility arises. In it, all dimensions, all universes, and all realities are gestated before birth.

In a twelve-petal, blue lotus throne—the *Indambaran Padmasimha*—Anma is forever joined with the one Father, Maha'Purusha. He rules as divine law, and She dreams the eternal dream.

Grandfather conveyed that this realm is not the end of things nor is it the place of beginnings. Our universe is merely one *indivaradala*—one petal—of Her lotus. Eleven more universes are Hers. And these too are not the full extent of what exists. For this great maha loka lotus is merely a trinket floating in an infinite sea filled with an endless number of lotuses.

When it seemed he had shown me all I could take in and our visit together was nearing an end, I asked, "Grandfather, I told you that I had hoped to see you also for all those I love and will yet come to love. What should I tell them about you when I see them?"

He answered, "Tell them very little about me, for I am not definable. Say to them that I am not here, but that I am everywhere. Then say it is better in life to be nothing than to strive to be anything.

Advise them to abandon their useless pursuits and accept what is given. How can the blind know what they want? Is it not true that the Great Mother, in her undying love, would give infinitely more to Her child than the child could ever imagine through limited pursuits? Receive in gratitude what is given and the heavens will open."

He continued, "Show them that they should bear no evil thoughts for another. All blame for wrongdoing must fall on the impure mind. Beneath the workings of the unclean intention is the same Self that lives in all. Is it possible to condemn that Self without condemning the One? To know this simple truth, forgiveness comes easily and compassion may finally dawn in the place of hatred. And then the evil that one might do will be no more.

"Say to them, meh priyatma, that to wake from the darkness of ignorance one must first learn to be still, then wait in silence until the great Will rouses the soul to move. Learn from the Great Mother who lives in the earth. See how Her oceans listen to the sky and then give their all to its call. See how Her flower listens to the sun and then blossoms without effort to reveal its hidden glory. She gives Herself willingly, endlessly. In silence, She waits. And when a need arises, the one Mother moves to bring fulfillment to life. Listen in this way before a word is spoken or an act is set in motion.

"And ask them to remember always that the aim of this great and noble path is not simply to lift the seeker above the shadows of illusion, nor to free the seeker from the misguided quests of the self-deceiving mind. Nor is the aim of this life to lose one's life in a sacrifice for God's sake. What use has God for those foolish sacrifices? If there must be a sacrifice, then sacrifice the shadow in the mind that obscures the great Will. That is all! The true aim of this path is to open the way for the light and power of truth-consciousness so that it might nourish a mastered life. This aim is to replace the misguided workings of the selfish mind with the real Self-Will that works for both the one and the many, so that it might transform this body and spirit and manifest a just divinity here on earth.

"And tell them this too, priyatma: If you choose to seek me, then first seek yourself. If you cannot sit still, then search near and far until you have exhausted your every effort. Then take your seat and enter silence. Then abandon your trivial wants and put your ear to the silent sea within. Relinquish all effort for the waiting streams of bliss, for surely they are there. And soon you will see it is my hand in yours that has come to bring you home, and your hand in mine that brings contentment."

In allowing me to truly see him, Grandfather Pitamah exposed me to the reach of his unlimited view. As a result, I was able to perceive him in a way I hadn't imagined possible. This was a master unlike any I had ever encountered, a truly great being of the old ways. In our contemporary world of pragmatic reasonability and adamantly affirmed limits, he could be imagined as convincingly impossible. And yet, here he is.

ABOUT THE AUTHOR

Aaravindha Himadra is a bestselling author and the founder of Sambodha, an international, nondenominational spiritual organization dedicated to elevating consciousness around the globe. Sambodha serves its vision through coaching the sacred art of compassion, spreading the study of dharma-oriented knowledge, supporting various *seva* activities, and providing numerous transcendental practices, including advanced meditation techniques. Sambodha also offers an extensive, seven-year training program for teachers.

In the Amartya tradition, Aaravindha has been designated the status of *jagad rishi*, a seer and world teacher. Aaravindha is currently the only publicly available master rishi in kinship with the highly reclusive *Surah Parampara*, the "never-ending tradition of the Sun." He regularly lectures and offers seminars in Europe, the United States, and Canada, and lives on an island in the Pacific Northwest with his wife, Ashayrah. To discover more about Aaravindha and Sambodha, please visit aaravindha.com and sambodha.org.

ABOUT SOUNDS TRUE

Sounds True is a multimedia publisher whose mission is to inspire and support personal transformation and spiritual awakening. Founded in 1985 and located in Boulder, Colorado, we work with many of the leading spiritual teachers, thinkers, healers, and visionary artists of our time. We strive with every title to preserve the essential "living wisdom" of the author or artist. It is our goal to create products that not only provide information to a reader or listener, but that also embody the quality of a wisdom transmission.

For those seeking genuine transformation, Sounds True is your trusted partner. At SoundsTrue.com you will find a wealth of free resources to support your journey, including exclusive weekly audio interviews, free downloads, interactive learning tools, and other special savings on all our titles.

To learn more, please visit SoundsTrue.com/freegifts or call us toll-free at 800.333.9185.

SOUNDS TRUE
many voices, one journey